HYBRID WARFARE UNDER INTERNATIONAL LAW

This book addresses the regulation of hybrid warfare under relevant branches of international law, beginning with the law on inter-state use of force (*jus ad bellum*).

The book looks at law enforcement action in response to hybrid warfare, both on land and on the high seas. It then assesses the extent to which forms of hybrid warfare comply with or violate the law of armed conflict before addressing hybrid warfare from the perspective of international counterterrorism law. It goes on to tackle the constraints applied to hybrid warfare under international human rights law, and looks at how hybrid warfare could be constrained under disarmament law. The final two chapters look at accountability for the conduct of hybrid warfare, leaving us with the question: can we move towards a less fragmented set of international legal rules that will govern hybrid warfare in the future?

Hybrid Warfare under International Law

Stuart Casey-Maslen

•HART•
OXFORD • LONDON • NEW YORK • NEW DELHI • SYDNEY

HART PUBLISHING

Bloomsbury Publishing Plc

Kemp House, Chawley Park, Cumnor Hill, Oxford, OX2 9PH, UK

1385 Broadway, New York, NY 10018, USA

29 Earlsfort Terrace, Dublin 2, Ireland

First published in Great Britain 2024

A catalogue record for this book is available from the British Library.

A catalogue record for this book is available from the Library of Congress.

ISBN: HB: 978-1-50997-957-8
ePDF: 978-1-50997-959-2
ePub: 978-1-50997-958-5

Typeset by Compuscript Ltd, Shannon

Contents

Table of Cases

International Tribunals

African Commission on Human and Peoples' Rights

European Commission on Human Rights

European Court of Human Rights

Inter-American Court of Human Rights

International Court of Justice

Contentious Cases

Advisory Opinions

International Criminal Court (ICC)

International Criminal Tribunal for Rwanda (ICTR)

International Criminal Tribunal for the former Yugoslavia (ICTY)

Arbitral Tribunal Awards

Domestic Courts

Canada

The Netherlands

New Zealand

United Kingdom

United States

Table of Materials

Treaties

1925

1945

1947

1948

1949

1950

1952

1966

1968

1969

1971

1977

Soft Law Instruments

Domestic Legislation

Introduction

THIS WORK EXPLORES how hybrid warfare is regulated under the relevant branches of public international law (generally delineated as just 'international law'). The first six chapters cover the substantive rules, assessing the application and interpretation to hybrid warfare of, respectively, international law on inter-State use of force (often referred to by its Latin moniker, *jus ad bellum*), the law of law enforcement, the law of armed conflict, international counterterrorism law, international human rights law, and disarmament law. In many instances, more than one branch of international law is applicable to any given situation and set of facts. The final two chapters look at accountability for violations of international law resulting from certain forms of hybrid warfare – first that of individuals under international criminal law for the commission of international crimes, and then of States under the law governing the responsibility of States for 'internationally wrongful acts'.

Despite the many legal complexities that are addressed, this book is written for non-lawyers as well as for experienced publicists. An annex on the basics of international law is included for those who might find it useful, along with a glossary of abbreviations and key terms. The book is also intended for those coming to the concept of hybrid warfare only recently and who join a burgeoning corpus of hybrid warfare experts. For, although the study of contemporary hybrid warfare boasts a vintage of less than 20 years, there is already considerable State practice to be analysed. All the major military powers are either currently engaged in, or are planning for, hybrid warfare, meaning that understanding how international law governs their actions is only going to grow in importance in the coming years.[1]

I. THE DEFINITION OF HYBRID WARFARE UNDER INTERNATIONAL LAW

A. The Origins of the Concept

Despite the plethora of debate, as yet no internationally agreed definition of hybrid warfare exists. That is so, even though, as Najžer suggests, the notion has

[1] At the time of writing, there were reports that ethnic Serbs in Bosnia and Herzegovina were being supported by Russia with a view to hybrid warfare being conducted against the majority administration, re-opening the ethnic wounds of the early 1990s. Milorad Dodik, the separatist president of Republika Srpska, has been accused of 'trying to use Russia's annexation playbook' by Ivana Stradner, research fellow at the Foundation for Defense of Democracies, headquartered in Washington DC. 'We're seeing the "little green men" as a tool in today's world of hybrid warfare',

indeed become a 'staple of national security discussions' and a 'household phrase in state capitals and general political discourse'.[2] Perhaps surprisingly given the term's etymology (as well as its currency), at the time of writing the United States (US) Department of Defense's influential *Dictionary of Military and Associated Terms* did not contain an entry for hybrid warfare. The North Atlantic Treaty Organization (NATO) also does not formally define hybrid warfare, although it does offer a general definition of a hybrid 'threat', as discussed below.

The US military analyst, Frank Hoffman, popularised the concept of hybrid warfare in an article for the Potomac Institute for Policy Studies published in 2007.[3] Two years earlier, Hoffman had written an article jointly with Lieutenant General James Mattis entitled 'Future Warfare: The Rise of Hybrid Wars', which warned of a merger – a 'synthesis' – of different modes and means of war with the addition of a fourth 'block' of psychological or information operations aspects to add to the three existing blocks of combat, humanitarian relief, and peacekeeping.[4] The article was marketed as 'a new way to look at the battlespace', although it passed largely under the radar at the time.

Hoffman himself credits a US Navy lieutenant, Robert G Walker, as the original source of the term hybrid warfare. In 1998, Walker had described the US Marine Corps as a 'hybrid force, capable of conducting operations within both the conventional and unconventional realms of warfare'. His 1998 master's thesis assessed the Corps' 'hybrid operations' in 'specific historical cases' with a view to rating its 'performance in such roles'.[5] But Walker cannot really be considered the instigator of the term either. Three years earlier, Thomas Mockaitis, an academic historian, was describing British counterinsurgency operations in Indonesia in the 1960s as a 'hybrid war, combining low intensity conventional engagements with insurgency'.[6]

she told *The Times* newspaper in November 2023. In July of the same year, at its summit meeting in Vilnius, the North Atlantic Treaty Organization (NATO) identified Bosnia as one of three 'vulnerable states', alongside Georgia and Moldova. C Bell-Davies, 'How Gaza and Ukraine are fuelling border tensions in Bosnia', *The Times*, 26 November 2023.

[2] B Najžer, *The Hybrid Age: International Security in the Era of Hybrid Warfare*, IB Tauris, London, 2022, p. 1.

[3] FG Hoffman, 'Conflict in the 21st Century: The Rise of Hybrid Wars', Research Paper, Potomac Institute for Policy Studies, Arlington VA, 2007, at: https://bit.ly/3R0PnuK, p 8. Hoffman had already referred to the phenomena as 'complex irregular warfare' in an article a year earlier that did not attract the same level of attention. FG Hoffman, 'Complex Irregular Warfare: The Next Revolution in Military Affairs' (2006) 50(3) *Orbis* 395–411.

[4] JN Mattis and FG Hoffman, 'Future Warfare: The Rise of Hybrid Wars' (November 2005) 131(11) *US Naval Institute Proceedings* 1, 233, at: https://bit.ly/3Rf9g39.

[5] RG Walker, 'The United States Marine Corps and Special Operations', Master's thesis, Naval Postgraduate School, Monterey CA, December 1998, available at: https://bit.ly/3sccRpN, Abstract. Hoffman also cites Alan Dupont's 2002 piece for the Australian National University's Strategic and Defence Studies Centre, 'Transformation or Stagnation?: Rethinking Australia's Defence' (2003) 57(1) *Australian Journal of International Affairs* 55, as reflecting new thinking on hybrid warfare. Hoffman, 'Conflict in the 21st Century: The Rise of Hybrid Wars', n 3 above, 11.

[6] See TR Mockaitis, 'A Hybrid War: The Indonesian Confrontation' in TR Mockaitis (ed), *British Counterinsurgency in the Post-imperial Era*, Manchester University Press, Manchester, 1995, pp 14–44.

Hoffman, who spent 30 years in the US Marines as an analyst and concept developer,[7] would go on to employ the term hybrid warfare using a wider lens than did both Walker and Mockaitis. In his view, hybrid warfare is certainly wrought by State armed forces and non-State actors alike.[8] But he understood the concept as denoting the decision not only to mix irregular and regular military forces in operational theatres but also to ensure that these actors employ a range of non-forcible as well as forcible actions. The aim of such hybrid action, he avers, is thereby to achieve 'synergistic effects in the physical *and* psychological dimensions of conflict'.[9] To attain this goal, hybrid warfare is to be exercised at all levels – from the tactical to the operational to the strategic.[10]

It is true that hybrid warfare remains to this day a contested concept.[11] That said, its contours are sketched out with reasonable clarity, such that when Solmaz talks of hybrid warfare as a 'dramatic example of conceptual stretch'[12] this is more a reflection of loose use of the term than of the term being necessarily loose in itself.[13] For, consonant with the ordinary meaning of the word *hybrid*, inherent in the notion of hybrid warfare is the calculated combination of different types of fighter using an array of means and methods of warfare with a view to attaining an overall political objective.[14] And while they may disparaged hybrid warfare as a 'bandwagon term', Jacobs and Kitzen nonetheless use it as the title for their entry in the *Oxford Bibliographies*, citing the earlier work by Mockaitis on Indonesia as 'an important piece of literature for understanding the history of hybrid warfare'.[15]

Further, although its heritage in contemporary warfare may be relatively recent,[16] most agree that the hybrid nature of combat dates back many centuries. The military historian Peter Mansoor, for instance, dates its historical pedigree to the Peloponnesian War of the fifth century BCE when Athens stirred up a

[7] Institute for National Strategic Studies (National Defense University), 'Francis G. Hoffman, Distinguished Research Fellow', https://bit.ly/3KK8Uie.

[8] Hoffman, 'Conflict in the 21st Century: The Rise of Hybrid Wars', n 3 above, p 14.

[9] FG Hoffman, 'Hybrid Warfare and Challenges' (2009) 52 *Joint Force Quarterly* 34–48, https://bit.ly/3dQxCzS, at 36.

[10] PR Mansoor, 'Introduction' in W Murray and PR Mansoor (eds), *Hybrid Warfare. Fighting Complex Opponents from the Ancient World to the Present*, Cambridge University Press, Cambridge, 2012, p 3.

[11] A Bilal, 'Hybrid Warfare – New Threats, Complexity, and "Trust" as the Antidote', *NATO Review*, 30 November 2021, at: https://bit.ly/3bTcV5M.

[12] T Solmaz, '"Hybrid Warfare": A Dramatic Example of Conceptual Stretching' (2022) 23(1) *National Security and the Future* 89–102, at: https://bit.ly/3sIwzK9.

[13] Solmaz gives the example of former US Secretary of State Rex Tillerson, who claimed that Russia's interference in the 2016 US presidential election was an act of hybrid warfare. Ibid, p 95, citing Euractiv with Agence France-Presse, 'Tillerson: Russian vote meddling was "hybrid warfare"', EURACTIV, 13 December 2017, at: https://bit.ly/3ugmVz0.

[14] Najžer, *The Hybrid Age: International Security in the Era of Hybrid Warfare*, n 2 above, p 22.

[15] JGLJ Jacobs and MWM Kitzen, 'Hybrid Warfare', *Oxford Bibliographies* (Last modified 22 September 2021), at: https://bit.ly/3ViBn2O, citing Mockaitis, 'A Hybrid War: The Indonesian Confrontation', n 6 above.

[16] Ibid, p ix.

Helot uprising in Sparta, causing its enemy to sue for peace fearful of a threat at its own backdoor.[17] Twenty-five centuries later, from Ukraine to Taiwan and beyond, hybrid warfare and hybrid threats are an integral component of State geopolitical strategy.

B. The Key Features of Hybrid Warfare

The concept of hybrid warfare is certainly more than just 'old wine in new bottles', to repeat the *cliché*. NATO has openly acknowledged that propaganda, deception, sabotage, and other non-military tactics have long been used to destabilise adversaries. But what is new about such attacks in recent years, it observes, is their speed, scale, and intensity. These developments have been facilitated by rapid technological change and global interconnectivity.[18] Accordingly, cyber operations, especially attacks in or through cyberspace, play an important role in hybrid warfare.

Indeed, hybrid warfare is typically wrought in multiple domains: on land, at sea, and in the air of course, but also in and through cyberspace and potentially even in outer space.[19] Its essence is the planned convergence across these domains of a range of actors, their means and methods of warfare, and their performance of non-military acts. Key features of hybrid warfare are usefully delineated in the widely cited International Institute for Strategic Studies definition of the term from 2015, which reads as follows:

> The use of military and non-military tools in an integrated campaign designed to achieve surprise, seize the initiative and gain psychological as well as physical advantages utilising diplomatic means; sophisticated and rapid information, electronic and cyber operations; covert and occasionally overt military and intelligence action; and economic pressure.[20]

This adaptive combination of manifold actors and diverse forms of conduct across multiple domains offers the ability to destabilise and, planners hope, ultimately overwhelm an adversary. Given the military hegemony of the United States and thus the asymmetry of the current international order, hybrid warfare is especially attractive to its rivals and adversaries.[21] Chief among them, of course, are China and Russia. As Weissmann and others have observed:

[17] Mansoor, 'Introduction' in Murray and Mansoor (eds), *Hybrid Warfare. Fighting Complex Opponents from the Ancient World to the Present*, n 10 above, 3–4.

[18] NATO, 'Countering hybrid threats', Last updated 18 August 2023, at: http://bit.ly/3KlVNnV.

[19] Hoffman, 'Hybrid Warfare and Challenges', n 9 above, 34–35.

[20] International Institute for Strategic Studies, *The Military Balance 2015*, IISS, London, 2015, p 5.

[21] Nyemann even attributes the rise of hybrid warfare to the 'success of traditional military deterrence from the West'. DB Nyemann, 'Hybrid warfare in the Baltics', ch 13 in M Weissmann, N Nilsson, B Palmertz and P Thunholm (eds), *Hybrid Warfare: Security and Asymmetric Conflict in International Relations*, IB Tauris, London, 2021, 195–213, at p 199.

> The fact that the combined military resources of the West remain vastly superior, certainly to those of Russia and for the time being also to those of China, has encouraged these and other actors to develop and combine other, less resource-consuming means for challenging the global hegemony of the West.[22]

Hybrid warfare is in this manner cast as 'a low-cost strategy with potentially high gains'.[23]

II. ALTERNATIVE TERMINOLOGY

Many alternative terms exist to that of hybrid warfare in contemporary military discourse, most notably hybrid 'threats', 'grey zone' conflicts, asymmetric warfare, and fourth generation warfare.[24] A further notion with similar features is 'compound warfare', a term proposed by Thomas Huber in 1996 as a descriptor for an alliance of conventional armies and irregular forces under strategic direction.[25] Less often employed are 'ambiguous warfare', 'non-linear warfare', and 'unconventional warfare'.[26] Weissmann suggests that the latter are terms 'more or less synonymous' with hybrid warfare.[27] This is, however, unpersuasive. A brief discussion of several terms follows, highlighting their distinctive features and comparing and contrasting their meaning with that of hybrid warfare.

A. Hybrid Threats

Perhaps unsurprisingly, the closest concept to hybrid warfare is that of 'hybrid threats', with a threat in this context understood as 'the combination of capability, intent and opportunity'.[28] In 2010, NATO defined a hybrid threat as 'one posed by any current or potential adversary, including State and non-State and

[22] M Weissmann, N Nilsson, B Palmertz, P Thunholm, and H Häggström, 'Security Challenges in the grey zone', ch 1 in M Weissmann, N Nilsson, B Palmertz, and P Thunholm (eds), *Hybrid Warfare: Security and Asymmetric Conflict in International Relations*, IB Tauris, London, 2021, 1–18, at p 3.

[23] Nyemann, 'Hybrid warfare in the Baltics', n 21 above, 210.

[24] See also on the issue of terminology: CS Chivvis, 'Understanding Russian "Hybrid Warfare" and What Can be Done About It', testimony of Christopher S Chivvis, The RAND Corporation, before the Committee on Armed Services, US House of Representatives, Washington DC, 22 March 2017, available at: https://bit.ly/3suaBL4.

[25] TM Huber, 'Napoleon in Spain and Naples: Fortified Compound Warfare', Combat Studies Institute (CSI), 1996. See also PR Mansoor, 'Introduction' in Murray and Mansoor (eds), *Hybrid Warfare. Fighting Complex Opponents from the Ancient World to the Present*, n 10 above, p 3 fn 4; and Hoffman, 'Conflict in the 21st Century: The Rise of Hybrid Wars', n 3 above, pp 20–22.

[26] Weissmann, Nilsson, Palmertz, Thunholm, and Häggström, 'Security Challenges in the grey zone', n 22 above, p 2.

[27] M Weissmann, 'Conceptualizing and countering hybrid threats and hybrid warfare', ch 5 in Weissmann, Nilsson, Palmertz and Thunholm (eds), *Hybrid Warfare*, n 21 above, 61–82, at p 63.

[28] Weissmann, Nilsson, Palmertz and Thunholm (eds), *Hybrid Warfare*, n 21 above, p viii.

terrorists, with the ability, whether demonstrated or likely, to simultaneously employ conventional and non-conventional means adaptively, in pursuit of their objectives'.[29] It would later refer to 'hybrid warfare threats', most notably in the 2014 Wales Summit Declaration.[30] Its terminology database included the following, rather cursory definition of a hybrid threat following internal approval in 2018: 'A type of threat that combines conventional, irregular and asymmetric activities in time and space'.[31]

Despite his close connection with the nomenclature of hybrid warfare, Hoffman is also attracted by the related label of hybrid threats, which he defined in 2014 as follows: 'Any adversary that simultaneously employs a tailored mix of conventional weapons, irregular tactics, terrorism, and criminal behaviour in the same time and battlespace to obtain their political objectives'.[32] Cast in this light, however, the distinction from hybrid warfare is rather hard to discern. In contrast, Nyemann seeks to differentiate between *hybrid threats* and *hybrid actions* on the one hand and *hybrid warfare* and *hybrid operations* on the other. Hybrid 'threats' she defines as 'deniable or covert actions by an aggressor in a target State involving instruments of power such as cyberattacks (not amounting to an armed attack), information operations, economic pressure, or other unfriendly activities often performed by third-party malign non-State actors'.[33] The clear blue water is thus the absence of war as such. 'Ideally', she affirms, 'States must react to hybrid threats *before* the situation evolves to a case of hybrid warfare'.[34] But there is also a perceived advantage for the attacker who remains below the legal threshold of armed conflict, perhaps with the consequence that he can 'get away with' certain hybrid operations, without actually being involved 'in a shooting war' or being held 'legally accountable'.[35]

Najžer complains that in ordinary parlance a threat is something that is yet to happen and is therefore an unsuitable alternative to hybrid warfare.[36] But the possibility of 'trouble, danger, or ruin', as the *Oxford English Dictionary* has it, certainly chimes with a burgeoning challenge to State and individual security – and one that reflects ongoing adverse circumstances and action rather than merely existing as a far-off menace.

[29] NATO, 'BI-SC Input to a New NATO Capstone Concept for the Military Contribution to Countering Hybrid Threats', 25 August 2010, accessed 1 May 2023 at: https://bit.ly/3AikFX8 (link no longer working), para 7.

[30] NATO, Wales Summit Declaration, Issued by the Heads of State and Government participating in the meeting of the North Atlantic Council in Wales, 5 September 2014, at: https://bit.ly/41pu5eU, para 13.

[31] NATO *Term*, 'Hybrid Threat', Record 37938, NATO Terminology Database, accessed 1 November 2023 at: https://bit.ly/3FZJ3jR.

[32] FG Hoffman, 'On Not-So-New Warfare: Political Warfare Vs Hybrid Threats', *War on the Rocks*, 28 July 2014, at: https://bit.ly/3AMrZuN.

[33] Nyemann, 'Hybrid warfare in the Baltics', n 21 above, p 196.

[34] Ibid, p 197.

[35] AW Dahl, 'Hybrid Warfare', Keynote speech, Conference on Hybrid Naval Warfare through the Lens of Maritime Security Law, Tallinn, 11 May 2023, p 2.

[36] Najžer, *The Hybrid Age: International Security in the Era of Hybrid Warfare*, n 2 above, 38.

B. 'Grey Zone' Conflicts

Other popular terms used instead of, or in addition to, hybrid warfare include the 'grey zone', which again Hoffman uses in his writings.[37] He decries broad conceptualisations of grey zone conflicts in other scholarship, preferring his own version:

> Those covert or illegal activities of non-traditional statecraft that are below the threshold of armed organized violence; including disruption of order, political subversion of government or non-governmental organizations, psychological operations, abuse of legal processes, and financial corruption as part of an integrated design to achieve strategic advantage.[38]

Here, the distinction from hybrid threats is hard to discern. But Hofmann also seeks to 'update our understanding' and distinguish hybrid conflict more clearly from irregular warfare, by offering a revised definition of the notion of hybrid warfare, namely:

> The purposeful and tailored violent application of advanced conventional military capabilities with irregular tactics, with terrorism and criminal activities, or combination of regular and irregular forces, operating as part of a common design in the same battlespace.[39]

The major distinction, he observes, 'is the addition of "violent" to the definition to clarify its placement in the continuum, and to further distinguish it from activities short of violent conflict'.[40] In contrast, Najžer is one of several authorities who consider *hybrid warfare* and *grey zone conflicts* as synonyms.[41] Certainly, in some US military circles, grey zone is a more popular term than hybrid to denote the same military concept. Nevertheless, grey zone conflict is not officially part of US military doctrine; it is even, in the words of one commentator, a 'sometimes loathed term'.[42]

In fact, the two terms are not to be equated. Grey zone conflicts are those violent operations and clashes that occur below the threshold of armed conflict, as that term is defined in international humanitarian law/the law of armed conflict.[43]

[37] FG Hoffman, 'Examining Complex Forms of Conflict: Gray Zone and Hybrid Challenges' (2018) 7(4) *Prism* 31–47, at: https://bit.ly/3QD6eH6.

[38] Ibid, p 36.

[39] Ibid, p 40.

[40] Ibid.

[41] Najžer, *The Hybrid Age: International Security in the Era of Hybrid Warfare*, n 2 above 31.

[42] J Willard, 'The US and hybrid challenges, Past, present and future', ch 11 in Weissmann, Nilsson, Palmertz and Thunholm (eds), *Hybrid Warfare*, n 21 above, 157–72, at p 158.

[43] Ibid. Armed conflict was defined by the International Criminal Tribunal for the former Yugoslavia (ICTY) in 1995 as existing as a matter of international humanitarian law 'whenever there is a resort to armed force between States or protracted armed violence between governmental authorities and organized armed groups or between such groups within a State'. ICTY, *Prosecutor v Tadić*, Decision on the Defence Motion for Interlocutory Appeal on Jurisdiction (Appeals Chamber), 2 October 1995, https://bit.ly/2YR8mzd, para 70.

In contrast, there is no requirement that hybrid warfare occupy solely this space. While low-intensity armed violence is often a feature of hybrid warfare, that is not necessarily the case, and the two notions should not be confused. Russia's invasion of Ukraine in late February 2022 and everything that has happened since in that conflict assuredly put paid to that notion. Accordingly, the claim that hybrid warfare is always a form of 'low-level conflict' must be rejected.[44]

C. Asymmetric Warfare

Asymmetric warfare should also not be conflated with hybrid warfare. The RAND Corporation defines the notion in straightforward terms as 'conflicts between nations or groups that have disparate military capabilities and strategies', giving as emblematic recent examples the 9/11 attacks against the United States and the war in Afghanistan leading up to the Taliban takeover in August 2021.[45] In contrast, hybrid warfare is about the collision of nation States, albeit (in part) through the medium of proxy armed groups. The other distinguishing feature of hybrid warfare is its integration of different actors, strategies, and tactics into a more coherent whole. The reference by the International Institute for Strategic Studies, in its definition of hybrid warfare cited above, to an 'integrated campaign' echoes NATO's use of the term 'integrated design' at the Wales Summit in September 2014.[46] On this basis, hybrid warfare should be contrasted with other, more opportunistic – or even chaotic – forms of asymmetric warfare.[47]

D. Fourth Generation Warfare

Fourth generation warfare (sometimes shortened to 4GW) is a longstanding term employed by a number of military analysts. In summary, 4GW holds that three generations of warfare – linear, firepower, and manoeuvre, respectively – have been supplanted by a complex form of insurgency that thrives in the absence or collapse of the State.[48] It was first proposed by William Lind and a number of serving US military figures in 1989[49] with the concept expanded by Thomas

[44] Najžer, *The Hybrid Age: International Security in the Era of Hybrid Warfare*, n 2 above, 29.

[45] The RAND Corporation, 'Asymmetric Warfare', accessed on 16 November 2023 at: https://bit.ly/3QDBx2V.

[46] NATO, 'We will ensure that NATO is able to effectively address the specific challenges posed by hybrid warfare threats, where a wide range of overt and covert military, paramilitary, and civilian measures are employed in a highly integrated design'. 2014 Wales Summit Declaration, n 30 above, para 13.

[47] Weissmann, 'Conceptualizing and countering hybrid threats and hybrid warfare', n 27 above, p 64.

[48] Najžer, *The Hybrid Age: International Security in the Era of Hybrid Warfare*, n 2 above, p 35.

[49] WS Lind, Col K Nightengale, Capt JF Schmitt, Col JW Sutton, and Lt-Col GI Wilson, 'The Changing Face of War: Into the Fourth Generation' (1989) 73(10) *Marine Corps Gazette* 22–26.

Hammes in 2005. Hammes observed that 'superior political will when properly employed can defeat greater economic and military power'.[50]

While the notion of fourth generation warfare has been persistently criticised for the flawed analysis that underpins it,[51] Hoffman himself has acknowledged that his definition of hybrid warfare is built on the focus of 4GW on the indistinct nature of conflicts to come and 'especially the blurring of war and peace'. The use of unconventional means, notably terrorism and information, also characterises 4GW (just as it does, in part, hybrid warfare).[52]

E. Working Definitions of Hybrid Warfare and Hybrid Threats

So where does that leave the key terminology? Without wishing to add unnecessarily to the burgeoning library of definitions, it is nonetheless important to clarify the working definition of both *hybrid warfare* and *hybrid threats*, as both are central to the discussion of the applicable international level regimes that follows. The two proposed definitions are as follows.

- Hybrid warfare is the integrated deployment by one State of regular and irregular armed forces using forcible and non-forcible measures against another State. The aim is to destabilise, and potentially overthrow, the adversary's government and critically weaken its armed forces. Hybrid warfare occurs in the context of an international armed conflict between two or more States and may involve an armed attack in violation of *jus ad bellum*.
- Hybrid threats are the use by one State against another of unlawful or unfriendly forcible and non-forcible measures, but which do not amount to an armed attack or an international armed conflict. Their aim is to destabilise and potentially overthrow its government and to undermine other State institutions. Hybrid threats, which may amount in certain circumstances to the threat or use of force under international law, may include (but are not limited to) cyberattacks, intimidation, disinformation and misinformation, and economic and military pressure.

III. LAYOUT OF THE BOOK

On the basis of these two working definitions, the remainder of the book is divided among eight chapters. Chapter one addresses the branch of international

[50] TX Hammes, 'Insurgency: Modern Warfare Evolves into a Fourth Generation' (2005) 214 *Strategic Forum* Institute for National Strategic Studies, Washington DC, 1–7, at: https://bit.ly/3YKArWQ.

[51] Najžer condemns it as 'misguided', for instance. Najžer, *The Hybrid Age: International Security in the Era of Hybrid Warfare*, n 2 above, p 36.

[52] Hoffman, 'Conflict in the 21st Century: The Rise of Hybrid Wars', n 3 above, p 18.

law that governs inter-State use of force. *Jus ad bellum*, its Latin descriptor, is already a contested legal space, but hybrid warfare adds further complexity into the mix. This is due, above all, to the important role that irregular, ostensibly non-State armed groups play in hybrid warfare, a fact which can muddy the legal waters.

The chapter initially considers when hybrid warfare falls to be regulated by *jus ad bellum* rules – in particular when one State is legally responsible for the use of force against another through the use of armed violence by proxy armed groups. It then discusses when hybrid warfare will amount to an act of aggression and when it may constitute an armed attack under the 1945 Charter of the United Nations and customary international law. In this regard, Russia has certainly used hybrid warfare on multiple occasions against former satellite members of the Soviet Union that are unwilling to once more fall under its influence, most notoriously against Ukraine, beginning in March 2014,[53] but also in 2008 in its actions towards and within Georgia. The remainder of the chapter examines the use of force in self-defence in response to an armed attack, concluding with analysis of the possible use of non-forcible countermeasures (where either the use of force is not permissible or where non-forcible measures are preferred as a matter of policy).

Chapter two considers the regulation of hybrid warfare and hybrid threats under the law of law enforcement. This is the branch of international law that governs State action, particularly policing, to ensure compliance with its domestic criminal law within its sovereign jurisdiction. The first section of the chapter considers the applicable international legal rules while the second explores the use of force in addressing hybrid threats, in particular when they emanate from individuals and groups supported by another State but where the conduct does not yet amount to an armed conflict. Two case studies are presented: the situation in Donetsk oblast in Ukraine in February–April 2014 with respect to the hybrid actions of Russia, and the situation in Taiwan with respect to the hybrid actions of China since 2018. China is highly likely to use hybrid threats ever more persistently in the near and medium term, with rivalry in the South China Sea and untamed animosity across the Taiwan Straits uppermost in its strategic thought.[54]

While, despite the terminology, the legality of certain forms of hybrid *warfare* falls to be governed by the law of law enforcement, more often it is the law of armed conflict[55] that governs the acts of organs or agents of one State

[53] *Munich Security Report 2015: Collapsing Order, Reluctant Guardians?*, Munich, 2015, at: http://bitly.ws/ScAz, pp 18, 34ff. Ironically, the term for hybrid warfare in Russian, *gibridnaya voyna*, was introduced into Russian discussion in the late 2000s only after it had gained currency in the West. M. Göransson, 'Understanding Russian thinking on *gibridnaya voyna*', ch 6 in Weissmann, Nilsson, Palmertz and Thunholm (eds), *Hybrid Warfare*, n 21 above, 83–94, at p 83.

[54] See, eg, G Haciyakupoglu and N Raska, 'China's political warfare in Taiwan', ch 12 in Weissmann, Nilsson, Palmertz and Thunholm (eds), *Hybrid Warfare*, n 21 above, 173–194, at pp 184–86.

[55] This body of international law is called international humanitarian law in many circles, or, by the United States in particular, the law of war.

intervening to support an armed group operating illegally on the territory of another. Chapter three considers first when an armed conflict is deemed generally to exist under international law and how specific forms of hybrid warfare may affect the specific classification of that armed conflict. The remainder of the chapter presents and examines two case studies. The first concerns what may be considered the archetypal case of hybrid warfare – Russian intervention through non-State actors in the Donbas in Ukraine in 2014. The second discusses the legal situation between Iran and Israel as it stood in October 2023 with respect to Gaza and the actions of Hamas.

There is a close relationship between hybrid warfare and international terrorism, as Chapter four explores. As noted, in 2010, NATO defined a hybrid threat as 'one posed by any current or potential adversary, including State and non-State *and terrorists*, with the ability, whether demonstrated or likely, to simultaneously employ conventional and non-conventional means adaptively, in pursuit of their objectives' (emphasis added).[56] This intertwining of approaches would become more evident in Russia's forcible interventions in Ukraine, most notably in 2014 through Russian government support for, and direction of, the actions of the 'People's Militia' of the self-proclaimed Luhansk People's Republic and Donetsk People's Republic (DPR).

The first part of the chapter explores the multiple definitions of terrorism in international law and their application to situations of hybrid warfare through the prism of terrorist bombings. The second part of the chapter discusses the application of the principles of international counterterrorism law to the conflicts in Ukraine since 2014 in two case studies. The first concerns the shooting down over Ukraine of Malaysian Airlines flight MH17 in 2014 by fighters of the People's Militia of the DPR. The second case study concerns the sabotage of the Nord Stream pipelines in September 2022 – explosive acts which have variously been ascribed to Russian, Ukrainian, or US entities or elements. All attempts at attribution were only allegations (though of varying degrees of credibility); none had been conclusively proven at the time of writing.

A range of fundamental human rights are impacted by the conduct of hybrid warfare, including cognitive warfare. Affected rights are, in particular, the right to life; the right to freedom from torture and other ill-treatment; the right to liberty; the right to private and family life; the right to property; and the right to freedom of opinion. As Chapter five discusses, however, the application of international human rights law to any given conduct depends on fulfilling critical jurisdictional requirements – geographical and personal as well as material and temporal. Only then can human rights be used to analyse the legality of hybrid warfare and efforts to counter it. In considering the four jurisdictional

[56] NATO, 'BI-SC Input to a New NATO Capstone Concept for the Military Contribution to Countering Hybrid Threats', 25 August 2010, accessed 1 May 2023 at: https://bit.ly/3AikFX8 (link no longer working), para 7.

bases, reference is made to the positions of Russia, the United States, and China. The chapter presents and discusses two case studies involving the application of fundamental human rights to hybrid warfare: the actions of Russia in Georgia in 2008 and through to the present day, and China's burgeoning cognitive warfare against the population of Taiwan.

Disarmament law – the body of international law that addresses the elimination of weapons – is the subject of Chapter six. Disarmament law in treaties applies first and foremost to the conduct of the organs of State in their respective States Parties. But under the law of State responsibility, a State is also responsible for the conduct of a 'person or group of persons' which is 'in fact' acting on its instructions or under its direction or control in carrying out that conduct.[57] The chapter argues that the notion of the prohibited conduct of a State Party to a disarmament treaty purposively includes conduct of all private companies or other non-State actors within the jurisdiction of that State, as well as that of any non-State actor which a State supports extraterritorially. This is so, irrespective of whether that State enjoys *effective control* over the actions of that non-State actor (as that term is understood in international law).

The chapter first considers disarmament and non-proliferation of weapons of mass destruction (WMD) in the context of hybrid warfare (in particular, chemical weapons) before turning to the disarmament of conventional weapons, ordinarily defined as all weapons other than WMD.[58] Disarmament treaties adopted in 1997 and 2008, respectively, comprehensively prohibit two specific types of conventional weapons – anti-personnel mines and cluster munitions. In addition, the 2013 UN Arms Trade Treaty prohibits the export of conventional weapons either where they undermine peace and security, or where they would be used to commit or facilitate a serious violation of the law of armed conflict (international humanitarian law) or international human rights law, an act of terrorism, or transnational organised crime.[59]

Chapter seven concerns the criminal responsibility of individuals for the commission of international crimes. For, in the words of the International Military Tribunal at Nuremburg, 'Crimes against international law are committed by men, not by abstract entities, and only by punishing individuals who commit such crimes can the provisions of international law be enforced'.[60] The chapter addresses the four 'core' international crimes that may occur in the course of hybrid warfare and hybrid threats: war crimes (the most common), crimes against humanity, genocide, and aggression. A brief overview of

[57] Art 8, Draft Articles on the Responsibility of States for Internationally Wrongful Acts, International Law Commission, UN doc. A/56/10, 2001.

[58] UN Office for Disarmament Affairs (UNODA), 'Conventional Arms', undated but accessed 1 October 2023 at: https://bit.ly/3rCvzH7.

[59] Art 7, Arms Trade Treaty; adopted at New York, 2 April 2013; entered into force, 24 December 2014.

[60] *Trial of the Major War Criminals before the International Military Tribunal*, Vol I, International Tribunal, Nuremberg, 1947, p 223.

international criminal law is offered before consideration moves to the specificities of the four different crimes in turn. The description of the law is buttressed by examples of the commission of international crimes in the context of hybrid warfare wrought over the past decade.

Finally, Chapter eight looks at the responsibility of States themselves for the unlawful perpetration of hybrid warfare. As the chapter explains, not all hybrid warfare violates international law, but many of its forms of conduct certainly do. These give rise to the duty on responsible States to repair the damage and compensate for the harm they have caused, measures that are explained and explored by reference to the law of State responsibility for internationally wrongful conduct. The chapter also reiterates the differing approaches to responsibility taken by the International Court of Justice and the European Court of Human Rights for the conduct of non-State armed groups that are being supported by a foreign State and/or that operate extraterritorially but in areas under that State's control.

Annex I to the book contains an introduction to and overview of international law for non-lawyers or those who specialise in domestic law. It may be helpful to read the annex before tackling the eight substantive chapters. Annex II provides a glossary of abbreviations and key terms.

1

Hybrid Warfare and Jus ad Bellum

THE INTERPRETATION AND application of the rules of *jus ad bellum*, the branch of international law that governs inter-State use of force, are often sharply contested. Among other issues, the threshold of violence necessary to constitute an 'armed attack', which gives rise to the right of a State to use force in self-defence, is much debated; whether a non-State armed group can perpetrate such an attack when acting independently of a State, even more so. Into that contested legal space comes hybrid warfare, a notion which, as we have seen, lacks precise definition in international law. What is certain is that the nature of hybrid warfare's relationship to *jus ad bellum* is of a complex, non-linear nature.

One of the principal reasons for the intricacy of the inter-relationship is that the international legal rules on attribution of conduct to States impede the application of *jus ad bellum* norms to certain forms of hybrid warfare. In its judgment in two key contentious cases, the International Court of Justice has made clear its view that a high wall shields States from international legal responsibility for the conduct of non-State actors they support. If I, operating as an executive organ of the State, send my armed forces to launch an attack of significant character against another State without any lawful exception or excuse, my State is responsible for an act of aggression. But if I decide to support a non-State actor already struggling against my enemy with the provision of a substantial quantity of weaponry, knowing – but not directing – that they will use it to attack the armed forces of my enemy State in a similar manner, my State would not bear equivalent responsibility under international law.[1]

[1] A different legal test – one of 'overall control' – applies under the law of armed conflict to determine whether my support for a non-State armed group has brought into being an international armed conflict between my State and the State against which that armed group is fighting. International Criminal Tribunal for the former Yugoslavia (ICTY), *Prosecutor v Tadić*, Judgment (Appeals Chamber) (Case No IT-94-1-A), 15 July 1999, para 131. This test, which is further addressed in Chapter 3 of this volume, is a markedly lower threshold than is the one set for State responsibility for the unlawful acts committed by that armed group. Thus, if the non-State actor I support uses the weapons I have provided it to commit war crimes, my State generally bears no responsibility for those crimes. That is so unless I, in my authority as a State organ or agent, directed the members of that non-State actor to commit those crimes or my State 'exercised effective control over the action during which the wrong was committed'. International Court of Justice, *Case Concerning Application of the Convention on the Prevention and Punishment of the Crime of Genocide* (*Bosnia and Herzegovina v Serbia and Montenegro*), Judgment, 26 February 2007, para 406. These issues of individual and State accountability are explored in detail in Chapters 7 and 8 of this volume, respectively.

It is thus the role of irregular, ostensibly non-State forces in hybrid warfare that complicates above all else the application of *jus ad bellum* rules. In 2018, Hoffman's updated description of 'hybrid challenges', noted in the Introduction to this book, reframed hybrid warfare as the 'purposeful and tailored violent application of advanced conventional military capabilities *with irregular tactics, with terrorism and criminal activities, or combination of regular and irregular forces*, operating as part of a common design in the same battlespace' (emphasis added).[2] This new definition, he explained, adds the notion of violence to the definition 'to clarify its placement in the continuum … and to further distinguish it from activities short of violent conflict'.[3]

Notwithstanding this application of violence through the medium of irregular forces and the consequent incidence of 'violent conflict', some consider hybrid warfare to operate only in the 'grey zone'[4] below the threshold of an 'armed attack' under *jus ad bellum*. The better view is that hybrid warfare operates at several levels: above the minimum threshold for the application of the international rules governing inter-State use of force and also, in certain cases, as an armed attack. In its July 2023 Vilnius Summit Communiqué, the Heads of State and Government of the North Atlantic Treaty Organization (NATO) reiterated their collective view that 'hybrid operations against Allies could reach the level of an armed attack and could lead the Council to invoke Article 5 of the Washington Treaty'.[5] But they also made clear that in situations short of a large-scale, forcible response, the NATO Alliance would 'continue to develop comprehensive preventive and response options and stand ready to apply them to enhance resilience and deter malign actors from engaging in hybrid operations'.[6]

The remainder of this chapter is in two main parts. The first considers when hybrid warfare falls to be regulated by *jus ad bellum* rules. It begins by recalling the fundamental rule – the general prohibition on inter-State use of force – to be found in the Charter of the United Nations[7] (hereafter, the UN Charter) and which is also applicable to all States under customary international law.[8] This

[2] FG Hoffman, 'Examining Complex Forms of Conflict: Gray Zone and Hybrid Challenges' (2018) 7(4) *Prism* 31–47, at: https://bit.ly/3QD6eH6, at p 40.

[3] Ibid.

[4] A Robertson, 'What is Grey Zone confrontation and why is it important?', *The Cove*, Australian Army, 18 July 2022, at: https://bit.ly/3Zbeh0a.

[5] Vilnius Summit Communiqué, issued by NATO Heads of State and Government participating in the meeting of the North Atlantic Council in Vilnius, 11 July 2023, at: https://bit.ly/3Et8Lwg, para 64.

[6] Ibid.

[7] Art 2(4), Charter of the United Nations; adopted at San Francisco, 26 June 1945; entered into force, 24 October 1945.

[8] Principle 1, Declaration on Principles of International Law concerning Friendly Relations and Co-operation among States in accordance with the Charter of the United Nations, annexed to UN General Assembly Resolution 2625 (XXV), adopted without a vote on 24 October 1970 (hereafter, 1970 Declaration on Principles of International Law concerning Friendly Relations and Co-operation among States). See also International Court of Justice, *Case Concerning Military and Paramilitary Activities in and against Nicaragua (Nicaragua v United States)*, Judgment (Merits), 27 June 1986 [1986] ICJ Rep 14 (hereafter, ICJ Nicaragua Merits Judgment), para 188.

prohibition only applies to hybrid warfare when one State is responsible at law for the use of force against another, although this responsibility also encompasses the use of armed violence by a State's proxy forces and not merely by its regular armed forces. The chapter moves to consider in turn when hybrid warfare amounts to an act of aggression and when it may constitute an armed attack under the UN Charter and customary law. The second part of the chapter discusses the use of force in self-defence in response to such an armed attack.

The chapter concludes with a discussion of the possibility to engage in non-forcible countermeasures. This could be either when the use of force is not available according to the rules of *jus ad bellum* or when force could lawfully be employed but the exercise of non-forcible measures is preferred as a matter of policy. The examination of the law governing countermeasures considers examples where certain forms of hybrid warfare could be undertaken lawfully.

I. HYBRID WARFARE AND THE RULES OF *JUS AD BELLUM*

Jus ad bellum rules determine when a State (or a group of States, such as within a military alliance) may lawfully use force against, or on the territory of, another State or when such action violates international law. The bedrock of the law is found in the UN Charter, but the interpretation and application of the relevant rules, particularly in the jurisprudence of the International Court of Justice, are either challenged or require greater clarity.

The fundamental rule of *jus ad bellum* is the general prohibition on inter-State threat or use of force codified in Article 2(4) of the UN Charter. Aggression is 'the most serious and dangerous form of the illegal use of force' according to the UN General Assembly's 1974 definition.[9] The prohibition of aggression is a peremptory rule of international law (*jus cogens*).[10] The peremptory nature of the rule means it is a higher species of customary norm that cannot be legislated away or circumvented by the negotiation of a treaty.[11] The prevention of aggression and the bringing to an end of an aggressive war are key tasks entrusted to the UN Security Council under the UN Charter, with its powers delineated in Chapter VII of the Charter.[12]

[9] Fifth preambular paragraph to the Definition of Aggression annexed to UN General Assembly Resolution 3314 (XXIX), adopted without a vote on 14 December 1974 (hereafter, 1974 UN Definition of Aggression).

[10] International Law Commission, 'Peremptory norms of general international law (*jus cogens*)', Texts of the draft conclusions and Annex adopted by the Drafting Committee on second reading, UN doc A/CN.4/L.967, 11 May 2022, Annex, norm (a).

[11] A peremptory norm of general international law 'is a norm accepted and recognized by the international community of States as a whole as a norm from which no derogation is permitted and which can be modified only by a subsequent norm of general international law having the same character'. Draft Conclusion 2, Fifth report on peremptory norms of general international law (*jus cogens*) by Dire Tladi, Special Rapporteur, International Law Commission, UN doc A/CN.4/747, 24 January 2022.

[12] Arts 24(1) and 39–51, UN Charter.

An armed attack involves the 'most grave forms of the use of force' – the use of armed violence on a significant scale that engenders substantial physical effects on people or *matériel*.[13] As set forth in Article 51 of the UN Charter and under customary law,[14] if and when an 'armed attack' occurs against a UN Member State, that State is entitled to use force in individual self-defence. The victim State may also request the assistance of others to help it repel the unlawful use of force (ie to engage in *collective* self-defence).[15]

A. The Prohibition of Inter-State Use of Force

Article 2(4) of the UN Charter articulates the general prohibition on inter-State use of force in the following manner: 'All Members shall refrain in their international relations from the threat or use of force against the territorial integrity or political independence of any State, or in any other manner inconsistent with the Purposes of the United Nations'. Although the codification of the rule in the Charter expressly binds only UN Member States (currently numbering 193),[16] its expression in customary international law applies to all States.[17] The reference in the rule to 'international relations' excludes from its purview the suppression by the executive branch of a State of purely domestic insurgencies and rebellions.[18]

The notion of force in Article 2(4) and customary law is limited to 'armed force'. As such, it does not encompass economic pressure, including as a result of the imposition of sanctions or following a cyberattack.[19] Similarly, misinformation, disinformation, and propaganda do not ordinarily amount to a use of force.[20] In other respects, however, the notion of armed force is understood broadly. It pertains not only to kinetic force (eg bullets, bombs, missiles, or shells) but also that which causes other forms of damage or physical injury, such as is achieved through use of directed energy weapons[21] or employment of

[13] ICJ Nicaragua Merits Judgment, n 8 above, paras 191, 195.

[14] Ibid, para 194.

[15] Ibid, para 199.

[16] The list is available on the UN website at: https://bit.ly/3Lgdoxj.

[17] Art I, 1974 UN Definition of Aggression, n 9 above; ICJ Nicaragua Merits Judgment, n 8 above, para 188. This includes the four other States recognised at the time of writing by the UN Secretary-General in his capacity as depositary of more than 550 treaties: the two UN Observer States – the Holy See and Palestine; and the two 'other' States, namely the Cook Islands and Niue.

[18] These would involve non-State armed groups that are not instructed, directed, or controlled by another State and which are not otherwise under its 'effective control'.

[19] See, eg, J Crawford, *Brownlie's Principles of Public International Law*, 9th edn, Oxford University Press, Oxford, 2019, p 717; and T Ruys, 'The Meaning of "Force" and the Boundaries of the *Jus ad Bellum*: Are "Minimal" Uses of Force Excluded from UN Charter Article 2(4)?' (2014) 108(2) *American Journal of International Law* 159–210, at p 163.

[20] International Group of Experts, *Tallinn Manual 2.0 on the International Law Applicable to Cyber Operations*, Cambridge University Press, Cambridge, 2017 (hereafter, Tallinn Manual 2.0), commentary para 29 on Rule 4.

[21] Directed energy weapons include laser weapons and millimetre wave weapons.

biological, chemical, or radiological weapons.[22] A cyberattack with resultant harmful consequences in the physical domain is also to be considered a use of force.[23] But the ordinary exercise of policing powers to enforce the criminal law – law enforcement – does not amount to an inter-State use of force. That is so, even when the subject of an arrest is a foreign national, as long as the arrest and any concomitant use of force are not politically motivated.

The threat of force is also prohibited under both customary ('general') international law and in Article 2(4) of the Charter. In its ordinary articulation, the so-called Brownlie formula holds that if a State declares that it will use force in conditions in which no justification for the use of force exists, the threat of force is itself illegal.[24] This position was effectively endorsed by the International Court of Justice in its 1996 Advisory Opinion on the Threat or Use of Nuclear Weapons.[25] While the notion of a threat of force is not formally defined in international law, it is generally understood as encompassing both overtly bellicose statements against one State by a political leader of another and the illicit penetration by the combat aircraft or warships of one State into the airspace or territorial waters of another with hostile intent.[26] It is generally agreed that threats may be implicit as well as explicit,[27] but to fall within the prohibition in international law a threat must be made by a State or State agent, not a non-State actor.

Indeed, the language instituting the general prohibitions in Article 2(4) is unequivocal: it pertains to one State threatening or using force against another. This is often conducted through use of its army, navy, or air force or, in the case of a threat, its political leaders. But it is also accepted that a State may use agents to threaten or use force rather than employ its own security forces to do so. This use of 'proxies' occurs often in hybrid warfare. Thus, where a person or group acts on the instructions of, or under the direction or effective control of,

[22] Thus, for example, the attempted murder of a Russian military intelligence defector in Salisbury in the United Kingdom in March 2018 by Russian operatives using the chemical agent Novichok was an unlawful inter-State use of force. 'Salisbury Incident', Statement by the UK Prime Minister (Mrs Theresa May), in *Hansard* HC Vol 637, 14 March 2018, at: https://bit.ly/3rqxXgv.

[23] Tallinn Manual 2.0, n 20 above, Commentary para 8 on Rule 69. The Tallinn Manual further decrees that in relation to cyber operations 'neither non-destructive cyber psychological operations intended solely to undermine confidence in a government, nor a State's prohibition of e-commerce with another State designed to cause negative economic consequences, qualify as uses of force'. Tallinn Manual 2.0, Commentary para 3 on Rule 69.

[24] I Brownlie, *International Law and the Use of Force by States*, Oxford University Press, Oxford, 1963, p 364.

[25] International Court of Justice, *Legality of the Threat or Use of Nuclear Weapons*, Advisory Opinion, 8 July 1996 (hereafter, Nuclear Weapons Advisory Opinion), para 47.

[26] Brownlie, *International Law and the Use of Force by States*, n 24 above, p 148. Brownlie would seem to have considered the latter category of conduct as amounting to an actual *use* of force and not merely a threat of its use.

[27] With respect to implicit threats, see, eg, Annex VII Arbitral Tribunal, *Award in the Arbitration Regarding the Delimitation of the Maritime Boundary Between Guyana and Suriname*, 17 September 2007, paras 432–39, at: https://bit.ly/3UNdvq0.

a State[28] in threatening or using force against another State, the State prompting the forcible action engages its own responsibility for that conduct under international law.[29]

But it is also the case that a State which provides weapons to an unauthorised non-State actor operating in or against another State is engaging in a threat or use of force. In the view of the International Court of Justice, the provision of weapons or 'logistical or other support', such as training or funding, 'may be regarded as a threat or use of force' or alternatively, it may amount only to unlawful intervention in the affairs of another State.[30] Later in its judgment on the merits in the *Nicaragua* case, however, the Court clarified its views, holding that 'the arming and training of the *contras* can certainly be said to involve the threat or use of force against Nicaragua' whereas the 'mere supply of funds' to them did 'not in itself amount to a use of force'.[31] Hence, the provision of weapons or other military support to non-State armed groups in Syria in the 2010s by agents of Qatar, Saudi Arabia, Türkiye, the United Kingdom, and the United States, which occurred without the consent of the Syrian government, was therefore an unlawful threat or use of force.[32] The argument sometimes employed, that these States were engaging in the collective defence of Iraq,[33] lacks legal merit.

B. Hybrid Warfare as an Act of Aggression

Under contemporary international law, aggression is an international crime.[34] Indeed, in 1946 the International Military Tribunal deemed the initiation of a war of aggression 'the supreme international crime differing only from other war crimes in that it contains within itself the accumulated evil of the whole'.[35]

[28] Art 8, *Draft Articles on the Responsibility of States for Internationally Wrongful Acts*, International Law Commission, UN doc A/56/10, 2001 (hereafter, 2001 Draft Articles on State Responsibility).

[29] See, on the issue of State responsibility under international law, Chapter 8 of this volume.

[30] ICJ Nicaragua Merits Judgment, n 8 above, para 195.

[31] Ibid, para 228. See for a critique of this distinction: KN Trapp, *State Responsibility for International Terrorism*, Oxford University Press, Oxford, 2012, § 2.1.2.

[32] C Gray, *International Law and the Use of Force*, 4th edn, Oxford University Press, Oxford, 2018, pp 113, 114, and 115.

[33] In November 2015, then British Prime Minister David Cameron stated: 'There is a clear legal basis for military action against ISIL [Islamic State] in Syria. The legality of UK strikes against ISIL in Syria is founded on the right of self-defence as it is recognised in Article 51 of the UN Charter. The right to self-defence may be exercised individually where it is necessary to the UK's own defence, and collectively in the defence of our friends and allies'. Memorandum to the Foreign Affairs Select Committee, Prime Minister's Response to the Foreign Affairs Select Committee's Second Report of Session 2015–16: The Extension of Offensive British Military Operations to Syria', London, November 2015, at: https://bit.ly/482o1xP, p 15.

[34] Art 5(2), 1974 UN Definition of Aggression, n 9 above.

[35] *Trial of the Major War Criminals before the International Military Tribunal*, Vol 22 (International Tribunal, Nuremburg, 1948), p 427.

In 1950, in its Resolution 380 (V), which was adopted by consensus, the UN General Assembly reaffirmed that 'whatever the weapons used, any aggression, whether committed openly, *or by fomenting civil strife in the interest of a foreign Power, or otherwise*, is the gravest of all crimes and security throughout the world' (emphasis added).[36] Thus, it was already implicit that a State could act forcibly through proxy armed groups instead of its armed forces and still commit an act of aggression. But an act of aggression only concerns the *use* of force and not merely the *threat* of its use.[37]

Substantial clarity was brought to the understanding of aggression in international law in 1974 when, after years of discussion,[38] the annex to UN General Assembly Resolution 3314 (XXIX) set out the definition of aggression that exists under customary law today. The preamble to the substantive definition refers to aggression as being 'the most serious and dangerous form of the illegal use of force', clearly signalling that certain, less serious forms of unlawful use of force do not amount to aggression. That said, the precise delineation between aggression and these lesser unlawful uses of force remains unsettled.

In its Article 3, the definition gave a non-exhaustive list of seven examples of acts of aggression. The first six involve the use of force directly by the armed forces of one State against another State in some manner. But the seventh and final example is of particular salience to hybrid warfare:

> The sending by or on behalf of a State of armed bands, groups, irregulars or mercenaries, which carry out acts of armed force against another State of such gravity as to amount to the acts listed above, or its substantial involvement therein.[39]

This brings within the scope of the international legal prohibition the acts of non-State armed groups which are 'sent' by one State to perpetrate aggression against another, or where one State has 'substantial involvement' in a grave use of force against another State by a non-State armed group. This 'may be taken' to be a specific rule of customary law according to the wording of the International Court of Justice's judgment on the merits in the *Nicaragua* case.[40] Substantial involvement is unquestionably a lower standard than is the 'sending' of a group. But alternate, lesser forms of support for a non-State armed group,

[36] UN General Assembly Resolution 380 (V) ('Peace through Deeds'), adopted by consensus on 17 November 1950, para 1.

[37] Art 1, 1974 UN Definition of Aggression, n 9 above.

[38] The resolution was 'a carefully negotiated instrument that reflected current customary international law' according to the Special Working Group on the Crime of Aggression established by States Parties to the International Criminal Court (ICC). See: ICC doc ICC-ASP/6/20/Add.1, Annex II: Report of the Special Working Group on the Crime of Aggression, June 2008, para 31. See also J Klabbers, 'Intervention, Armed Intervention, Armed Attack, Threat to Peace, Act of Aggression, and Threat or Use of Force: What's the Difference?', ch 22 in M Weller (ed), *The Oxford Handbook of the Use of Force in International Law*, Oxford University Press, Oxford, 2015, 488–506, at pp 498–99.

[39] Art 3(g), 1974 UN Definition of Aggression, n 9 above.

[40] ICJ Nicaragua Merits Judgment, n 8 above, para 195.

such as 'assistance to' or 'collaboration in', which were considered prior to the passage of the 1974 resolution, were ultimately rejected by the community of States. As such, Trapp concludes, 'no form of indirect aggression made its way into the UN Definition of Aggression'.[41]

It is also specified in the UN definition that 'nothing therein', and in particular Article 3 of the definition, could 'in any way' prejudice the right to self-determination, derived from the UN Charter, of peoples 'forcibly deprived of that right' (Article 7). This concerns especially those peoples forced to live under colonial or racist regimes or other forms of foreign domination. Their right 'to struggle to that end and to seek and receive support, in accordance with the principles of the Charter' endures.[42] Hence, national liberation movements were considered to be incapable of committing the crime of aggression (as were, one must conclude, also the States that supported them).

In sum, hybrid warfare will constitute an act of aggression when one State sends any armed group to engage in an unlawful and significant use of force against another State or where it is 'substantially involved' in such conduct. That is so, unless that armed group is struggling on behalf of a people's legitimate right to self-determination against a colonial dominant, an alien State occupier, or a racist regime.[43] An act of aggression could be perpetrated on the territory of the victim State (the use of force against 'the territorial integrity' of a State), as well as against its armed forces or political leaders anywhere else (the use of force against a State's 'political independence', in the wording of paragraph 4 of Article 2 of the UN Charter). As the UN Definition of Aggression makes explicit, 'Aggression gives rise to international responsibility'.[44]

C. Hybrid Warfare as an Armed Attack

Article 51 codifies the customary rule whereby a State is entitled to resort to armed force in response to an armed attack that is occurring.[45] Reference to an 'armed attack' appears only once in the UN Charter, but this in no way minimises the significance of the concept. It is not incidental that the provision uses

[41] Trapp, *State Responsibility for International Terrorism*, n 31 above, p 27.

[42] Art 7, 1974 UN Definition of Aggression, n 9 above.

[43] Promoting respect for the self-determination of peoples is a purpose of the United Nations according to the UN Charter (Arts 1(2) and 55) and customary international law. In the 1970 Declaration on Principles of International Law concerning Friendly Relations and Co-operation among States, it is stipulated under the 'principle of equal rights and self-determination of peoples' that: 'By virtue of the principle of equal rights and self-determination of peoples enshrined in the Charter of the United Nations, all peoples have the right freely to determine, without external interference, their political status and to pursue their economic, social and cultural development, and every State has the duty to respect this right in accordance with the provisions of the Charter'.

[44] Art 5(2), 1974 UN Definition of Aggression, n 9 above. See further Chapter 8 of this volume on this issue.

[45] ICJ Nicaragua Merits Judgment, n 8 above, para 176.

a different terminology not only from that of 'aggression' but also from the general prohibition on inter-State 'use of force'.

(i) Defining 'Armed Attack'

An armed attack is certainly a serious violation of that prohibition. What is not settled, however, is the precise threshold at which an armed attack may be deemed to have been perpetrated.[46] In this regard, the claim by the International Court of Justice in its judgment on the merits in the *Nicaragua* case that, already in the 1980s, 'general agreement' existed on 'the nature of the acts which can be treated as constituting armed attacks' does not correspond to legal reality, even today.[47]

The Court confirmed that an armed attack was limited to 'the most grave forms of the use of force' and was thus to be distinguished from other 'less grave' forms. That said, the threshold between a use of force *simpliciter* and a use of force equating to an armed attack may still be quite low. Famously, in its 2003 judgment on the merits in the *Oil Platforms* case, the Court would 'not exclude' the possibility that the mining of 'a single military vessel' might be sufficient to 'bring into play' the inherent right of self-defence.[48] But it also stated that even if it were true that the mine that hit the US-flagged ship and the alleged firing on US helicopters from Iranian gunboats at issue in the case were attributable to Iran, it did not believe this would have constituted an armed attack on the United States of the kind it had qualified as a 'most grave' form of the use of force in *Nicaragua*.[49]

The notions of 'aggression' and 'armed attack' are not synonyms but they are certainly closely related. In this regard, the authentic French version of the UN Charter uses the term '*agression armée*' in Article 51.[50] Aggression is thus the broader of the two terms, meaning that not every act of aggression is to be considered an armed attack.[51] The 1947 Rio Treaty, for instance, referred to the situation where 'any American State should be affected by an aggression, which is not an armed attack'.[52] In a declaration cited by the International Court of Justice in the *Nicaragua* case, El Salvador spoke of being 'the victims of aggression and armed attack from Nicaragua'.[53]

[46] Y Dinstein, *War, Aggression and Self-defence*, 6th edn, Cambridge University Press, Cambridge, 2017, para 548.

[47] ICJ Nicaragua Merits Judgment, n 8 above, para 195.

[48] International Court of Justice, *Case Concerning Oil Platforms* (*Iran v United States*), Judgment (Merits), 6 November 2003 (hereafter ICJ Oil Platforms Judgment), para 72.

[49] Ibid, para 64.

[50] A certified copy of the UN Charter in all UN languages is available at: http://bit.ly/30HXCBF.

[51] Independent International Fact-Finding Mission on the Conflict in Georgia, Report, September 2009, Vol II, available at: https://bit.ly/3hI6Nek, p 244.

[52] Art 6, Inter-American Treaty of Reciprocal Assistance; signed at Rio de Janeiro, 2 September 1947; entered into force, 3 December 1948.

[53] ICJ Nicaragua Merits Judgment, n 8 above, para 132.

In reaffirming that an armed attack is to be more narrowly construed than aggression,[54] in 2009 the Independent International Fact-Finding Mission on the Conflict in Georgia cited an earlier edition of Yoram Dinstein's *War, Aggression and Self-defence*. In the last edition of this leading work (the sixth), Dinstein affirmed that the two concepts 'may at least partly coincide'.[55] In their legal commentary of Article 51 of the UN Charter, Randelzhofer and Nolte concur that an armed attack is a narrower concept than is aggression, but aver that 'the difference between the two is so small that it is overlooked'.[56] One possible substantive distinction is that a disproportionate use of force in response to an armed attack may be an act of aggression, but it would not be an armed attack.[57] Another, more controversial distinction is that an armed attack may be perpetrated by a non-State actor operating independently of any State (an issue considered below), but an act of aggression demands the responsibility of a State where its own armed forces are not engaged. As Dinstein acknowledged, though, this would serve to broaden, not narrow, the notion of an armed attack.[58]

(ii) An Armed Attack by a Non-State Actor

It is settled law that the level of violence corresponding to an armed attack against a State may be effected by a non-State actor, as long as that non-State actor has been 'sent' for this purpose by a State. Thus, in its judgment in *Nicaragua*, the International Court of Justice declared that 'it may be considered to be agreed' that an armed attack pertains not only to action by regular armed forces across an international border, but also the sending by a State of armed groups, including mercenaries, to 'carry out acts of armed force against another State of such gravity' as to amount to an armed attack conducted by regular forces. This element of the provision,[59] which as noted above comes from the 1974 UN Definition of Aggression, has been taken by the Court not only to reflect customary international law with respect to aggression but also to delineate one of the possible contours of an armed attack.

[54] Almost alone among States, the United States has 'long taken the position that the inherent right of self-defense potentially applies against any illegal use of force'. See US Department of Defense, *Department of Defense Law of War Manual*, June 2015 (Updated December 2016), Washington DC, 2016, §1.11.5.2. It thus believes that the notion of aggression has a higher threshold than does an armed attack.

[55] Dinstein, *War, Aggression and Self-defence*, 6th edn, n 46 above, para 549.

[56] A Randelzhofer and G Nolte, 'Article 51' in B Simma et al (eds), *The Charter of the United Nations: A Commentary*, Oxford Commentaries on International Law, 3rd edn (Vol II), Oxford University Press, Oxford, 2012, p 1408.

[57] S Casey-Maslen, *Jus ad Bellum*, Hart Publishing, Oxford, 2020, p 61.

[58] Dinstein, *War, Aggression and Self-defence*, 6th edn, n 46 above, para 548.

[59] Notably, the Court did not refer also to a State's 'substantial involvement' in a grave use of force by a non-State actor, indicating another possible area of clear blue water between aggression and armed attack.

The Court thus considered that, similarly in customary law,

> the prohibition of armed attacks may apply to the sending by a State of armed bands to the territory of another State, if such an operation, because of its scale and effects, would have been classified as an armed attack rather than as a mere frontier incident had it been carried out by regular armed forces.[60]

The notion of 'sending' of a group has been described as 'coming close' to a relationship whereby the group is a 'de facto' State organ.[61] In contrast, the Court has expressly rejected the suggestion that the concept also extended to assistance to armed non-State actors manifested by the provision of weapons or logistical or other support.[62] *A fortiori*, therefore, where a non-State armed group acts independently of a State it may not, in the view of the Court, perpetrate an armed attack. Despite the Court's holding, this is perhaps the single most contested issue in *jus ad bellum* today.

In its *Palestinian Wall* Advisory Opinion in 2004, the International Court of Justice declared: 'Article 51 of the Charter *thus* recognizes the existence of an inherent right of self-defence in the case of armed attack by one State against another State' (emphasis added).[63] While this wording can be read in contrasting manners, the Court's implicit position – and that of general international law – was that only a State could perpetrate an armed attack. This is certainly how Judge Simma interpreted the affirmation of the Court.[64] Many commentators have criticised the Court's stance on this critical issue. Trapp, for example, has called starkly for the Court's reading of Article 51 to 'be laid to rest'.[65] In more nuanced opposition, Ruys argues that 'exceptionally' and in the absence of State imputability, attacks by non-State actors may qualify as 'armed attacks' in the legal sense and give rise to the right to use force in self-defence.[66]

Al-Qaeda was not operating under the direction or instruction of Afghanistan and it was not under the effective control of the Taliban government when it launched the attacks on 11 September 2001. As a consequence, several authorities consider that preambular references to the right of self-defence in UN Security Council Resolutions 1368 and 1373 constitute recognition that an armed attack under Article 51 of the UN Charter may be perpetrated by other entities than

[60] ICJ Nicaragua Merits Judgment, n 8 above, para 195.

[61] Randelzhofer and Nolte, 'Article 51', n 56 above, p 1415.

[62] ICJ Nicaragua Merits Judgment, n 8 above, para 195.

[63] International Court of Justice, *Legal Consequences of the Construction of a Wall in the Occupied Palestinian Territory*, Advisory Opinion, 9 July 2004, para 139.

[64] International Court of Justice, *Case Concerning Armed Activities on the Territory of the Congo* (*Democratic Republic of Congo v Uganda*), Judgment, 19 December 2005, Separate Opinion of Bruno Simma, para 11.

[65] Trapp, *State Responsibility for International Terrorism*, n 31 above, p 59.

[66] T Ruys, *'Armed Attack' and Article 51 of the UN Charter: Evolutions in Customary Law and Practice*, Cambridge Studies in International and Comparative Law, Series No 74, Cambridge University Press, Cambridge, 2010, p 531. Ruys sets out a long and restrictive set of criteria for this exceptional situation.

a State.[67] In this regard, in his separate opinion to the Court's judgment in the *Armed Activities* contentious case in 2005, Judge Simma declared that: 'Security Council resolutions 1368 (2001) and 1373 (2001) cannot but be read as affirmations of the view that large-scale attacks by non-State actors can qualify as "armed attacks" within the meaning of Article 51'.[68] That claim remains subject to contestation. First and foremost, it must be recalled that the Security Council with its 15 members does not create customary law for all 197 States; only general practice backed by legal opinion can do that. Second, the reference to the right of self-defence in the two resolutions cited was only contained in a preambular paragraph not an operative paragraph, lowering its normative significance.[69] Third, it was uncertain at the time precisely who had attacked the United States, let alone whether it was perpetrated by a non-State actor acting alone.[70] Moreover, the impact of the attacks was very significant, giving rise to great sympathy among the international community of States and perhaps a lesser attention to legal detail than would otherwise have been the case.

Hence, no instant change of customary rules governing self-defence occurred in the aftermath of the 9/11 attacks, despite occasional claims to the contrary.[71] Nevertheless, subsequently a number of leading military powers have sought to bypass the apparent dictates of international law, including in the aggression perpetrated by the United States against Iraq in 2003. This has led, according to Tams, to a situation where States have been 'pressured' into admitting other, non-written, exceptions to Article 2(4) of the UN Charter.[72] This, though,

[67] See, eg, JD Ohlin, 'The Unwilling and Unable Test for Extraterritorial Defensive Force', ch 4 in C Kreß and R Lawless (eds), *Necessity and Proportionality in International Peace and Security Law*, Lieber Studies Vol 5, Oxford University Press, New York, 2021, 113–30, at p 114; Dinstein, *War, Aggression and Self-defence*, 6th edn, n 46 above, para 647. See also K Trapp, 'Can Non-state Actors Mount an Armed Attack?', ch 30 in Weller (ed), *The Oxford Handbook of the Use of Force in International Law*, n 38 above, 679–96, at p 690.

[68] International Court of Justice, *Case Concerning Armed Activities on the Territory of the Congo (Democratic Republic of Congo v Uganda)*, Judgment, 19 December 2005, Separate Opinion of Bruno Simma, para 11.

[69] Ruys' description of the inclusion of a reference to the right of self-defence in the two resolutions as 'remarkable' thus overeggs the significance. Ruys, *'Armed Attack' and Article 51 of the UN Charter: Evolutions in Customary Law and Practice*, p 530.

[70] The significance of the attacks could legitimately have militated against such a reality in the minds of many diplomats at the time.

[71] M Byers, 'The Intervention in Afghanistan – 2001', ch 48 in Ruys and Corten (eds), *The Use of Force in International Law: A Case-Based Approach*, 1st edn, 625–38, at p 631. Ruys cites in this regard Langille's 2003 piece: B Langille, 'It's "instant custom": how the Bush doctrine became law after the terrorist attacks of September 11, 2001' (2003) 26 *Boston College International and Comparative Law Review* 145–56, at: https://bit.ly/489HaOq. In fact, Langille was arguing that the Bush doctrine, which equated harbouring terrorists with terrorism itself, was not custom and not a change in the rules governing use of force per se. The element of preventive use of force under the so-called Bush doctrine has been widely discredited following the aggression against Iraq and is certainly not reflective of international law. See, eg, on the details of the Bush doctrine: 'The Bush Doctrine', *Frontpagemagazine.com*, 7 October 2002 at: https://bit.ly/3sH7xLb.

[72] CJ Tams, 'Light Treatment of a Complex Problem: The Law of Self-Defence in the Wall Case' (2006) 16(5) *The European Journal of International Law* 963–78, https://bit.ly/40MtTGs.

implies that when certain States cannot do what they want to do legally, they must be permitted either to change the rules of their own accord or simply to ignore them. In 2001, it was always open to the United States to secure due authorisation to use force against al-Qaeda in Afghanistan from the Security Council – authorisation it would undoubtedly have received had it sought it. The world's most powerful nation, however, decided on a different path.

Dinstein argues that action by foreign States in Syria amounts to State practice that 'prominently upholds' the 'unable or unwilling' test for forcible action in self-defence against non-State actors operating on the territory of another State.[73] But as two other leading publicists conclude, 'the preferable view still seems to be that attacks by organized armed groups need to be attributed to a State in order to enable the affected State to exercise its right of self-defence'.[74] This does mean that some forms of hybrid warfare involving irregular non-State actors will not give rise to the right to use force in self-defence. Nor does it mean that the victim State is either powerless or deprived of the means to protect itself. Domestically, State sovereignty means the right to pursue law enforcement action (consonant with the principles of the law of law enforcement and international human rights law). Effective law enforcement by the relevant US agencies, for instance, would have prevented the 9/11 attacks, none of which was launched from outside US territory.[75] On the international plane, it is still open to a victim State to: pursue other political, diplomatic, and economic measures; have recourse to the UN Security Council seeking an authorisation to use force; undertake law enforcement measures that do not breach Article 2(4) of the UN Charter; and apply targeted countermeasures against a responsible State. The choice of response to international terrorism is not a binary one between massive use of force against another State and/or a non-State armed group and no possibility to use any forcible measures at all.

II. RESPONSES TO HYBRID WARFARE UNDER *JUS AD BELLUM*

Even if one were to admit that international law has changed so markedly as to accept that an armed attack may be perpetrated by a non-State actor operating independently of any State, the question arises as to where and against whom the resultant right to use force applies. Would it, for example, justify forcible action against a government that did not support a non-State armed group present on its territory? Would a massive attack such as the one initiated by the United States against the Taliban government in Afghanistan be lawful?

[73] Dinstein, *War, Aggression and Self-defence*, 6th edn, n 46 above, para 768.

[74] Randelzhofer and Nolte, 'Article 51', n 56 above, p 1417.

[75] As the Final Report of the 9/11 Commission recalls, the director of the Central Intelligence Agency stated in the summer of 2001 that 'the system was blinking red'. See The 9/11 Commission Report, at: https://bit.ly/3LbEJRt, esp pp 259–66. See further C Whipple, 'What the CIA knew before 9/11: New details', *Politico*, 13 November 2015, at: https://bit.ly/485XKhQ.

In any event, all forcible action in lawful self-defence is subject to two, cumulative principles of international law *ad bellum*: necessity and proportionality. The following section describes their application and interpretation under international law.

A. Hybrid Warfare and the Use of Force in Self-defence

Under customary law, even if a State has been the victim of an armed attack and therefore is entitled to exercise its right of self-defence, the use of force must be necessary in the circumstances and the force actually used must observe the principle of proportionality *ad bellum*. This was acknowledged by both parties to the *Nicaragua* case in their pleadings before the International Court of Justice and endorsed by the Court itself in its judgment.[76] The Court reiterated these twin conditions in its Advisory Opinion on the Legality of the Threat or Use of Nuclear Weapons,[77] and again in its later judgment in the contentious *Oil Platforms* case.[78] The conditions apply to the exercise of both individual and collective self-defence.[79]

(i) Necessity for the Use of Force in Self-Defence

The principle of necessity in relation to self-defence dictates that force be required in the circumstances 'because no practicable alternative means of redress are within reach'.[80] Thus, non-forceful measures, such as diplomacy, economic sanctions, and law enforcement, must all be insufficient to address the situation.[81] Some argue that the attack must be 'ongoing' in order to justify the use of force in self-defence.[82] If that were true, this could be taken to discount any right to attack Afghanistan in the aftermath of 9/11. In fact, what necessity does is to signify that the time-lag between the armed attack and the exercise of self-defence in response must not be an undue one.[83] Relevant factors include the temporal proximity between the armed attack and the forcible response; the period needed to identify the attacker (with certainty); and the time required to

[76] ICJ Nicaragua Merits Judgment, n 8 above, para 194.
[77] ICJ Nuclear Weapons Advisory Opinion, n 25 above, para 41.
[78] ICJ Oil Platforms Merits Judgment, n 48 above, para 74.
[79] ICJ Nicaragua Merits Judgment, n 8 above, para 195.
[80] Dinstein, *War, Aggression and Self-defence*, 6th edn, n 46 above, para 656, citing R Ago, 'Addendum to the Eighth Report on State Responsibility', *Yearbook of the International Law Commission 1980*, Vol II, Pt 1, p 69, para 120.
[81] Tallinn Manual 2.0, n 20 above, commentary para 2 on Rule 72.
[82] Randelzhofer and Nolte, 'Article 51', n 56 above, p 1420.
[83] Dinstein uses these words in relation to his discerned principle of 'immediacy' but the temporal issue is better considered as an element of necessity. Dinstein, *War, Aggression and Self-defence*, 6th edn, n 46 above, para 659. See C Kreß, 'The International Court of Justice and the "Principle of Non-Use of Force"' in Weller (ed), *The Oxford Handbook of the Use of Force in International Law*, n 38 above, 561–604, at p 587.

prepare a forcible response.[84] Moreover, as the soft law document, the *Tallinn Manual on the International Law Applicable to Cyber Operations*, observes specifically with respect to cyber operations, the fact that a cyber armed attack has occurred or is occurring may not be apparent for some time.[85]

Attribution has two aspects. The first is the need to identify precisely and reliably the author of a use of force. The second is whether an attack can be attributed to a State under the law governing State responsibility. In their commentary on Article 51 of the UN Charter, Randelzhofer and Nolte discuss attribution only in the context of cyber operations.[86] But there are broader issues to consider, as the attacks by al-Qaeda on the United States on 11 September 2001 clearly demonstrated. On 7 October 2001, Ambassador John D Negroponte, the US Permanent Representative to the United Nations in New York, wrote a letter to the President of the UN Security Council in which he stated that the US Government had obtained 'clear and compelling information' that al-Qaeda, 'which is supported by the Taliban regime in Afghanistan', had 'a central role in the attacks'.[87] Resolution 1373 had been passed by the Council more than a week prior to that letter being sent.

Dinstein defines as an element of the principle of necessity that a State invoking the right of self-defence (the victim State) must 'establish in a definite manner' that an armed attack was launched by a particular State against which it is responding.[88] In its judgment in the *Oil Platforms* case, the International Court of Justice held that the attack must have been 'aimed specifically' at the victim State.[89] Accordingly, the burden of proof on the State alleging it is acting in self-defence is exceptionally high. In fact, where inter-State force is concerned, the international rule of law should demand certainty and not only a reasonable suspicion, much less a claim pressed ardently by the victim State.

UN Security Council Resolution 1530 is a salutary lesson in this regard. The resolution, which was adopted within hours of the Madrid train bombings on 11 March 2004, unequivocally attributed responsibility for the bombings that killed 193 people and injured more than 2,000 others to the non-State armed group, ETA.[90] It later emerged, though, that this was a case of mistaken identity and that in fact a group with links to al-Qaeda was responsible for the atrocity.[91]

[84] Tallinn Manual 2.0, n 20 above, commentary para 12 on Rule 73.

[85] Ibid, commentary para 14 on Rule 73.

[86] Randelzhofer and Nolte, 'Article 51', n 56 above, p 1420.

[87] Letter to the President of the UN Security Council from John D Negroponte, US Permanent Representative to the United Nations in New York, UN doc S/2001/946, 7 October 2001, p 1.

[88] Dinstein, *War, Aggression and Self-defence*, 6th edn, n 46 above, para 654.

[89] ICJ Oil Platforms Merits Judgment, n 48 above, para 64.

[90] UN Security Council Resolution 1530, adopted by unanimous vote in favour on 11 March 2004. ETA – Euskadi Ta Askatasuna (Basque Homeland and Liberty) – was the Basque separatist group active in Spain between 1959 and 2018.

[91] See on this issue, eg, T O'Donnell, 'Naming and Shaming: The Sorry Tale of Security Council Resolution 1530 (2004)' (November 2006) 17(5) *European Journal of International Law* 945–68.

More infamously, the United States declared that without doubt the Iraqi regime had produced and stockpiled weapons of mass destruction prior to its invasion of Iraq in March 2003 and that the United States *knew* where these weapons were – claims that would prove to be false. US Secretary of State, Colin Powell, told the UN Security Council – and the whole world – that

> the facts and Iraq's behaviour show that Saddam Hussein and his regime are concealing their efforts to produce more weapons of mass destruction … [E]very statement I make today is backed up by sources, solid sources. These are not assertions. What we're giving you are facts and conclusions based on solid intelligence.[92]

Given the risk of the loss of thousands and even hundreds of thousands of lives, the standard of evidence justifying the use of force against another State should therefore be an objective one of *beyond reasonable doubt*.[93]

(ii) Proportionality in the Use of Force in Self-Defence

Proportionality in the use of force in self-defence means that the force actually employed must be limited to force of such nature and extent as to repel the threat – to drive out forces engaged in a belligerent occupation of sovereign territory, or to cause an attack on territory and/or an aerial bombardment to cease. This means that regime change in the attacking State is almost invariably an unlawful objective for the use of force in self-defence, as is the annihilation of the enemy's armed forces. Purely retaliatory or punitive actions are also unlawful.[94]

According to Ago, 'what matters in this respect is the result to be achieved by the "defensive action", and not the forms, substance and strength of the action itself'.[95] Hence, when the use of force is necessary in self-defence, such force as is reasonably necessary to halt and repel the attack will not be disproportionate.[96] The position of the United States is that force may be used in self-defence, 'but only to the extent that it is required to repel the armed attack and to restore the security of the party attacked'.[97] Or, as the Independent International Fact-Finding

[92] Remarks by US Secretary of State Colin Powell, UN Security Council, New York, 5 February 2003, at: https://bit.ly/3LCN1Cf. Secretary of State Powell later declared: 'I, of course, regret the UN speech that I gave, which became the prominent presentation of our case. But we thought it was correct at the time. The President thought it was correct. Congress thought it was correct. … Of course I regret that a lot of it turned out be wrong'. Television interview with Jon Stewart, *The Daily Show*, 13 June 2012, available in certain jurisdictions at: https://bit.ly/489tdje.

[93] In the *Oil Platforms* case, the International Court of Justice rejected as insufficient the evidence supplied by the United States that the mine that hit the USS *Samuel B. Roberts* was Iranian, ruling that it was 'highly suggestive, but not conclusive'. ICJ Oil Platforms Merits Judgment, n 48 above, para 71.

[94] A Randelzhofer, 'Article 51' in B Simma et al (eds), *The Charter of the United Nations: A Commentary*, 2nd edn (Vol I), Oxford University Press, Oxford, 2002, para 42.

[95] Ago, 'Addendum to the Eighth Report on State Responsibility', n 80 above, p 69, para 121.

[96] Gray, *International Law and the Use of Force*, 4th edn, n 32 above, p 159.

[97] US Department of Defense, *Department of Defense Law of War Manual*, December 2016, § 1.11.1.2.

Mission on the Conflict in Georgia framed it, a 'reaction is proportionate if there is a reasonable relationship between the measures employed and the objective, the only permissible objective being the repulsion of the armed attack'.[98]

The principle of proportionality thus limits the 'scale, scope, duration, and intensity of the defensive response' to that required to end the situation which has given rise to the right to act in self-defence.[99] This may require use of 'considerably more force than was used by the attack itself'.[100] That said, in its judgment in the *Oil Platforms* case, the International Court of Justice found that Operation Praying Mantis, a response by the United States to an alleged Iranian armed attack, would have been found to be disproportionate (had that issue been formally adjudicated by the court). This was on the basis that it involved, among other things, the destruction of two Iranian frigates and a number of other naval vessels and aircraft, all conducted in response to the mining of a single US warship, which was severely damaged but not sunk, and which occurred without loss of life.[101]

But when the target is a non-State armed group, particularly one spread out over numerous territories, what is a proportionate forcible response? May all these territories be attacked if the territorial States are unable to ensure their members' neutralisation or expulsion or agree to a demand for their extradition? What if extradition is blocked by the international rule of *non-refoulement*? Furthermore, what is the recourse for the territorial State where a mistake is made as to attribution? In 1998, following the al-Qaeda bomb attacks on the US embassies in Dar es Salaam and Nairobi, the United States launched Operation Infinite Reach, bombing training camps in Afghanistan as well as a pharmaceutical plant at Al-Shifa in Sudan, claiming that it was an al-Qaeda-supported chemical weapons factory. The attack on the Sudanese plant was widely condemned by the international community[102] as it appeared to be – just as the Government of Sudan declared it was at the time – a civilian pharmaceutical plant.[103]

B. Hybrid Warfare and Countermeasures

Where force is used against a State in contravention of Article 2(4) of the UN Charter and customary law, but does not, in its significance, also amount to

[98] Independent International Fact-Finding Mission on the Conflict in Georgia, Report, Vol II, p 249: https://bit.ly/3hI6Nek.

[99] Tallinn Manual 2.0, n 20 above, commentary para 5 on Rule 72.

[100] Randelzhofer and Nolte, 'Article 51', n 56 above, p 1426. See similarly Tallinn Manual 2.0, n 20 above, commentary para 5 on Rule 72.

[101] ICJ Oil Platforms Merits Judgment, n 48 above, para 77.

[102] Trapp, *State Responsibility for International Terrorism*, n 31 above, p 52.

[103] See, eg, J Copelyn and J Sassoon, 'The US and Sudan: Two acts of terror, but only one act of compensation', Op-Ed, *The Daily Maverick*, 15 November 2020, at: https://bit.ly/3EwCWmk.

an armed attack, alternative responses to the use of force must be applied.[104] Possible responses include countermeasures, which are non-forcible measures taken by one State against another to stop or repair a breach of international law.[105] They are, as one international lawyer has noted, 'an important tool for States that are victims of violations of international law'.[106]

Ordinarily classed as illegal acts, countermeasures may be lawful if conducted not to punish the commission of a prior internationally wrongful act, but rather with a view to bringing the unlawful conduct to an end and/or in order to secure reparation for its consequences.[107] They may be of a military (but not forcible) nature as well as a non-military nature. But the key restraint, which is of course especially relevant to hybrid warfare, is that, as a matter of law, countermeasures only exist between States, not between a State and a non-State armed group. Naturally, the UN Security Council can impose sanctions on non-State actors, as it has done many times in its history.[108]

Ordinarily, countermeasures are acts that would be violative of international law.[109] But when the measures taken are in accord with a set of conditions, they constitute a lawful form of 'self-help'.[110] Reprisals used to be considered under international law as a forcible or non-forcible form of self-help, but the term is no longer widely employed in this manner. In modern parlance, reprisals (or 'belligerent reprisals', as they often described) are generally associated with violent action during and in connection with an ongoing armed conflict. Belligerent reprisals involve acts that would ordinarily be unlawful – indeed they would typically amount to war crimes – but which may exceptionally be licit as a proportionate response to a prior and serious violation of the law of armed conflict. That is so when they are conducted *primarily* with a view to returning the enemy to compliance with

[104] ICJ Oil Platforms Merits Judgment, n 48 above, Separate Opinion of Judge Simma; and see TD Gill, 'The Forcible Protection, Affirmation and Exercise of Rights by States under Contemporary International Law' (1992) XXIII *Netherlands Yearbook of International Law* 105–73.

[105] Art 22, 2001 Draft Articles on State Responsibility, n 28 above.

[106] C Krass, 'Implementing Integrated Deterrence in the Cyber Domain: The Role of Lawyers', Blog post, *Articles of War*, Lieber Institute for Law & Warfare at West Point, United States, 18 April 2023, at: https://bit.ly/44nloVa.

[107] Commentary to Chapter II (Countermeasures), 2001 Draft Articles on State Responsibility, n 28 above, para 1. Countermeasures are therefore to be distinguished from sanctions on the basis that the latter have a punitive and 'exemplary' character. E Zoller, *Peacetime Unilateral Remedies: An Analysis of Countermeasures*, Transnational Publishers, New York, 1984, 106.

[108] See, eg, the Security Council Committee pursuant to Resolutions 1267 (1999), 1989 (2011), and 2253 (2015) concerning Islamic State (ISIL, Da'esh), al-Qaeda, and associated individuals, groups, undertakings and entities.

[109] Countermeasures must be distinguished from *retorsion*, which is 'unfriendly' conduct that does not violate an international obligation binding the State engaging in it, even though the conduct may be a response to an internationally wrongful act. Commentary to Chapter II (Countermeasures), 2001 Draft Articles on State Responsibility, n 28 above, para 3. That the measures taken do not contravene international law is the distinguishing feature of acts of retorsion. Examples of acts of retorsion are the prohibition of or limitations upon normal diplomatic relations; embargoes of various kinds; and the withdrawal of voluntary aid programmes.

[110] Crawford, *Brownlie's Principles of Public International Law*, 9th edn, n 19 above, 572.

that body of international law.[111] Belligerent reprisals are prohibited against a wide range of targets according to general international law (in particular, military or civilian detainees) and law-of-armed-conflict treaty provisions.

(i) The form and Legality of Countermeasures

Critical in the lawful exercise of countermeasures is the due assessment of a prior breach of international law.[112] In practice, this is likely to be a subjective determination by the Executive branch of a State, whereas under international law it would be adjudged objectively before a competent court or tribunal. In the *Air Services Agreement* case, for instance, the Arbitral Tribunal held that France was incorrect in determining that the United States had violated their mutual agreement and therefore was unentitled under international law to take countermeasures.[113]

As noted, countermeasures may not involve the threat or use of force in violation of Article 2(4) of the UN Charter.[114] In its judgment on the merits in the *Nicaragua* case in 1986, the International Court of Justice thus clarified that: 'While an armed attack would give rise to an entitlement to collective self-defence, a use of force of a lesser degree of gravity cannot … produce any entitlement to take collective countermeasures involving the use of force'.[115] This categorical position was reflected in 2001 in the International Law Commission's Draft Articles on State Responsibility.[116]

Four basic conditions for the lawful exercise of non-forcible countermeasures were set down by the Court in its 1997 judgment in the *Gabčikovo-Nagymaros Project* case:

- The measure(s) must be taken in response to a previous internationally wrongful act of another State.[117]
- The measure(s) must be directed against that State.[118]

[111] The International Committee of the Red Cross (ICRC), in its treatment of the customary international humanitarian law governing reprisals, describes a belligerent reprisal as consisting of 'an action that would otherwise be unlawful but that in exceptional cases is considered lawful under international law when used as an enforcement measure in reaction to unlawful acts of an adversary'. ICRC Customary International Humanitarian Law (IHL) Rule 145: 'Reprisals', at: https://bit.ly/2OUWdae.

[112] ND White and A Abass, 'Countermeasures and Sanctions', ch 18 in MD Evans (ed), *International Law*, 4th edn, Oxford University Press, Oxford, 2014, 537–62, at p 541.

[113] *Air Service Agreement of 27 March 1946 between the United States of America and France*, Arbitral Award, 9 December 1978, 446–47: https://bit.ly/3I2T1BZ.

[114] Crawford, *Brownlie's Principles of Public International Law*, 9th edn, n 19 above, p 573. Action that falls below a de minimis threshold or which is taken for a legitimate law enforcement purpose will not amount to a prohibited use of force.

[115] ICJ Nicaragua Merits Judgment, n 8 above, para 249. See further on this issue para 211 of the judgment.

[116] Art 50(1)(a), 2001 Draft Articles on State Responsibility, n 28 above.

[117] International Court of Justice, *Case Concerning the Gabčikovo-Nagymaros Project (Hungary/Slovakia)*, Judgment (Merits), 25 September 1997 (hereafter, ICJ Gabčikovo-Nagymaros Project Judgment), para 83. See similarly Art 49, 2001 Draft Articles on State Responsibility, n 28 above.

[118] ICJ Gabčikovo-Nagymaros Project Judgment, n 117 above, para 83.

- The injured State must have called upon the culpable State to discontinue its wrongful conduct and/or to make reparation for it.[119]
- The effects of a countermeasure must be 'commensurate'[120] with the injury suffered, 'taking account of the rights in question'.[121]

It is thus critical to bear in mind that countermeasures apply to another State and not to an armed group. Accordingly, a State that is targeted with countermeasures must have been responsible under international law for the prior violation.[122] As such, the independent conduct of a non-State armed group will not give rise to the possibility of countermeasures, even if that conduct involves the breach of a *jus cogens* norm.[123]

In addition, if the victim of a cyberattack is a private company, the right to take countermeasures vests in the relevant injured State or States. Thus, when Sony was the victim of malicious cyber operations in 2014 that were allegedly conducted by, or attributable to, North Korea, Sony was not entitled under international law to 'hack back' as a countermeasure. Instead, the right was reserved to the United States, to the extent that the cyberattack could be considered a violation of its sovereignty.[124]

Further conditions for the lawful exercise of countermeasures were identified by the International Law Commission in its 2001 Draft Articles on State Responsibility:

- The injured State must notify the responsible State of any decision to take countermeasures, and offer to negotiate with that State.[125]
- The countermeasures may not breach obligations for the protection of fundamental human rights, obligations of a humanitarian character

[119] Ibid, para 84.

[120] In its judgment in the *Nicaragua* case, the Court had used the term 'proportionate'. ICJ Nicaragua Merits Judgment, n 8 above, para 249. See similarly Art 51, 2001 Draft Articles on State Responsibility, n 28 above.

[121] ICJ Gabčikovo-Nagymaros Project Judgment, n 117 above, para 85. See similarly Art 52, 2001 Draft Articles on State Responsibility, n 28 above.

[122] Tallinn Manual 2.0, n 20 above, commentary para 7 on Rule 20.

[123] Whether any State is entitled to take countermeasures in respect of the breach of an obligation *erga omnes* – that is to say, one that is of interest to the community of States as a whole as a peremptory norm of international law – is not settled. In the words of James Crawford, the Special Rapporteur of the International Law Commission for the issue, the Draft Articles on State Responsibility left the matter open following 'strong reactions from many States'. Crawford, *Brownlie's Principles of Public International Law*, 9th edn, n 19 above, p 575. White and Abass find that the State and institutional practice in support of an entitlement is 'inconsistent, making the drawing of any conclusions as to *opinio juris* extremely difficult, if not impossible'. White and Abass, 'Countermeasures and Sanctions', n 112 above, p 547.

[124] Tallinn Manual 2.0, n 20 above, commentary paras. 2 and 3 on Rule 24.

[125] Art 52(1)(b), 2001 Draft Articles on State Responsibility, n 28 above. The majority, but not all, of the International Group of Experts who elaborated the second edition of the Tallinn Manual rejected the purported requirement whereby an injured State is to seek negotiations before undertaking countermeasures. Tallinn Manual 2.0, n 20 above, commentary para 13 on Rule 21.

prohibiting (belligerent) reprisals, or other peremptory (*jus cogens*) rules of international law.[126]

– A State taking countermeasures is not relieved from fulfilling its obligations under any dispute settlement procedure applicable between it and the responsible State.[127]
– A State taking countermeasures must respect the inviolability of diplomatic or consular agents, premises, archives, and documents.[128]

The principle of necessity applies to the exercise of countermeasures. Thus, where the wrongful acts against the victim State have ceased or the matter is pending before an international court or tribunal, countermeasures must cease (if they have already been implemented) or must not be taken.[129] This indicates that countermeasures should ordinarily be reversible.[130] In general, countermeasures must not breach the rights of third States.[131] While 'anticipatory' countermeasures are unlawful,[132] an injured State is still entitled to 'take such measures as are necessary to preserve its rights'.[133]

In its judgment in the *Gabčikovo-Nagymaros Project* case, the International Court of Justice held that the unilateral assumption of control over a large section of the waters of the Danube river by the erstwhile Czechoslovakia was disproportionate to the original offence.[134] Disproportionate measures give rise to the responsibility of the State executing them.[135] That said, there is no stipulation in general international law that countermeasures must concern the same obligation breached by the State that has acted wrongfully (see section II.C below).[136]

(ii) Available Countermeasures

While, under contemporary international law, countermeasures must not be forcible in nature – or at least they must not infringe the prohibition on inter-State use of force – this does not, however, mean that countermeasures may not be military in nature. Where, for instance, a cyberattack is directed against a State's military infrastructure or personnel, either by another State directly or by

[126] Art 50(1)(b), (c), and (d), 2001 Draft Articles on State Responsibility, n 28 above.
[127] Art 50(2)(a), 2001 Draft Articles on State Responsibility, n 28 above.
[128] Art 50(2)(b), 2001 Draft Articles on State Responsibility, n 28 above.
[129] Art 53, 2001 Draft Articles on State Responsibility, n 28 above.
[130] Art 49(2) and (3), 2001 Draft Articles on State Responsibility, n 28 above; ICJ Gabčikovo-Nagymaros Project Judgment, n 117 above, para 87.
[131] P Gaeta, JE Viñuales, and S Zappalà, *Cassese's International Law*, 3rd edn, Oxford University Press, Oxford, 2020, p 301.
[132] OY Elagab, *The Legality of Non-Forcible Counter-Measures in International Law*, Clarendon Press, Oxford, 1988, p 63.
[133] M Shaw, *International Law*, 8th edn, Cambridge University Press, Cambridge, 2018, p 603.
[134] ICJ Gabčikovo-Nagymaros Project Judgment, n 117 above, paras 85–87.
[135] J Crawford, *The International Law Commission's Articles on State Responsibility*, Cambridge University Press, Cambridge, 2002, p 294.
[136] Shaw, *International Law*, 8th edn, n 133 above, p 602.

a non-State actor under its effective control, but where the cyber operation does not amount to an armed attack, the victim State is likely to be entitled to take countermeasures.[137] Unilateral termination of a bilateral military cooperation agreement, without adequate justification under that agreement, could amount to a lawful countermeasure of a military nature even where the hybrid threat did not itself contravene the agreement. The countermeasure(s) taken in response to a cyberattack may themselves be cyber in nature but they do not need to be.[138] To date, most countermeasures taken under international law involve non-military measures.

C. Responding to Hybrid Threats Other than by Use of Force

(i) Responding to the Provision of Weapons to an Unauthorised Non-State Actor

One of the most common forms of hybrid warfare involves the provision of weapons to an unauthorised non-State actor that is struggling against the territorial authorities of another State. Where there is no armed group already engaged in violent action against the State itself, if the intent is to undermine the government in power, an alternative is to supply criminal groups with weapons with a view to fomenting broader violence and social strife. Such a criminal group may be engaged, eg, in armed robbery, racially motivated attacks on civilians, drug smuggling, and/or human trafficking. In 2015, Galeotti observed thus that organised criminal networks in the Baltics likely had ties with Moscow and could be used 'as an instrument to gather intelligence and exert influence abroad'.[139]

In September 2022, China complained about the proposed supply of arms worth US$1.1 billion from the United States to Taiwan. The proposed package included 60 anti-ship missiles and 100 air-to-air missiles to help Taiwan 'modernize its armed forces'.[140] The statement by China concerned its consistent view of Taiwan as a renegade province without the autonomous legal authority to import weapons. China declared that it would adopt countermeasures in response to the arms shipment and that the measures to be taken would be 'legitimate and necessary' in light of 'the development of the situation'.[141] It did not elaborate on the nature and extent of those countermeasures.

Given that countermeasures do not need to be of the same order as the original breach of international law, their form and nature are potentially very broad indeed. Obvious examples are trade embargoes in breach of World Trade

[137] Tallinn Manual 2.0, n 20 above, Rule 20.
[138] Ibid, commentary para 6 on Rule 20.
[139] M Galeotti, 'Organized Crime in the Baltic States', *Baltic Review*, 24 March 2015.
[140] J Abrahams, 'China threatens "counter-measures" as US prepares arms package for Taiwan', *Daily Telegraph*, 3 September 2022.
[141] TRT World, 'China demands US cancel $1.1B Taiwan arms sales or face "counter-measures"', 3 September 2022, at: https://bit.ly/3cIRYLi.

Organization rules or at least the imposition of heavy and discriminatory tariffs on the import of goods from the responsible State. Even though the original breach concerns the threat or use of force, as discussed above, countermeasures may not themselves involve the threat or use of force. This might appear to some to be unjust, but it is the law. If one accepts the distinction made by the International Court of Justice, it does, though, allow the *funding* of a non-State armed group in the responsible State, just not its arming or training.

(ii) Responding to Advising of an Unauthorised Non-State Actor on Military Strategy or Operations

Individuals within the jurisdiction of a State who are providing advice to an illegal armed group or advice to other individuals on the commission of illegal acts are themselves engaged in a criminal conspiracy. Domestic law ordinarily gives law enforcement agencies far-reaching powers to address these individuals, including through arrest and prosecution. Where the individuals providing advice have diplomatic immunity, they can of course be expelled. But countermeasures that infringe diplomatic or consular inviolability are prohibited. The Tallinn Manual gives the possible example of a lawful countermeasure of the launching of ransomware against an embassy's computer system accompanied by a demand that the embassy's sending State discontinue its wrongful act.[142]

(iii) Responding to Multiple Hybrid Threats

Finally, multiple hybrid threats falling short of a use of force that amounts to an armed attack, even when considered in combination, similarly allow for non-forcible countermeasures by an injured State or States.[143] Moreover, repeated attacks of the same nature may be perpetrated by one State against another. As the Tallinn Manual has observed, when a cyber operation is only one in a 'series' of ongoing actions which, according to State responsibility under international law, constitute a single internationally wrongful act, countermeasures remain available.[144] The Manual cited directed denial-of-service attacks against the US banking system from late 2012 to early 2013, which was allegedly the work of Iranians.[145] It was unknown whether this was the work of State organs or agents.

[142] Tallinn Manual 2.0, n 20 above, commentary para 8 on Rule 22.
[143] Tallinn Manual 2.0, n 20 above, Rule 24.
[144] Tallinn Manual 2.0, n 20 above, commentary para. 7 on Rule 21.
[145] N Perth and Q Hardy, 'Bank Hacking Was the Work of Iranians, Officials Say', *The New York Times*, 8 January 2013.

2

Hybrid Warfare and the Law of Law Enforcement

LAW ENFORCEMENT IS the dedicated work of State organs or agents to protect members of the public (as well as other law enforcement officials) from violence, to prevent the perpetration of a crime, to arrest a person suspected of having committed a criminal offence, or to detain a convicted criminal pursuant to a lawful sentence.[1] This involves legislative action – as regulated by international human rights law – as well as potentially forcible action by a law enforcement official and law enforcement agency.

In turn, the law of law enforcement is the branch of international law that governs State action to ensure compliance with its domestic criminal law in its own sovereign jurisdiction. Extraterritorially, this branch of international law will also regulate the use of force in policing areas that the State effectively controls and with respect to persons over whom it exercises effective control in any other place. While one ordinarily thinks of the police as a generic law enforcement entity, under international law the terms 'law enforcement official' and 'law enforcement agency' are broader, encompassing also the military as well as other State security forces, whenever and wherever they exercise such so-called policing or 'constabulary' powers.[2]

In considering how the law of law enforcement governs hybrid warfare, the first part of the chapter considers the international legal rules that restrain State use of force to enforce its domestic criminal law. As Chapter one noted, the use of force in ordinary law enforcement does not contravene the prohibition on inter-State use of force codified in the Charter of the United Nations[3] or customary international law. That is ordinarily so even if the target of law enforcement is a foreign national[4] or the action takes place abroad, so long as the action is not politically motivated. The two fundamental principles of necessity and

[1] Adapted from *United Nations Human Rights Guidance on Less-Lethal Weapons in Law Enforcement*, Office of the United Nations High Commissioner for Human Rights (OHCHR), New York and Geneva, 2020, p 44.

[2] Formal commentary to Art 1, Code of Conduct for Law Enforcement Officials; adopted at New York by UN General Assembly Resolution 34/169, adopted without a vote on 17 December 1979.

[3] Art 2(4), Charter of the United Nations; adopted at San Francisco, 26 June 1945; entered into force, 24 October 1945.

[4] If law enforcement action involves racial discrimination or animus, this would still amount to law enforcement for the purpose of its regulation under international law, but it would also violate

proportionality apply to all use of force in law enforcement, but their interpretation and application in this branch of international law differ materially from the identically named principles governing the use of force in self-defence *ad bellum* (see Chapter one).

The second part of the present chapter discusses the use of force in addressing hybrid threats, in particular when these threats are carried out by individuals and groups supported by another State where the conduct does not amount to an armed conflict. Two case studies are presented: the situation in Donetsk Oblast in Ukraine in February to April 2014 with respect to the hybrid threats from Russia, and the situation in Taiwan with respect to hybrid threats from China since 2018. The term 'hybrid threats' is generally used in this chapter given that *warfare* – as that term is understood and governed in the law of armed conflict – does not generally fall to be considered by the law of law enforcement.[5]

I. THE LAW OF LAW ENFORCEMENT

The rules of international law governing policing and other law enforcement constitute a framework of general and dedicated principles and norms. The content of the law of law enforcement is found by reference to the three primary sources of international law: treaty, custom, and general principles of law.[6] While certain aspects of law enforcement are referenced in human rights treaties, most of the important elements of the law originated in so-called soft law (politically binding) instruments, notably the 1979 UN Code of Conduct for Law Enforcement Officials and the 1990 UN Basic Principles on the Use of Force and Firearms by Law Enforcement Officials.[7] But what were once soft law standards

a peremptory norm of international human rights law. The UN Charter does not detail the various human rights to be respected but it does stipulate that one of the purposes of the United Nations is to promote and encourage respect for human rights and fundamental freedoms for all 'without distinction as to race'. Arts 1(3) and 55(c), UN Charter. The prohibition of racial discrimination is considered a norm of *jus cogens* by the International Law Commission. International Law Commission, 'Peremptory norms of general international law (*jus cogens*)', Texts of the draft conclusions and Annex adopted by the Drafting Committee on second reading, UN doc A/CN.4/L.967, 11 May 2022, Annex, norm (e).

[5] As noted in the Introduction to this book, the following working definition of hybrid threats is used throughout: 'the use by one State against another of unlawful or unfriendly forcible and non-forcible measures, but which do not amount to an armed attack or an international armed conflict. Their aim is to destabilise and potentially overthrow its government and to undermine other State institutions. Hybrid threats, which may amount in certain circumstances to the threat or use of force under international law, may include (but are not limited to) cyberattacks, intimidation, disinformation and misinformation, and economic and military pressure'.

[6] Art 38(1)(a)–(c), Statute of the International Court of Justice; adopted at San Francisco, 26 June 1945; entered into force, 24 October 1945 (hereafter, ICJ Statute).

[7] The 1990 UN Basic Principles were adopted by the Eighth UN Congress on the Prevention of Crime and the Treatment of Offenders, Havana, Cuba, 27 August to 7 September 1990. In December 1990, the UN General Assembly welcomed the Basic Principles and invited governments to respect them. UN General Assembly Resolution 45/166, adopted without a vote on 18 December 1990, para 4.

have since become legally binding rules, in particular through their crystallisation as customary international law. Also pertinent to the evolution of the law of law enforcement are the two subsidiary sources used by the International Court of Justice to determine rules of international law: judicial decisions and the writings of leading international lawyers ('publicists').[8]

A. The Fundamental Principles of the Law of Law Enforcement

As signalled above, the two fundamental principles governing the use of force for law enforcement purposes are necessity and proportionality. These principles are used to determine whether any given use of force by a law enforcement official, at the moment of its application, is lawful. They are also used to test whether the exercise of State authority complies with international human rights law. This involves especially the dictates of the right to life – specifically the prohibition on arbitrary deprivation of life and the duty to protect life – as well as those of the prohibitions on torture and other forms of cruel, inhuman, or degrading treatment or punishment (hereafter denoted by the umbrella term 'ill-treatment').

The principles of necessity and proportionality, whose content is explained below, are applied sequentially in adjudging the legality of State action in law enforcement: in order to apply the principle of proportionality, the requirements of the principle of necessity must first be met. If not, the use of force will already be unlawful and the proportionality test will be superfluous. The twin principles apply directly to all action to confront hybrid threats outside the confines of an armed conflict as well as in the course of an armed conflict where the conduct addressed is not directly related to that conflict.[9]

A similar approach exists with respect to maritime law enforcement operations, including with respect to hybrid threats. On the high seas, the International Tribunal for the Law of the Sea, which oversees the application and implementation of the 1982 UN Convention on the Law of the Sea,[10] has examined how much force may lawfully be used by States when they conduct law enforcement operations under the aegis of international maritime law. In its judgment in the *M/V 'Saiga' (No 2)* case, the Tribunal stated that international

[8] Art 38(1)(d), ICJ Statute.

[9] This latter scenario is because, of course, ordinary policing persists during an armed conflict: individuals still attack other individuals and destroy, damage, or steal property for reasons entirely unrelated to the fighting. Even a bank robbery that is mounted owing to the relative absence of police officers, some of whom may have been drafted to support the army in combat, is still an issue of law enforcement, not of the law of armed conflict. That is the case, as long as the perpetrators are not seeking unlawfully to secure funds for military action on behalf of one party to the ambient armed conflict against another.

[10] UN Convention on the Law of the Sea; adopted at Montego Bay, 10 December 1982; entered into force, 16 November 1994.

law 'requires that the use of force must be avoided as far as possible and, where force is unavoidable, it must not go beyond what is reasonable and necessary in the circumstances'.[11] The notion of reasonableness, a general standard in many common law contexts constraining what may be deemed permissible force, is to be equated here with the notion of proportionality under international law, but at national level it also pertains to the view of the individual law enforcement official as to whether force was necessary.[12]

For the most part, neither of the two principles appears in international human rights treaties with respect to the use of force by State agents. The exception to this general rule is the 1950 European Convention on Human Rights.[13] In its Article 2, the Convention stipulates that deprivation of life shall not be regarded as inflicted in contravention of the right to life 'when it results from the use of force which is *no more than absolutely necessary*' (emphasis added).[14] In contrast, proportionality is not mentioned in the article (or indeed anywhere in the Convention). Instead, the application of the principle of proportionality to police use of force has been determined by the European Court of Human Rights to inhere in the concept of 'absolute' necessity.[15]

[11] International Tribunal for the Law of the Sea, *M/V 'Saiga' (No 2)* case (*Saint Vincent and the Grenadines v Guinea*), Judgment, 1 July 1999, para 155. The Tribunal's findings are considered to articulate customary international law on use of force on the high seas. The Permanent Court of Arbitration also 'accepts the argument that in international law force may be used in law enforcement activities provided that such force is unavoidable, reasonable and necessary'. Permanent Court of Arbitration, *Guyana v Suriname*, Award of 17 September 2007, para 445.

[12] The term is also used in common law contexts as an additional principle supplementing necessity and proportionality. Cyr suggests that, in Canadian law, the principle 'requires the officer to act "on reasonable grounds"', which he takes to mean 'that the officer must believe, on reasonable grounds, that the police intervention is both necessary in the circumstances and proportionate to the threat faced'. K Cyr, 'Police Use of Force: Assessing Necessity and Proportionality' (2016), 53(3) *Alberta Law Review* 663–79, available at: https://canlii.ca/t/6sc, at p 674. In England and Wales, the College of Policing stated that: 'Police officers only use force to the extent that it is necessary, proportionate and reasonable in all the circumstances'. College of Policing, 'Legal framework', updated 8 September 2023, at: https://bit.ly/47N7BrY. As the College of Policing recalls, in *R (on the application of Bennett) v HM Coroner for Inner South London* [2006] EWHC 196 (Admin), the Administrative Court held that the reasonableness test does not differ from the right to life test of absolute necessity under the right to life as protected under Article 2 of the European Convention on Human Rights – 'they are one and the same'. In the 2006 decision the Court held that: 'In truth, if any officer reasonably decides that he must use lethal force, it will inevitably be because it is absolutely necessary to do so. To kill when it is not absolutely necessary to do so is surely to act unreasonably. Thus, the reasonableness test does not in truth differ from the Article 2 test as applied in McCann'. (Opinion of Justice Collins, para 25). An honest and objectively reasonable belief as to the need for the use of force on the part of a law enforcement official obviates a violation of the law of law enforcement and relevant human rights with respect to necessity, and, if it would not be excessive based on the honest and reasonable belief of that official, also proportionality.

[13] Convention for the Protection of Human Rights and Fundamental Freedoms; adopted at Rome, 4 December 1950; entered into force, 3 September 1953 (hereafter, European Convention on Human Rights).

[14] Art 2(2), European Convention on Human Rights.

[15] This flexible interpretation by the Court is discussed below.

B. The Principle of Necessity for Use of Force in Law Enforcement

The principle of necessity dictates that, in order to be lawful, any police use of force must be necessary in the prevailing circumstances in order to achieve a legitimate law enforcement purpose. Any force that is applied must be no more than the minimum necessary in those circumstances as the police officer(s) concerned honestly and reasonably believed them to be. Furthermore, once the need for force to be used has passed (for instance, because a suspect has ceased to resist arrest), the application of additional force will be unlawful.

In particular, any punitive use of force by a police officer will violate the human rights law prohibition of ill-treatment. Should any unlawful force by the law enforcement authorities be life-threatening, such as by unnecessary use of a firearm, the right to life may also be violated. That is so even when the victim survives. In any event, compliance with the right to life must be assessed when police action causes loss of life.[16]

(i) Use of Force Only for a Legitimate Law Enforcement Purpose

An integral part of the principle of necessity is the rule that force may only be applied when it is applied for a legitimate law enforcement purpose.[17] Preventing the perpetration of a crime whose commission is reasonably believed to be imminent or arresting a criminal suspect are legitimate purposes; in contrast, police officers seeking to punish suspected offenders for their prior actions are in violation of the law. Thus, in its 2020 judgment in the *Kukhalashvili* case, the European Court of Human Rights held that 'the use of lethal force for purely punitive, retaliatory purposes, even if those purposes target alleged members of the criminal underworld, cannot be justified'.[18]

The same principle applies in exactly the same manner to enforcement action addressing hybrid threats: members of any group supported by a foreign State who engage in violent action against the territorial authorities or the public of the victim State should be arrested, using force only where and to the extent necessary, and then charged with the relevant criminal offences. Punitive use of force against those engaging in hybrid threats is a breach of international law which engages the responsibility of the State in whose name that force is exercised.

[16] Human Rights Committee, General Comment No 36 – Article 6: Right to Life, UN doc CCPR/C/GC/36, 3 September 2019, paras 10–12.

[17] The 2001 European Code of Police Ethics, for instance, stipulates that the police may use force 'only to the extent required to obtain a legitimate objective'. European Code of Police Ethics, adopted by the Committee of Ministers of the Council of Europe on 19 September 2001, available at: https://bit.ly/3CuSbLM, para 37.

[18] European Court of Human Rights, *Kukhalashvili v Georgia*, Judgment (Fifth Section), 2 April 2020, para 151.

(ii) *The 'Minimum Necessary Force'*

When some measure of force is justified, the force that is applied must be no more than the minimum necessary.[19] The use of excessive or gratuitous force is therefore unlawful. The lawfulness of a police intervention is, though, judged at the moment of the use of force in the circumstances as the relevant officer or officers honestly and reasonably believed them to be.[20] This means that mistakes can be and are made – some resulting in tragedies – but without necessarily violating the principle of necessity (or proportionality). In the *McCann* case, the Grand Chamber of the European Court of Human Rights (its highest chamber) held that use of force by agents of the State may be justified where it is based on an honest belief which is perceived, for good reasons, to be valid at the time but which subsequently turns out to be mistaken. To hold otherwise, the Court stated, 'would be to impose an unrealistic burden on the State and its law-enforcement personnel in the execution of their duty, perhaps to the detriment of their lives and those of others'.[21]

This is certainly true. But the Court also deemed it critical to take into account the broader context in assessing the legality of any use of force in law enforcement. What may have been necessary at the instant of use of force could perhaps have been avoided by more sage action upstream in the planning of a law enforcement operation. This was certainly the reality in the *McCann* case, where the decision by the British authorities not to arrest three Irish Republican Army (IRA) operatives as they watched them cross the border from Spain into Gibraltar increased the likelihood of a fatal outcome for all concerned both materially and significantly. Accordingly, in its judgment in the case, the European Court buttressed the understanding of the principle of necessity by adding a human rights duty of *precaution* on the authorities. This requires them to both plan and control an operation 'so as to minimise, to the greatest extent possible, recourse to lethal force'.[22] The duty to respect the right to life of the suspects included an obligation on the authorities 'to exercise the greatest of care in evaluating the information at their disposal before transmitting it to soldiers whose use of firearms automatically involved shooting to kill'.[23]

[19] Art 3, 1979 UN Code of Conduct for Law Enforcement Officials; and see also 'Report of the Special Rapporteur on extrajudicial, summary or arbitrary executions, Christof Heyns', UN doc A/HRC/26/36, 1 April 2014, paras 59–60.

[20] The margin of discretion accorded to police officers can extend to judgements they make at a specific instant but which, in hindsight, could have been better. Thus, for instance, the US Supreme Court held in its landmark 1989 judgment in *Graham v Connor* that: 'The calculus of reasonableness must embody allowance for the fact that police officers are often forced to make split-second judgments in circumstances that are tense, uncertain, and rapidly evolving – about the amount of force that is necessary in a particular situation'. US Supreme Court, *Graham v Connor*, 490 US 386 (1989), Decided 15 May 1989, at pp 396–97.

[21] European Court of Human Rights, *McCann and others v United Kingdom*, Judgment (Grand Chamber), 27 September 1995, para 200; approved, inter alia, in *Armani da Silva v United Kingdom*, Judgment (Grand Chamber), 30 March 2016, para 244 *et seq*.

[22] *McCann*, para 194.

[23] *McCann*, para 211.

This principle of precaution should have been litigated in the application to the European Court of Human Rights by Ms Armani da Silva, the cousin of Jean-Charles de Menezes, a Brazilian national shot to death by Metropolitan Police officers in the Underground on 22 July 2005 in a tragic case of mistaken identity. The police wrongly believed that he was carrying a bomb which he could be, or was, about to detonate. In a botched surveillance operation,[24] Mr de Menezes, an electrician working in London, had been misidentified for an ostensibly Somali national, Hussain Osman, a terrorist living in the same block of flats and who had sought to detonate a bomb composed of hydrogen peroxide[25] on the capital's transport infrastructure the day before. Mr Osman – in reality an Ethiopian national whose real name is believed to be Hamdi Isaac Adus – had in fact already fled the jurisdiction.[26]

Had the July 2005 bombings been an instance of hybrid warfare rather than a home-grown plot, the same three principles (necessity, proportionality, and precaution) would have applied in order to determine legality. The use of force by the Metropolitan Police would not, however, have amounted to a use of force *ad bellum* against either Somalia or Ethiopia, just as Mr de Menezes' avoidable death did not amount to a use of force *ad bellum* against Brazil. That is so, even though the police killing of Mr de Menezes led to protests in Brazil, with the Landless Workers' Movement demonstrating outside British diplomatic missions in Brasília and Rio de Janeiro in the days following his fatal shooting.[27] The Brazilian government released a statement expressing its shock at the killing, declaring that it looked forward 'to receiving the necessary explanation from the British authorities on the circumstances which led to this tragedy'.[28]

C. The Principle of Proportionality of Force in Law Enforcement

If any given use of force complies with the principle of necessity, it has then also to comply with the principle of proportionality. Failure to comply with both principles means that the force used will have been unlawful. The principle of proportionality acts as a ceiling on lawful force, adjudging whether the force used was reasonable when considering the threat posed by a suspect or the harm

[24] Surveillance of the apartment buildings had been compromised as the officer most familiar with the suspect was relieving himself into a bottle in his surveillance van when Mr de Menezes came out of his home on the morning of 22 July 2005, and thus did not postively identify the suspect. 'The catalogue of errors that killed Jean Charles de Menezes', *The Conversation*, 21 July 2015, at: https://bit.ly/3z3osX6.

[25] On the use of this material by terrorists, see, eg, Associated Press, 'Tiny, cheap, deadly: hydrogen peroxide bombs', *NBC News*, 23 September 2009, at: https://bit.ly/3sYFwPz.

[26] He was later detained in Italy and returned to the United Kingdom where he was convicted with three other men of conspiracy to murder and sentenced to life imprisonment with a minimum tariff of 40 years in prison. BBC, 'Four 21/7 bomb plotters get life', 11 July 2007, at: https://bit.ly/3EG7d1R.

[27] BBC, 'Protest in Brazil after shooting', 26 July 2005, at: https://bit.ly/3Zkccik.

[28] BBC, 'Family condemns police shooting', 24 July 2005, at: https://bit.ly/3sYHQWJ.

sought to be avoided. According to the 1990 UN Basic Principles on the Use of Force and Firearms: 'Whenever the lawful use of force and firearms is unavoidable, law enforcement officers shall … act in proportion to the seriousness of the offence and legitimate objective to be achieved'.[29] Hence, while a certain level of force may be necessary in the circumstances in order to achieve a legitimate law enforcement objective (such as to secure a lawful arrest of a person suspected of unlawful hybrid action), it may nonetheless be deemed unlawful as it exceeds what is appropriate in those circumstances. In the words of the UN Special Rapporteur on extrajudicial, summary, or arbitrary executions:

> If necessity can be visualized as a ladder, proportionality is a scale that determines how high up the ladder of force one is allowed to go. The force used may not go above that ceiling, even if it might otherwise be deemed 'necessary' to achieve the legitimate aim.[30]

The principle of proportionality is not set forth in human rights treaties but exists as a customary rule and a longstanding general principle of law. As the Code of Conduct issued in 1979 recalled at the time, national law ordinarily restricts the use of force by law enforcement officials in accordance with a principle of proportionality.[31] In its judgment in the *McCann* case, the European Court's Grand Chamber interpreted the wording of Article 2(2) of the European Convention – that the use of force must be 'no more than absolutely necessary' for listed purposes – as meaning that the force used must also be *strictly proportionate* to the achievement of those purposes.[32]

Other regional mechanisms have adopted the same approach. Concerning arbitrary deprivation of life, as prohibited under the 1969 Inter-American Convention on Human Rights, the Inter-American Court of Human Rights thus held in its 2015 judgment in the *Cruz Sánchez* case that a violation of the right to life will occur when the use of force is 'illegitimate, excessive or disproportionate'.[33] In its interpretation of the right to life, the African Commission on Human and Peoples' Rights has similarly held that the use of force by law enforcement officials must comply with the principles of both necessity and proportionality.[34]

[29] Principle 5, 1990 UN Basic Principles.

[30] Report of the Special Rapporteur on extrajudicial, summary or arbitrary executions, UN doc A/HRC/26/36, 1 April 2014, para 66.

[31] Commentary para (b) on Art 3, 1979 Code of Conduct.

[32] European Court of Human Rights, *McCann and others v United Kingdom*, Judgment (Grand Chamber), para 149.

[33] Inter-American Court of Human Rights, *Cruz Sánchez and others v Peru*, Judgment (Merits), 17 April 2015, para 261. In the original Spanish: 'no cualquier privación de la vida será reputada como contraria a la Convención, sino solo aquella que se hubiera producido de manera arbitraria, por ejemplo por ser producto de la utilización de la fuerza de forma ilegitima, excesiva o desproporcionada'.

[34] African Commission on Human and Peoples' Rights, General Comment No 3 on Article 4: the Right to Life, November 2015, para 27: https://bit.ly/4bLxpYf.

D. The Use of Firearms in Law Enforcement Operations

The restrictions imposed by international law on the use of firearms in law enforcement operations represent the practical application of the twin principles of necessity and proportionality. The rules, which are of a customary law nature,[35] are set out in Principle 9 of the 1990 UN Basic Principles on the Use of Force and Firearms. The default rule is that law enforcement officials 'shall not use firearms against persons except in self-defence or defence of others against the imminent threat of death or serious injury' and even then 'only when less extreme means are insufficient to achieve these objectives'. The latter element of the rule evidently reflects the principle of necessity while the former component embodies the principle of proportionality.[36] Imminence is not defined in the 1990 Basic Principles, but as the UN Special Rapporteur on extrajudicial, summary or arbitrary executions has indicated, an 'imminent or immediate threat' should be considered 'a matter of seconds, not hours'.[37]

In truly exceptional circumstances, a firearm may be used when the threat posed by a criminal suspect is not imminent. Basic Principle 9 thus allows the use of firearms by law enforcement officials, when strictly necessary, 'to prevent the perpetration of a particularly serious crime involving grave threat to life, to arrest a person presenting such a danger and resisting their authority, or to prevent his or her escape'. Hence, three distinct scenarios pertain to such circumstances where a threat to life is not imminent: to prevent the perpetration of a particularly serious crime involving grave threat to life; to enable a suspect resisting arrest to be arrested if he or she is about to commit a particularly serious crime that involves grave threat to life; and to prevent a suspect resisting arrest from escaping in circumstances where he or she is about to commit a particularly serious crime that involves a grave threat to life.

In contrast to the default scenario for potentially lawful use of firearms by the police (which involves 'shooting to stop'), the threat justifying shooting to kill must be to life alone and not merely a threat of serious injury. The threat to life must also be 'grave', meaning that it must be both temporally proximate and constant,[38] even though its manifestation in violence does not need to be imminent. Thus, the mere fact that a suspect flees arrest or escapes from custody does not justify the use of a firearm, 'unless this person presents an ongoing grave

[35] Inter-American Court of Human Rights, *Montero-Aranguren and ors (Detention Centre of Catia) v Venezuela*, Judgment (Merits), 5 July 2006, para 69.

[36] NS Rodley with M Pollard, *The Treatment of Prisoners under International Law*, 3rd edn, Oxford University Press, Oxford, 2011, p 499.

[37] Report of the Special Rapporteur on extrajudicial, summary or arbitrary executions, UN doc A/HRC/26/36, 1 April 2014, para 59.

[38] UN Office of Drugs and Crime (UNODC) and OHCHR, *Resource Book on the Use of Force and Firearms in Law Enforcement*, Criminal Justice Handbook Series, United Nations, New York, 2017, p 21.

threat to the life of another person that can be realized at any time'.[39] Examples of a threat that could amount to a grave threat to life might include a suspected terrorist, believed to have already committed murder and who was reasonably expected to be seeking to kill again in the very near future. Thus, in 1997, in a Turkish case, the erstwhile European Commission on Human Rights considered that the shooting of an escaping – but unarmed – terrorist bombing suspect fell within the exception set out in Article 2(2)(b) of the European Convention on Human Rights 'to prevent the escape of a person lawfully detained'.[40]

In its 2012 decision in the *Noah Kazingachire* case, the African Commission on Human and Peoples' Rights duly cited the 1979 Code of Conduct for Law Enforcement Officials and the 1990 UN Basic Principles on the Use of Force and Firearms in establishing the international standards to be used for assessing the legality of police use of firearms. Applying these standards to the facts before them, the Commission found that the right to life of the two unarmed complainants who were shot and killed by the police had been violated.[41] In any event, the defence of property alone or the discharge of a firearm with a view to preventing the escape of a thief (even one making off with goods of great value) never justifies police recourse to the use of firearms under international law.[42]

A significantly higher international standard applies when a law enforcement official is shooting with intent to kill. Principle 9 of the 1990 Basic Principles thus stipulates that: 'In any event, intentional lethal use of firearms may only be made when strictly unavoidable in order to protect life'. Thus, the aim of preventing serious injury will not allow the intentional taking of life during a law enforcement operation; only the preservation of life (of either a law enforcement official or a member of the public) can suffice. Inhering in the phrase *strictly unavoidable* are the notions of imminence and of absolute necessity. No other means must realistically be open to law enforcement officials to prevent loss of life.

The heightened international legal standard for intentional killing typically concerns two scenarios: a hostage taker who is perceived to be on the verge of killing his or her hostage or a bomber just about to detonate an explosive device, whether or not it is body borne. Consequently, if a suspect is not honestly and reasonably believed to be about to pull the trigger of a gun aimed at a hostage's head, or to detonate a bomb, intentional lethal use of force cannot be said to be strictly unavoidable to protect life. In the *McCann* case, the four British soldiers who shot to death three IRA operatives in Gibraltar had acknowledged at an earlier inquest that their intent, once they opened fire, was to kill. 'They

[39] Amnesty International, *Use of Force. Guidelines for Implementation of the UN Basic Principles on the Use of Force and Firearms by Law Enforcement Officials*, AI Dutch Section, Amsterdam, 2015, at: https://bit.ly/2LROt61, p 31, Guideline 2(c).

[40] European Commission on Human Rights, *M.D. v Turkey*, Decision, 30 June 1997.

[41] African Commission on Human and Peoples' Rights, *Noah Kazingachire, John Chitsenga, Elias Chemvura and Batanai Hadzisi (represented by Zimbabwe Human Rights NGO Forum) v Zimbabwe*, Views (Comm No 295/04), Banjul, The Gambia, 18 April to 2 May 2012, paras 111, 114, 115, and 116–23.

[42] Human Rights Committee, General Comment No 36 – Article 6: right to life, para 12.

considered that it was necessary to continue to fire at the suspects until they were rendered physically incapable of detonating a device'.[43] The Grand Chamber accepted that the soldiers

> honestly believed, in the light of the information that they had been given, that it was necessary to shoot the suspects in order to prevent them from detonating a bomb and causing serious loss of life … The actions which they took, in obedience to superior orders, were thus perceived by them as absolutely necessary in order to safeguard innocent lives.[44]

II. THE USE OF FORCE IN LAW ENFORCEMENT TO TACKLE HYBRID THREATS

Based on the law set forth above, this section looks at the use of force in law enforcement in response to hybrid threats in two domains: first on land and then at sea. Both domains are potentially fertile areas for such hybrid action. The principles governing the use of force by the police and other law enforcement agencies apply directly to all interventions outside the sphere of armed conflict. The first case study concerns the reaction of the Ukrainian authorities who came to power after the Maidan Revolution to the proclamation of the independence of the Donetsk People's Republic in 2014. The second case concerns the ongoing hybrid threats by China against the island of Taiwan, which may one day lead to a massive use of force.[45]

A. Tackling Hybrid Threats on Land

(i) The Law Enforcement Response to the Proclamation of the Donetsk People's Republic in 2014

If one looks at the early days of the self-proclaimed Donetsk People's Republic in March and April 2014, there was widespread criminal action and the use of

[43] European Court of Human Rights, *McCann and others v United Kingdom*, Judgment (Grand Chamber), para 199.

[44] Ibid, para 200. Nonetheless, the Court did mitigate that position in its finding that the United Kingdom had failed in its duty of precaution towards the applicants' deceased relatives, when referring to 'the automatic recourse to lethal force when the soldiers opened fire'. Ibid, para 213.

[45] In mid-November 2023, in a summit between Chinese President Xi Jinping and US President Joe Biden, discussions inevitably focused on the situation in Taiwan. President Xi reportedly insisted that Beijing's preference was for peaceful reunification, 'but then moved immediately to conditions that the potential use of force could be utilised', according to an unnamed US official. This included the reported statement that 'peace is all well and good, but at some point we need to move towards resolution more generally'. At the same time, the president also said that he had seen reports and assessments in the United States that China was planning to take military action by a given year, and expressed 'exasperation' at such reports, insisting no such plans existed. J Borger, 'Joe Biden hails progress after Xi Jinping talks but Taiwan still the sticking point', *The Guardian*, 16 November 2023, at: https://bit.ly/3QFYoLg.

unlawful violence by the paramilitaries who seized power from the Constitutional authorities before an armed conflict came into existence. Following the Maidan Revolution that began in February 2014 and which led to the ouster of Prime Minister Viktor Yanukovych, pro-Russian protesters seized the regional government building in the city of Donetsk and declared a 'people's republic'.[46] Interim Ukrainian President, Oleksandr Turchynov, called the unrest an attempt by Russia to 'dismember' Ukraine, declaring in an address on national television that this was 'the second wave' of a Russian operation to destabilise Ukraine, overthrow the government, and disrupt planned elections. In a more circumspect statement, then US Secretary of State, John Kerry, said that the events 'did not appear to be spontaneous'.[47]

Local separatists, some of whom were said to be already funded and even directed by the Russian security services,[48] occupied government buildings in Donetsk Oblast in the first few days of March 2014. But action by the authorities reporting to the Ukrainian government in Kyiv was able to remove the separatists by 10 March.[49] On 13 March, a pro-Ukrainian protester was stabbed and killed during the ongoing violence.[50] A report by the Organization for Security and Co-operation in Europe (OSCE)'s Office for Democratic Institutions and Human Rights (ODIHR) stated that local police forces had failed to take adequate measures to protect the pro-Maidan assembly, and reported claims by witnesses that the police 'could be observed treating the anti-Maidan protesters in a favourable manner'.[51]

In April 2014, in a second phase of hybrid action, armed groups again seized government buildings across Donetsk Oblast and launched an insurgency in several areas across the Donbas region. Between 6 and 23 April, the separatists used armed men to capture and hold the administration buildings that had been lost in early March. In the view of experts at The RAND Corporation: 'It is unclear whether these assaults were coordinated with Russian authorities'.[52]

[46] S Pifer, 'Ukraine: Looking forward, five years after the Maidan Revolution', *Commentary*, The Brookings Institution, 22 February 2019, at: https://bit.ly/44Yr1Zb.

[47] BBC, 'Ukraine crisis: Protesters declare Donetsk "republic"', 7 April 2014, at: https://bit.ly/3EI7gKM.

[48] T Kuzio, *Putin's War against Ukraine. Revolution, Nationalism, and Crime*, CreateSpace Independent Publishing Platform, North Charleston SC, 2017, p 252.

[49] M Kofman, K Migacheva, B Nichiporuk, A Radin, O Tkacheva, and J Oberholtzer, *Lessons from Russia's Operations in Crimea and Eastern Ukraine*, Report, The RAND Corporation, Santa Monica CA, 2017, at: https://bit.ly/3Pozwa2, pp 37–38.

[50] Reuters, 'One dead in Ukraine clash in eastern city', 13 March 2014, at: https://bit.ly/3Zk5I30.

[51] OSCE ODIHR, 'Human Rights Assessment Mission in Ukraine: Human Rights and Minority Rights Situation', Report, March–April 2014, The Hague/Warsaw, 12 May 2014, at: https://bit.ly/3PIvDyn, paras 20, 41, and 44.

[52] Kofman et al, *Lessons from Russia's Operations in Crimea and Eastern Ukraine*, n 49 above, p 39.

To seek to suppress the burgeoning insurgency, the Ukrainian government initiated an 'Anti-Terrorist Operation'[53] using its armed forces to confront the paramilitary forces.[54] The operation did not go well:

> Most of the deployed units in the east were halted outside the captured cities by a handful of crude checkpoints and several pro-Russian civilian mobs. Ukrainian security forces were ineffective for two reasons. First, at the time, the Ukrainian army existed largely on paper, with perhaps only 6,000 combat-capable troops available.[55] Second, Ukrainian army commanders spoke Russian and were disinclined to fight against fellow Russian speakers or order troops into civilian areas. As a whole, the Ukrainian military was completely unprepared for the launch of combat operations. The local police in Donetsk, Luhansk, Slovyansk, and Kramatorsk were either intimidated by the separatists or defected to them.[56]

At the initial stages of the operation, the involvement of the Ukrainian military was still to be adjudged according to law of law enforcement rules, despite the heavily armed nature of some of the insurgents. This meant the use of force by the authorities had to be in full accord with the principles of necessity and proportionality and their planning of interventions was further to respect the principle of precaution with a view to minimising injury.

Long before late August 2014, however, when Ukraine had re-taken most separatist-held territory and nearly regained control of the Russia–Ukraine border, the situation of armed violence had become a fully-fledged non-international armed conflict.[57] The use of force was now subject to the more permissive dictates of the rules of the law of armed conflict. In response, Russia covertly sent in heavy artillery and tanks to the separatists along with tens of thousands of 'volunteers'[58] (the so-called 'little green men'),[59] transforming the fighting into an international armed conflict. The same body of international law (the law of armed conflict) was applicable, but a more complex and detailed framework regulated that international armed conflict, as Chapter three analyses.

[53] D Sandford, 'Ukraine says Donetsk "anti-terror operation" under way', BBC, 15 April 2014, at: https://bit.ly/3EJmm2K.

[54] PJ D'Anieri, *Ukraine and Russia: From Civilized Divorce to Uncivil War*, Cambridge University Press, Cambridge, 2019, p 234.

[55] J Whalen and A Cullison, 'Ukraine Battles to Rebuild a Depleted Military', *The Wall Street Journal*, 25 March 2014; and L Kinstler, 'Why Is Ukraine's Army So Appallingly Bad?', *New Republic*, 9 May 2014.

[56] Kofman et al, *Lessons from Russia's Operations in Crimea and Eastern Ukraine*, n 49 above, pp 40–41.

[57] Ibid, p 44.

[58] MR Gordon, 'Russia Moves Artillery Units into Ukraine, NATO Says', *The New York Times*, 22 August 2014, at: https://bit.ly/48hcRoU.

[59] BBC, '"Little green men" or "Russian invaders"?', 11 March 2014, at: https://bit.ly/3RqFbPM. See also, eg, K Walczuk, 'Flight MH17 and Russia's "little green men"', Blog post, *The Conversation*, 19 July 2014, at: https://bit.ly/3rgnjfK. See further on this issue Chapter 3 of this volume.

(ii) Chinese Hybrid Threats Against Taiwan

China has repeatedly made clear its intention to bring Taiwan under its effective control. Although the Beijing regime has never exercised authority over the island, Chinese policymakers consider it an integral part of the People's Republic of China (PRC).[60] In November 2023, Tsai Ing-wen, the president of Taiwan, told international media:

> Taiwan is facing mounting military intimidation, grey-zone campaigns, cyberattacks and information manipulation. It is crucial for us to demonstrate the strength and resolve to defend ourselves. At the same time, it is also crucial to remember that it takes concerted efforts by all partners and allies to fend off the aggression of extremism, terrorism and authoritarianism.[61]

In January 2023, the PRC had renewed its threat to use force against Taiwan and warned that foreign politicians who interact with the self-governing island are 'playing with fire'. Ma Xiaoguang, a spokesperson for China's Taiwan Affairs Office, said the State was recommitted to 'safeguarding sovereignty and territorial integrity' and 'smashing plots for Taiwan independence'.[62] In early November 2023, People's Liberation Army General Zhang Youxia, vice chairman of the Central Military Commission of the Chinese Communist Party, declared: 'No matter who wants to separate Taiwan from China in any form, the Chinese military will never agree and will show no mercy'.[63]

Assuredly, though, China's violent repression of protesters in Hong Kong has substantially lessened the desire of the Taiwanese public for reunification with the mainland. In 2021, one commentator had even suggested that the longstanding 'one country, two systems' principle has 'come to a closure' and that the Chinese government 'is running out of diplomatic options to reserve Taiwan's drift towards independence'.[64] This assertion is open to question. Nevertheless, the PRC has certainly been exerting military and diplomatic pressure on Taiwan. Thus, in the first nine months of 2020 alone, Taiwan had to scramble its air force nearly 3,000 times against Chinese combat aircraft, reportedly costing Taiwan almost US$900 million in fuel costs, pilot fatigue, and 'wear and tear'.[65]

On 18 September 2023, Taiwan's Ministry of National Defense called on China to immediately halt its 'unilateral military harassment', after a record 103

[60] S Singh, 'Is China-Taiwan moving to hybrid warfare?', *The Kootneeti*, 6 April 2021, at: https://bit.ly/3PIbGrq.

[61] R Lloyd Parry, 'Xi Jinping "too busy with internal affairs" to invade Taiwan', *The Times*, 30 November 2023.

[62] Associated Press, 'China renews threat against Taiwan as island holds drills', 11 January 2023, at: https://bit.ly/3RkehJe.

[63] X Xiaoshan, 'Chinese General: Military Will "Show No Mercy" on Taiwan Independence', *Voice of America*, 4 November 2023, available at: https://bit.ly/47ilbn8.

[64] Singh, 'Is China-Taiwan moving to hybrid warfare?' n 60 above.

[65] Reuters, 'Taiwan says has spent almost $900 million scrambling against China this year', 7 October 2020, at: https://bit.ly/3PGd91b.

Chinese military aircraft were detected around Taiwan in a 24-hour period.[66] Of this total, 40 aircraft crossed the median line of the Taiwan Strait and entered the south-western and south-eastern parts of Taiwan's air defence identification zone (ADIZ).[67] The ministry said it scrambled planes to monitor the Chinese aircraft, issued radio warnings, mobilised combat air and naval patrols, and deployed defence missile systems to track the Chinese warplanes. In a statement, the Taiwanese Ministry of National Defense said that, in addition to the 103 warplanes, nine warships were also spotted in areas close to Taiwan between 6am Sunday, 17 September and 6am the following morning.[68] In this way, and without firing a single shot, China has been depleting and exhausting Taiwan's defensive resources.[69]

Taiwan's status under international law is not that of a distinct State but a de facto authority. The PRC took over China's seat in the UN Security Council in 1971, displacing the Republic of China (namely, Taiwan, earlier referred to as Formosa). Only the ever-diminishing number of a dozen UN Member States recognise Taiwan as a State today; Honduras withdrew its recognition of the Republic of China in March 2023.[70] The list does not include the United States.[71] Of further note is that the Constitution of Taiwan itself does not proclaim its own independence from the mainland but only its existence as a 'republic'.[72]

[66] Republic of China (ROC) Central News Agency, 'Taiwan reports record number of military incursions, urges China to stop "harassment"', *Global Security*, 18 September 2023, at: https://bit.ly/3EJbDoQ. The number of Chinese military aircraft detected near Taiwan in a 24-hour-period broke the previous record set in April 2023, when 91 warplanes flew close to Taiwan in a 24-hour period.

[67] The ADIZ is a self-declared area in which a country claims the right to identify, locate, and control approaching foreign aircraft but is not part of its territorial airspace as defined by international law.

[68] ROC Central News Agency, 'Taiwan reports record number of military incursions, urges China to stop "harassment"'.

[69] Singh, 'Is China-Taiwan moving to hybrid warfare?', n 60 above.

[70] 'Honduras snaps ties with Taiwan in favour of China: Which countries recognise Taiwan currently?', *The Indian Express*, 28 March 2023, at: https://bit.ly/44UCOaT. The following 12 UN Member States were reported still to recognise Taiwan at the time of writing: Belize, Eswatini, Guatemala, Haiti, Marshall Islands, Nauru, Palau, Paraguay, St Kitts and Nevis, St Lucia, and St Vincent and the Grenadines, and Tuvalu. UN Observer State, the Holy See, also recognises Taiwan as a nation State.

[71] The US Department of State declares that: 'Though the United States does not have diplomatic relations with Taiwan, we have a robust unofficial relationship'. It further states that: 'The United States has a longstanding one China policy … We oppose any unilateral changes to the status quo from either side; *we do not support Taiwan independence*; and we expect cross-Strait differences to be resolved by peaceful means. We continue to have an abiding interest in peace and stability across the Taiwan Strait. Consistent with the Taiwan Relations Act, the United States makes available defense articles and services as necessary to enable Taiwan to maintain a sufficient self-defense capability—and maintains our capacity to resist any resort to force or other forms of coercion that would jeopardize the security, or the social or economic system, of Taiwan' (emphasis added). US Department of State, 'U.S. Relations With Taiwan', Fact Sheet, Bureau of East Asian and Pacific Affairs, Washington DC, 28 May 2022, at: https://bit.ly/3EJ5QzK.

[72] 'The Republic of China … shall be a democratic republic of the people, to be governed by the people and for the people'. Art 1, 1947 Constitution of the Republic of China (Taiwan),

Chinese 'lawfare' seeks to exploit the uncertainty of Taiwan's status under international law 'to make strategic gains – maximally, "to win without fighting."'[73] This is one of the 'Three Warfares' concept China has developed, a form of influencing constituting aspects of what the West considers hybrid warfare or hybrid threats.[74] China has also been engaging in two other forms of cognitive warfare against Taiwan, weaponising disinformation and manipulating public opinion to influence perceptions, while using intimidation to wage psychological warfare.[75] Thus, in 2018, in an article in *The Diplomat*, it was suggested that:

> In a crisis situation in the Taiwan Strait, an interim government might be set up by pro-China elements cooperating from within the island. They would announce that the interim government has taken over the military and replaced the current government. The announcement, regardless of its legitimacy, could create considerable turbulence and even reduce the will of the military to fight. With cooperation from certain media outlets, the interim government could announce to local people that it has control of the whole country while declaring to the international community that the current government has surrendered. Such measures are meant to disrupt people's will to rebel and to reduce the willingness of other countries to intervene. In such a scenario, the media – not military might – is likely to become the final winning factor. Whether Taiwan's existing crisis management mechanism is capable of restoring media functions in a chaotic situation and ensuring the legitimacy of the current government remains to be seen. The military should not make light of a war scenario of this kind. Publicity through the media, not direct warfare, is now the main field for competition between nations.[76]

To respond to the legal warfare being wrought by mainland China, Taiwan has adopted a number of amendments to its domestic laws. These were necessary in part because the PRC is not considered in Taiwanese law – at least not explicitly – a separate country. These legislative changes (i) criminalise acts such as establishing an organisation in Taiwan for the official use of foreign countries or the mainland; (ii) regulate investments in Taiwanese companies; (iii) widen the offences concerning classified information to include information stored in Taiwanese servers; (iv) expand legal surveillance powers to cover the internet; and (v) adjust and even abolish the statute of limitations in relation to offences committed by retired military personnel and former government employees. The 2020 Anti-Infiltration Act, the 'cornerstone' of these reforms, defines

at: https://bit.ly/46aaymh (hereafter, Constitution of Taiwan). 'Persons possessing the nationality of the Republic of China shall be citizens of the Republic of China'. Art 2, Constitution of Taiwan. 'The territory of the Republic of China according to its existing national boundaries shall not be altered except by resolution of the National Assembly'. Art 4, Constitution of Taiwan.

[73] MJ West and A Insisa, 'Reunifying Taiwan with China through Cross-Strait Lawfare' (2023) *The China Quarterly* 1–16, available at: https://bit.ly/47qGtiX.

[74] Ibid, pp 2, 5.

[75] National Institute for Defense Studies (NIDS), *China Security Report 2022*, Tokyo, 2022, at: https://bit.ly/48m4Pv8, pp 82–86.

[76] L Ying-Yu, 'China's Hybrid Warfare and Taiwan', *The Diplomat*, 13 January 2018, at: https://bit.ly/3PI8Xyb.

'sources of infiltration' broadly to include political organisations of external hostile forces (ie the PRC) or their agents, with harsh penalties incurred where infiltration occurs.[77]

There have already been law enforcement interventions and subsequent prosecutions under the 2020 law. In November 2022, prosecutors raided the homes and offices of three people based on the provisions of the Anti-Infiltration Act, searching for evidence of vote-buying using alleged Chinese funds. These were said to be the first since the Act took effect in January 2020. Prosecutors and Investigation Bureau agents searched four locations on the grounds the suspects were engaged in buying votes at the behest of Chinese backers.[78] In August 2023, three people connected with PRC-funded organisations were indicted for contravening the Anti-Infiltration Act. The Gong He Party allegedly received money from officials in China to put up pro-Beijing candidates, one of whom received 316 votes in Taipei. The three defendants were the first people Taipei prosecutors had charged for contravening the Act since its passage.[79]

A year earlier, the visit of US House Speaker, Nancy Pelosi, to Taiwan triggered a flurry of denial-of-service attacks on the websites of the Taiwanese president, the Ministry of National Defense, and the Ministry of Foreign Affairs, as well as that of Taiwan Taoyuan International Airport. Convenience store chain 7-Eleven, local railway stations, and government facilities using Chinese software in their digital signage systems were hacked and displayed messages slandering Speaker Pelosi. This escalation occurred in a broader context of increasing cyber hostility. According to local media reports, cyberattacks against Taiwan's Ministry of Foreign Affairs increased forty-fold between 2018 and 2020, reaching 2,100 intrusions per day.[80]

In October 2022, Taiwan claimed that China was looking at the experience of the war in Ukraine to develop hybrid warfare strategies against it, including using drones and psychological pressure. A senior Taiwanese security official said that the island has been carefully studying the lessons of the Ukraine war to inform how it may react should China ever make good on threats to use force to enforce its sovereignty claim.[81] Certainly, Taiwan's army needs to be strengthened significantly in order to deter an armed attack. Commentary in August 2023

[77] West and Insisa, 'Reunifying Taiwan with China through Cross-Strait Lawfare', n 73 above, pp 11–12.

[78] F Wang and P Hsio, 'Prosecutors raid premises over alleged vote-buying with Chinese funds', *Central News Agency*, 24 November 2022.

[79] C Li-chung and J Pan, 'Three indicted for "united front" work', *Taipei Times*, 10 August 2023, at: https://bit.ly/3raXMVk. Already in June, political commentators had been asking whether further legislative strengthening would be pursued by the new parliament in 2024. B Hioe, 'Will the Government Strengthen Measures Against Chinese Infiltration?', *New Bloom*, 18 June 2023, at: https://bit.ly/3Plou5A.

[80] D Impiombato, Y Lau, and F Hunter, 'China's escalating coercion of Taiwan holds lessons for the international community', *The Strategist*, 10 August 2022, at: https://bit.ly/46hvIOD.

[81] B Blanchard, 'Taiwan says China looking at Ukraine war to develop "hybrid" strategies', *Reuters*, 12 October 2022, at: https://bit.ly/45LMNAB.

suggested that many of the structural problems in the Russian army similarly feature in Taiwan's, such as a rigidly hierarchical command structure, an ineffective reservist system, and poor training of recruits. From December 2022, compulsory military service now lasts for an extended period of one year, an increase of eight months on what it had been before. Recruits used to describe military service as a kind of summer camp at which instructors were primarily concerned with cleanliness and ensuring their trainees did not injure themselves. No one knows how many tanks and weapon systems in Taiwan's army are actually combat-ready. The military also suffers from logistical issues.[82] Topography and defensive posture will only go so far towards protecting Taiwan against a Chinese invasion.

In May 2023, the Institute for the Study of War claimed that the 'dominant but contested domestic framing of the 2024 Taiwanese presidential election as a choice between peace and war' probably supports the efforts of the Chinese Communist Party to 'coerce Taiwan into supporting cross-strait engagement'.[83] By August 2023, one commentator was reporting that 'Ukraine today, Taiwan tomorrow' had become an oft-heard phrase on the island.[84] The Swedish research institute V Dem found that Taiwan is more exposed to disinformation from a foreign State than anywhere else in the world. A recurring theme has been the attempt by the PRC to sow doubt among Taiwanese as to whether the United States would really stand by them in the event of an invasion. The visit from Speaker Pelosi in August 2022 had, though, dispelled some of this doubt, Köckritz observes.[85]

Whether Donald Trump, if re-elected president in November 2024, would protect Taiwan in the event of hostilities from China is very much open to question. In March 2022, the former president said that he believes China will invade Taiwan 'sooner rather than later'.[86] Writing a year later, one Taiwanese commentator argued:

> Taiwan must be ready for a second Trump term unfavourable to Taiwan's security. The new Trump administration would resume the economic-centred relationship with China as it did in the first term, likely at the cost of Taiwan's international status and sovereignty.[87]

[82] A Köckritz, 'How tomorrow never comes: Russia's war against Ukraine and its impact on Taiwan', Commentary, European Council on Foreign Relations, 8 August 2023, at: https://bit.ly/45Sz1vT.

[83] N Peterson and R Eakin, 'China-Taiwan Weekly Update, 26 May 2023', Institute for the Study of War, 26 May 2023, at: https://bit.ly/48k0tUZ.

[84] Köckritz, 'How tomorrow never comes: Russia's war against Ukraine and its impact on Taiwan', n 82 above.

[85] Ibid.

[86] C Vakil and L Kelly, 'Trump says he believes China will invade Taiwan', *The Hill*, 2 March 2022, at: https://bit.ly/3QUUC0z.

[87] D Jia, 'What a 2nd Trump Term Would Mean to Taiwan (and the US)', Blog post, Taiwan Research Hub, University of Nottingham, 11 April 2023, at: https://bit.ly/3Gcc241.

The US Central Intelligence Agency has claimed that President Xi has instructed the armed forces to be ready to invade Taiwan by 2027.[88] The outcome of the Taiwanese presidential election in January 2024 might be influential in affecting future cross-Straits policy. The opposition Kuomintang and Taiwan People's Party, both of whom advocated renewing talks with China, had failed to agree on a joint presidential ticket.[89] On 13 January 2024, and despite persistent interference by China in the run-up, the ruling Democratic Progressive Party (DPP) candidate, Lai Ching-te, was elected as Taiwan's new president. Responding to the news, China said it would not give up on achieving 'reunification'.[90] *The Economist* warned that China would be keen to make Taiwanese citizens feel that they have entered more dangerous waters by electing Mr Lai.[91]

B. Tackling Hybrid Threats at Sea

The maritime environment is a potentially fruitful domain for hybrid threats within and outside of armed conflict, as the situation in Taiwan has illustrated. It is especially difficult to interdict such actions using traditional law enforcement action. An adversary could, for instance, use a non-State armed group to target offshore oil-platforms using bomb-laden fast boats. Identifying such a threat amid a dense shipping and fishing environment has always been a major challenge. Hybrid action could involve foreign military personnel in some form.

Mirroring the 'little green men' of Russia present in Ukraine from 2014, retired US Navy Admiral James Stavridis has used the term 'little blue sailors' to denote individuals who are 'not exactly uniformed personnel'. These little blue sailors 'will not have any markings on their clothing, will not carry passports, and, if captured, will deny being part of any organized military'.[92] He further argues that in order to maintain plausible deniability,

> maritime hybrid warfare generally will be conducted in the coastal waters of the littorals. Instead of using force directly from identifiable 'gray hull' navy platforms, hybrid warfare will feature the use of both civilian vessels (tramp steamers, large fishing vessels, light coastal tankers, small fast craft, and even 'low slow' skiffs with outboard engines). It also will be conducted and likely command-and-controlled from so-called white hulls assigned to the coast guards of given nations. Both the

[88] G Torode, 'Why the Indian Ocean could be China's Achilles' heel in a Taiwan war', *Reuters*, 14 December 2023, at: https://bit.ly/3RlsfJg.

[89] W Yang, 'Taiwan Presidential Election Heats Up After Opposition Parties Announce VP Candidates', *Voice of America*, 24 November 2023, available at: https://bit.ly/3QRIBJn.

[90] Y Lee and S Wu, 'Taiwan voters rebuff China, ruling party gets third presidential term', *Reuters*, 13 January 2024, at: https://bit.ly/3TWwuh9.

[91] 'Defying China, Taiwan elects William Lai Ching-te as president', *The Economist*, 13 January 2024, at: https://bit.ly/3HkzkVQ.

[92] Admiral (ret.) J Stavridis, 'Maritime Hybrid Warfare Is Coming', (December 2016) 142(12) *US Naval Institute Proceedings*, at: https://bit.ly/3Nq0y1A, p 1366.

> Chinese and the Iranians are using their coast guards (and revolutionary guards in the case of Iran) in this fashion in the South China Sea and Arabian Gulf, respectively.[93]

Khurana suggests that impeding maritime domain awareness through cyberattacks against coastal surveillance measures and command, control, communications and intelligence networks could precede kinetic military action. Such disruption could also precede a strike from the sea against critical littoral infrastructure, such as nuclear installations. Coastal infrastructure and assets are also susceptible to hybrid threats in the form of clandestine underwater attacks by irregular personnel trained in diving operations. Achieving even limited sub-surface maritime domain awareness is, he notes, extremely challenging. Advances in underwater technology, including employing robotics, compound the threat.[94]

But a law enforcement response compliant with international law is certainly possible. Stavridis recommends that the US government use its Coast Guard to maximum advantage. 'Involving it in a leadership role in combating maritime hybrid warfare is crucial', he affirms, using the systems and platforms it has already developed in the context of counternarcotics, counterpiracy, and counterterrorism operations at sea. 'What remains is to think through how to leverage it against a much more sophisticated, national-level opponent'.[95] In the case of Taiwan, Taipei has warned that it will counterattack if Chinese armed forces enter its territorial waters or airspace.[96] Should such a scenario come to pass, this would in all likelihood be the end of law enforcement action by Taiwan and the beginning of all-out war with China.

[93] Ibid.

[94] GS Khurana, 'Maritime Dimension of Hybrid Warfare – The Indian Context', National Maritime Foundation (28 December 2017), https://bit.ly/42eVJfx.

[95] Stavridis, 'Maritime Hybrid Warfare Is Coming'.

[96] Y. Nakamura, 'Taiwan report sounds alarm over China hybrid warfare capabilities', *Nikkei Asia*, 1 September 2022, at: https://bit.ly/3Rl9lDX.

3

Hybrid Warfare and the Law of Armed Conflict

WHILE THE LEGALITY of hybrid threats typically falls to be governed by the law of law enforcement, in the case of hybrid warfare it is usually the law of armed conflict that governs the acts of organs or agents of one State intervening to support an armed group fighting illegally on the territory of another. This body of international law is also called international humanitarian law in many circles, or – by the United States in particular – the law of war.

This chapter considers first when an armed conflict is deemed generally to exist under international law and how specific forms of hybrid warfare may affect the legal classification of that armed conflict. The remainder of the chapter is divided into two sections. The first concerns what may be considered the archetypal case of hybrid warfare – Russian intervention through non-State actors in the Donbas in Ukraine in 2014. Russia's supply of weapons to both the People's Militia of the Donetsk People's Republic and the People's Militia of the Luhansk People's Republic in Ukraine certainly contravened the general prohibition on inter-State use of force that is codified in the Charter of the United Nations[1] and forms part of customary international law.[2] But the fact that this fundamental *ad bellum* rule is violated in any instance does not necessarily imply that an armed conflict also exists.[3]

The final section of the chapter discusses the legal situation between Iran and Israel as it stood in October 2023, with respect to Gaza and Hamas. It remained unclear at the time of writing whether Iran had in any manner directed or controlled Hamas's attack on Israel on 7 October 2023 or even if it had known of the group's plans to do so.

[1] Art 2(4), Charter of the United Nations; adopted at San Francisco, 26 June 1945; entered into force, 24 October 1945 (hereafter, UN Charter).

[2] International Court of Justice, *Case Concerning Military and Paramilitary Activities in and against Nicaragua* (*Nicaragua v United States*), Judgment (Merits), 27 June 1986 (hereafter, ICJ Nicaragua Merits Judgment), para 228.

[3] As noted in Chapter 1, for instance, the poisoning in Salisbury in 2018 of Sergei Skripal, a Russian defector, by Russian military intelligence operatives, was an inter-State use of force. 'Salisbury Incident', Statement by then UK Prime Minister (Mrs Theresa May), in *Hansard* HC Vol 637, 14 March 2018, https://bit.ly/3rqxXgv. Nevertheless, there was no armed conflict between Russia and the United Kingdom.

I. THE DEFINITION AND CLASSIFICATION OF ARMED CONFLICT IN INTERNATIONAL LAW

International law knows only two classifications of armed conflict: international armed conflict and armed conflict 'not of an international character' (hereafter, non-international armed conflict). These two classifications or 'typologies' were first set out in international law in Common Article 2 and Common Article 3, respectively, of the four 1949 Geneva Conventions.[4] For several years now every State in the world has been bound by all four of the Conventions.[5]

Other classificatory formulations sometimes seen in scholarship, such as 'transnational' armed conflict[6] or 'internationalised' armed conflict,[7] are not recognised by treaty or customary law and confuse rather than clarify complex military-political situations. They do not reflect extant international law. That said, it is possible for a non-international armed conflict to be transformed into an international armed conflict by the involvement of a third State in hybrid warfare,[8] as this chapter illustrates. It is also possible to have an international armed conflict and a non-international armed conflict occurring on the same territory at the same time.[9] There may even be multiple armed conflicts of both typologies, as was the case, for instance, in Syria at various points in the 2010s.

Below, the different forms of international and non-international armed conflicts are described in turn.

A. The Definition of International Armed Conflict

(i) An 'Active' International Armed Conflict

Common Article 2 stipulates that any armed conflict between two or more States Parties[10] to the Geneva Conventions is an international armed conflict

[4] These are termed 'common' articles because the text of the two provisions is identical across each of the four 1949 Conventions. See, eg, Arts 2 and 3, Convention (III) relative to the Treatment of Prisoners of War; adopted at Geneva, 12 August 1949; entered into force, 21 October 1950.

[5] The last of the 197 States to adhere was Palestine in 2014. In fact, 196 States are party to the Convention while Niue remains bound through New Zealand's ratification in 1959, before Niue became recognised as a State in its own right. See International Committee of the Red Cross (ICRC), 'States Party to the Following International Humanitarian Law and Other Related Treaties as of 25-September-2023', at: https://bit.ly/494sPTK.

[6] See, eg, GS Corn, 'Hamdan, Lebanon, and the Regulation of Armed Conflict: The Need to Recognize a Hybrid Category of Armed Conflict' (March 2007) 40(2) *Vanderbilt Journal of Transnational Law* 295–355, available at: https://bit.ly/3QaXcix.

[7] JG Stewart, 'Towards a Single Definition of Armed Conflict in International Humanitarian Law: A Critique of Internationalized Armed Conflict' (2003) 85(850) *International Review of the Red Cross* 313–49, available at: https://bit.ly/3rVDoI9.

[8] S Vite, 'Typology of armed conflicts in international humanitarian law: legal concepts and actual situations' (2009) 91(873) *International Review of the Red Cross* 69–94, at: https://bit.ly/3cl95gh, at p 71.

[9] ICJ Nicaragua Merits Judgment, n 2 above, para 219.

[10] The nomenclature is in fact 'High Contracting Parties', but there is no substantive difference from the more common term used in international law of 'States Parties'.

even if a state of 'war' is not recognised by one of them. An active international armed conflict exists most obviously where one State uses military force against another or the armed forces of two States clash. This can occur, for instance, through bombardment of a State's sovereign territory but it may also be a result of military action against another State's armed forces in any other place, such as on the high seas or on the territory of a third State (or even in outer space).

What matters in the classification of any situation are the facts. An international armed conflict between Armenia and Azerbaijan lasted for six weeks from September to November 2020, which resulted in thousands of casualties on both sides. The descriptors used by any of the protagonists may be duly considered, but they are certainly not determinative. Thus, a major international armed conflict between Ukraine and Russia, which began with the Russian invasion on 24 February 2022, was ongoing at the time of writing. This is despite the Russian president, Vladimir Putin, terming his war of aggression a 'special military operation'.

While massive use of force characterises the Ukraine–Russia conflict, for an international armed conflict to exist the law of armed conflict demands relatively little violence between enemy armed forces. According to the International Committee of the Red Cross (ICRC), for example, 'factors such as duration and intensity are generally not considered to enter the equation'. Indeed, the ICRC suggests that 'the mere capture of a soldier or minor skirmishes between the armed forces of two or more States may spark off an international armed conflict and lead to the applicability of IHL [international humanitarian law]', at least 'insofar as such acts may be taken as evidence of genuine belligerent intent'.[11] This 'first shot' theory is, though, questionable.[12] The better view is that while only minimal violence is necessary, it must be more than a limited exchange of fire over an international border.

(ii) Military Occupation

In contrast, no use of violence is needed for a belligerent military occupation to exist (and for the rules of the law of armed conflict to apply). This is where one State sends its armed forces onto even a small area of the territory of another without the valid consent of the territorial State it is entering.[13] In this regard, Common Article 2 provides that each Convention shall apply to all cases of partial or total occupation of the territory of a State Party, 'even if the

[11] ICRC, 'International Humanitarian Law and the Challenges of Contemporary Armed Conflicts', Report for the 32nd International Conference of the Red Cross and Red Crescent, Geneva, October 2015, at: http://bit.ly/2Mzrxch, p 8.

[12] GD Solis, *The Law of Armed Conflict: International Humanitarian Law in War*, 3rd edn, Cambridge University Press, Cambridge, 2021, p 132.

[13] On the vexed issue of consent where the legitimate authority representing the territorial State is contested, see, eg, S Casey-Maslen, *Jus ad Bellum: The Law on Inter-State Use of Force*, Hart Publ[illegible] Oxford, 2020, ch 2.

said occupation meets with no armed resistance'. That military occupation is indeed a form of international armed conflict was confirmed by States in the elaboration of the 'elements of crimes'[14] under the 1998 Rome Statute of the International Criminal Court.[15]

(iii) A 'Proxy' International Armed Conflict

One of the defining features of hybrid warfare is the use by one State of irregular forces against a foreign enemy State. But not all support to irregular forces operating illegally abroad causes an international armed conflict to come into being. The generally accepted test is that the supporting State must exercise overall control over the conduct of the – ostensibly – *non-State* armed group. The 'overall control' test was proposed by the International Criminal Tribunal for the former Yugoslavia (ICTY) in its judgment on appeal in the *Tadić* case in 1999. In the words of the Tribunal:

> In order to attribute the acts of a military or paramilitary group to a State, it must be proved that the State wields overall control over the group, not only by equipping and financing the group, but also by coordinating or helping in the general planning of its military activity.[16]

Without formally endorsing this understanding, in its 2007 judgment in the *Bosnian Genocide* case the International Court of Justice declared that 'it may well be that the test is applicable and suitable'.[17] Five years later, a trial chamber of the International Criminal Court expressly 'concluded' that the overall control test 'is the correct approach'. This will, the Court declared, 'determine whether an armed conflict not of an international character may have become internationalised due to the involvement of armed forces acting on behalf of another State'.[18]

But while the applicability of the overall control test has been generally endorsed, the legal consequences that result are more fraught and may justly be contested. As per the citation above, the International Criminal Court implies that an existing non-international armed conflict is extinguished when

[14] 'Elements of Crimes' under the Rome Statute of the International Criminal Court, reproduced from Official Records of the Assembly of States Parties to the Rome Statute of the International Criminal Court, First Session, New York, 3–10 September 2002, Article 8(2)(a)(i), fn 34: https://legal.un.org/icc/asp/1stsession/report/english/part_ii_b_e.pdf.

[15] Rome Statute of the International Criminal Court; adopted at Rome, 17 July 1998; entered into force, 1 July 2002.

[16] ICTY, *Prosecutor v Tadić*, Judgment (Appeals Chamber) (Case No IT-94-1-A), 15 July 1999, para 131.

[17] International Court of Justice, *Case Concerning Application of the Convention on the Prevention and Punishment of the Crime of Genocide* (*Bosnia and Herzegovina v Yugoslavia (Serbia and Montenegro)*), Judgment (Merits), 26 February 2007 (hereafter, ICJ Bosnian Genocide Judgment), para 404.

[18] International Criminal Court, *Prosecutor v Lubanga Dyilo*, Judgment (Trial Chamber I) (Case No ICC-01/04-01/06), 14 March 2012, para 541.

it becomes an international armed conflict through overall control of a non-State armed group. In its most recent expert commentary of the 1949 Geneva Convention III, which it published in 2020, the ICRC was overt in this regard:

> In such a situation, there will no longer be parallel non-international and international armed conflicts, but only an international armed conflict between the intervening State and the territorial State, even though one of them makes use of a non-State armed group.[19]

One problem with this 'extinction' approach is that the legal responsibility of a State under international law for the acts of the armed group it is supporting is believed only to operate when the States exercises a heightened level of control over the group. Thus, in 1986, in its judgment on the merits in the *Nicaragua* case, the International Court of Justice identified a different, higher threshold for State responsibility for the unlawful acts of the armed group fighting against another State – one of 'effective' control. According to this test, 'it would in principle have to be proved that that State had effective control of the military or paramilitary operations in the course of which the alleged violations were committed'.[20]

The Court explicitly reaffirmed its 'effective control' standard in its judgment in the *Bosnian Genocide* case, reiterating that such control is manifested by the foreign State giving instructions 'in respect of each operation in which the alleged violations occurred, not generally in respect of the overall actions taken by the persons or groups of persons having committed the violations'.[21] As I have written elsewhere with Annyssa Bellal:

> The differential with the overall control test – and the awkward fragmentation of international legal order – has potentially unfortunate consequences. Thus, there may be actions by a proxy armed group in the context of an international armed conflict that violate IHL and even, in certain circumstances, amount to war crimes, but for which the foreign State which is party to the armed conflict has no responsibility in international law. This is so, even though the armed group is acting as its proxy.[22]

The difficulties this creates notwithstanding, the International Court of Justice has sought to downplay the consequences of the legal gap between the two tests (ie overall control versus effective control). In 2007, it averred that:

> The degree and nature of a State's involvement in an armed conflict on another State's territory which is required for the conflict to be characterized as international, can very well, and without logical inconsistency, differ from the degree and nature of involvement required to give rise to that State's responsibility for a specific act committed in the course of the conflict.[23]

[19] ICRC Commentary on Article 2 of 1949 Geneva Convention III, at: https://bit.ly/3tNwWU3, para 299.
[20] ICJ Nicaragua Merits Judgment, n 2 above, para 115.
[21] ICJ Bosnian Genocide Judgment, n 17 above, paras 399–400.
[22] S Casey-Maslen and A Bellal, *The Additional Protocols to the Geneva Conventions in Context*, Oxford University Press, Oxford, 2022, para 1.19.
[23] ICJ Bosnian Genocide Judgment, n 17 above, para 405.

This is unpersuasive. The better view is that the two armed conflicts – non-international armed conflict and international armed conflict – exist side by side with each other.[24] This should be so *at the least* until the threshold of effective control is reached and the armed group becomes both in fact and in law an agent of the State, no longer an independent entity with its own decision-making power.

The ICRC is on much stronger ground when it further asserts that, for a proxy international armed conflict to exist, there is no need for a prior non-international armed conflict on which it must be based. Where a State uses an armed group instead of its armed forces to attack another State and the requisite 'effective' control is exercised over that group, at a low level of violence an international armed conflict may be initiated directly.[25] It is thus not necessary for the existence of a proxy international armed conflict that a State send an armed group to carry out 'acts of armed force against another State of such gravity' as to amount to an act of aggression under *jus ad bellum*.[26]

(iv) A National Liberation Movement

Exceptionally, where a State is party to the 1977 Additional Protocol I, and is deemed to be engaged in either 'colonial domination' or foreign ('alien') occupation or where the government is a 'racist' regime (such as *apartheid* South Africa), a national liberation movement fighting against that oppressive power for the right of a people to self-determination may make a formal declaration to the Swiss Federal Council that it will respect the Additional Protocol I and the 1949 Geneva Conventions. If the Council accepts the declaration as valid, this transforms what would otherwise be a non-international armed conflict into an international armed conflict.[27]

To date, this possibility has only been successfully invoked once in the history of the Protocol, in the case of Morocco and Western Sahara, where the longstanding conflict between the Moroccan armed forces and the Polisario Front has been considered an international armed conflict since 2015.[28] The Polisario Front is accepted to be the armed group fighting on behalf of the Sahrawi people's right to self-determination as an independent State in the territory of Western Sahara.[29] (In the past, it has received significant assistance from neighbouring States.)

[24] S Casey-Maslen and T Vestner, *International Law and Policy on the Protection of Civilians*, Cambridge University Press, Cambridge, 2022, p 295.

[25] ICRC Commentary on Article 2 of 1949 Geneva Convention III, para 299, fn 111.

[26] Art 3(g), Definition of Aggression annexed to UN General Assembly Resolution 3314 (XXIX), adopted without a vote on 14 December 1974.

[27] Arts 1(4) and 96(3), Protocol Additional to the Geneva Conventions of 12 August 1949, and relating to the Protection of Victims of International Armed Conflicts (Protocol I); adopted at Geneva, 8 June 1977; entered into force, 7 December 1978 (hereafter, 1977 Additional Protocol I).

[28] See on this issue K Fortin, 'Unilateral Declaration by Polisario under API accepted by Swiss Federal Council', *Armed Groups and International Law* blog, 2 September 2015, at: http://bit.ly/2NcA0lb.

[29] Indeed, the Sahrawi Arab Democratic Republic is a Member State of the African Union, but it is not similarly recognised by the Secretary-General of the United Nations in his capacity as the depositary of more than 550 treaties.

The provision in the 1977 Additional Protocol I allowing for indirect adherence by a national liberation movement is not, though, reflective of customary international law. Hence, while the treaty's application to the situation in Gaza might be considered possible at some stage, given both that Israel is not a State Party to the Protocol and that, even if it were, Hamas has shown no inclination whatsoever to comply with the fundamental rules of the law of armed conflict, the most recent armed conflict between the two parties that began on 7 October 2023 remains non-international in character.[30]

B. The Definition of Non-International Armed Conflict

The concept of a non-international armed conflict was first incorporated in Common Article 3 of the four Geneva Conventions of 1949 but it was not defined in that provision. It was only in 1995 that a definition was offered by an international tribunal – the ICTY. In its landmark decision on jurisdiction, it declared that a non-international armed conflict existed whenever there is 'protracted armed violence between governmental authorities and organized armed groups or between such groups within a State'.[31] Despite the ordinary meaning of the word 'protracted', the ICTY subsequently clarified at trial that this pertained to the *intensity* of the violence rather than its *duration*.[32]

The notion of an 'organised' armed group is one that reflects certain qualities of a State armed force, such as having in place a functioning chain of command and possessing a reasonable degree of logistical capacity in addition to having the ability to conduct sustained military operations.[33] It is not necessary, however, that the armed group control or hold territory or that its fighters be in uniform for a non-international armed conflict to exist. Moreover, the provision of weapons, training, and/or funding to an organised armed group by a foreign State does not, in and of itself, transform a non-international armed conflict into an international armed conflict.

It is arguable, but not certain, that this two-part test for a non-international armed conflict – 'organisation' of the armed group (or groups) and a relatively high intensity of violence against State authorities (or another armed group) – reflects customary international law. If so, once both criteria are met simultaneously, a non-international armed conflict comes into being as a matter of international law. Thereafter, however, if either criterion is not sustained, the

[30] In contrast, Israel's continuing occupation of Gaza in November 2023 amounted to a separate international armed conflict between Israel and Palestine.

[31] ICTY, *Prosecutor v Tadić*, Decision on the Defence Motion for Interlocutory Appeal on Jurisdiction (Appeals Chamber) (Case No IT-94–1), 2 October 1995, at: http://bit.ly/2JkqZ5z, para 70.

[32] 'The test applied by the Appeals Chamber to the existence of an armed conflict for the purposes of the rules contained in Common Article 3 focuses on two aspects of a conflict: the intensity of the conflict and the organization of the parties to the conflict'. ICTY, *Prosecutor v Tadić*, Judgment (Trial Chamber) (Case No IT-94-1-T), 7 May 1997, para 562.

[33] Casey-Maslen and Bellal, *The Additional Protocols to the Geneva Conventions in Context*, n 22 above, para 1.33.

non-international armed conflict is deemed to have ended. On this issue, therefore, the ICTY was wrong to assert that a non-international armed conflict only ends when 'a peaceful settlement is achieved'.[34] While this is possible, most non-international armed conflicts do not end in this manner.

All non-international armed conflicts are regulated by Common Article 3 of the 1949 Geneva Conventions as well as by customary law rules on the conduct of hostilities (the term used in the law for combat/the fighting).[35] In 1995–2005, the ICRC conducted a detailed study of the customary rules of the law of armed conflict applicable to both international and non-international armed conflicts. The resultant database describes both the rules and the State practice that underpins them.[36]

Persons fall into the power of the enemy (whether that be an organised armed group or its State adversary) when they are detained. In any such scenario, treaty and custom demand that they be humanely treated at all times.[37] This rule applies in 'the whole territory under the control of a party, whether or not actual combat takes place there'.[38] So moving detainees far away from the front lines does not remove their law-of-armed-conflict protections. But with respect to the fighting itself, 'some of the provisions are clearly bound up with the hostilities and the geographical scope of those provisions should be so limited'.[39] This means that the more permissive rules of the law of armed conflict only apply to fighting between the State armed forces and those of the non-State armed group. Other policing tasks remain governed by the more restrictive rules of the law of law enforcement and the human rights to life and to freedom from inhuman treatment.

II. HYBRID WARFARE IN THE DONBAS AND THE LAW OF ARMED CONFLICT

A. The Evolution of the Violence into Armed Conflict

Following the Maidan Revolution that began in February 2014 and which led to the ouster of Prime Minister Viktor Yanukovych, pro-Russian protesters seized regional government buildings in the cities of Donetsk and Luhansk and declared a 'people's republic' in each case. The force used to oust them was governed by the law of law enforcement, as the previous chapter discussed. In

[34] ICTY, *Prosecutor v Tadić*, Decision on the Defence Motion for Interlocutory Appeal on Jurisdiction (Appeals Chamber), n 31 above, para 70.

[35] ICRC, 'Customary International Humanitarian Law', Article, 29 October 2010, at: http://bit.ly/33UmyIL.

[36] The rules are available at: http://bit.ly/2ZecVG4.

[37] This demands that they be protected against all forms of violence and given food, water, shelter, and medical treatment for injuries or illness.

[38] ICTY, *Prosecutor v Tadić*, Decision on the Defence Motion for Interlocutory Appeal on Jurisdiction (Appeals Chamber), n 31 above, para 70.

[39] Ibid, para 68. Although the remark was made in connection with an international armed conflict, it pertains a fortiori to a non-international armed conflict.

April 2014, however, in a second phase of hybrid action, armed groups again seized government buildings across the Donbas region and initiated military action in numerous areas. To seek to suppress what became a swiftly burgeoning insurgency, the Ukrainian government initiated an 'Anti-Terrorist Operation'[40] using its armed forces to confront the paramilitary forces.[41] Very soon thereafter the situation snowballed into a non-international armed conflict.[42] The use of force by all parties was now subject to the salient rules of the law of armed conflict.

In response to the secessionist groups being pushed back by Ukraine's military, Russia covertly sent in heavy artillery and tanks to aid the separatists along with tens of thousands of 'volunteers'[43] (the so-called 'little green men' who first appeared at checkpoints in the Crimea).[44] No longer was the Russian Federation merely a State supplying arms, funding, and training to the People's Militia of the Donetsk People's Republic (DPR) and the People's Militia of the Luhansk People's Republic (LPR); it was also actively participating in fighting and dictating strategy for their military operations. This exercise of overall control transformed the indirect fighting between Russia and Ukraine into an international armed conflict between the two.[45] Still, at least for a short while, this left intact the two non-international armed conflicts, respectively, between Ukraine and the People's Militia of the DPR and between Ukraine and the People's Militia of the LPR.[46]

In rendering its decision on jurisdiction at the end of November 2022 in the inter-State case of *Ukraine and The Netherlands v Russia*, the European Court of Human Rights' Grand Chamber acknowledged that the 'precise boundaries of the areas of operation as well as the allegiances and chains of command of the different separatist armed groups active at the outset of hostilities in eastern Ukraine have not been clearly established'.[47] That said, as the decision

[40] D Sandford, 'Ukraine says Donetsk "anti-terror operation" under way', *BBC*, 15 April 2014, at: https://bit.ly/3EJmm2K.

[41] PJ D'Anieri, *Ukraine and Russia: From Civilized Divorce to Uncivil War*, Cambridge University Press, Cambridge, 2019, p 234.

[42] Ibid, p 44.

[43] MR Gordon, 'Russia Moves Artillery Units into Ukraine, NATO Says', *The New York Times*, 22 August 2014, at: https://bit.ly/48hcRoU.

[44] S Pifer, 'Watch Out for Little Green Men', Commentary, Opinion Editorial, The Brookings Institution, 7 July 2014, at: https://bit.ly/40egpEH; BBC, '"Little green men" or "Russian invaders"?', 11 March 2014, at: https://bit.ly/3RqFbPM.

[45] On 17 November 2022, the district criminal court in The Hague delivered its verdict in the trial for the downing of flight MH17. The court found that the Russian Federation had had 'overall control' over the DPR from mid-May 2014 at least until the crash of flight MH17 (on 17 July 2014) and that thus the conflict had become an international armed conflict. District Court of The Hague, Case ref ECLI:NL:RBDHA:2022:14036, at: https://bit.ly/44jokkt, § 4.4.3.1.3.

[46] This was not the view of the District Court, which followed the ICRC approach insofar as it held that 'the armed conflict, which was non-international in geographic terms, was internationalised and was therefore an international armed conflict'. Ibid.

[47] European Court of Human Rights, *Ukraine and The Netherlands v Russia*, Decision on admissibility (Grand Chamber), 30 November 2022, para 132.

makes clear, a key figure in the orchestrated violence in the Donbas was Igor Vsevolodovich Girkin (*aka* Igor Ivanovich Strelkov), a Russian national who served as the first Minister of Defence of the DPR. Mr Girkin held the rank of colonel in the Russian Federal Security Service (FSB), although he claimed to have retired from this post prior to his involvement in the conflict in Ukraine.[48] (Ironically, at the time of writing, he had been arrested by the Russian authorities and charged with extremism.[49])

The European Court considered it significant that the evidence establishes that Mr Girkin travelled to eastern Ukraine in early April 2014 with a group of men and shortly afterwards took control of Ukrainian government buildings in Slovyansk, a city in Donetsk Oblast in the north of the Donbas. This fact was not contested by Russia. Russia did, however, deny that he was operating on their instructions, and repeated the claim that he had resigned from the Russian military before entering eastern Ukraine. These assertions, the Court observed, 'could easily have been corroborated by the submission of evidence of Mr Girkin's previous employment and his resignation. However, no such documents were provided.[50] In the absence of evidence to the contrary, the Court found it established 'that Mr Girkin travelled to eastern Ukraine as an extension of his activities in Crimea, to act there under the general authority of the Russian Federation and to carry out that State's interests'.[51]

In stark contrast to this analysis, Russia's position was unequivocal: the Russian Federation was not involved in the conflict in eastern Ukraine.[52] The people whom Ukraine identified as agents of the Russian Federation were not, in fact, agents, it said. Furthermore, there was no basis whatsoever for regarding separatist government figures or separatist commanders as Russian agents. In particular, it averred, Mr Girkin was not a State agent of the Russian Federation.[53] These blanket denials did not persuade the Grand Chamber, which declared that

> the evidence of the situation on the ground supports the conclusion that increasing military participation from the Russian Federation occurred over the summer of 2014. It reveals that control initially acquired by the separatists over vast swathes of land in Donbass in April and early May 2014 was gradually being lost over the course of that summer in the face of an increasingly professional and organised Ukrainian military response in the context of the ATO [Anti-Terrorist Operation]. By July and into August 2014, the separatists were in real danger of being defeated.[54]

[48] Ibid, para 108.

[49] A Osborn, 'Pro-war nationalist Putin critic Girkin charged with inciting extremism', *Reuters*, 22 July 2023, at: https://bit.ly/47ynd2u.

[50] European Court of Human Rights, *Ukraine and The Netherlands v Russia*, Decision on admissibility (Grand Chamber), n 47 above, para 590.

[51] Ibid, para 591.

[52] Ibid, para 355.

[53] Ibid, para 365.

[54] Ibid, para 605.

The Court did not consider it established beyond reasonable doubt that Russia had exercised effective control over the territory of the DPR and the LPR from April 2014 'solely by virtue of the military presence of its own *de jure* soldiers'.[55] But when taken together with the decisive degree of influence and control Russia had enjoyed over the areas under separatist control in eastern Ukraine as a result of its military, political, and economic support to the separatist entities, the Court concluded that 'these areas were, from 11 May 2014 and subsequently, under the effective control of the Russian Federation'. This met the threshold, the Court decided, 'for establishing Russian jurisdiction in respect of allegations concerning events which took place within these areas'.[56]

Russian actions in Ukraine over the summer of 2014 certainly did stir some response from the North Atlantic Treaty Organization (NATO). On 4 September 2014, General Philip M Breedlove, the then Commander of NATO's Supreme Allied Command, Europe, declared:

> What we see in Russia now in this hybrid approach to war is to use all of the tools that they have … to reach into a nation and cause instability, use their energy tools, use their finance tools, use what I think is probably the most amazing information warfare blitzkrieg we have ever seen in the history of informational warfare, using all these tools to stir up problems that they can then begin to exploit with their military tool – through coercion … or through, what we see now in Crimea, what we've seen in Eastern Ukraine, Russian regular and irregular forces, these little green men without badges inside of nations stirring trouble.[57]

The following day, the NATO leaders at the Summit in Wales issued a declaration expressing deep concern 'that the violence and insecurity in the region caused by Russia and the Russian-backed separatists are resulting in a deteriorating humanitarian situation and material destruction in eastern Ukraine'.[58] But NATO's position was not yet that – outside Crimea – Russia was exercising effective control of the actions of the separatists in eastern Ukraine.

B. The Applicable Rules of the Law of Armed Conflict

Whether the conflict was a non-international or an international armed conflict from May 2014 onward has little bearing on the rules governing the conduct of hostilities, often referred to collectively as the Hague Law branch of the law of armed conflict. Broadly speaking, the same rules apply to a situation of armed conflict whether that conflict is one between States or between a State and an organised armed group.

[55] Ibid, para 611.

[56] Ibid, para 695.

[57] Remarks of PM Breedlove on 4 September 2014, cited in Munich Security Conference, *Munich Security Report 2015*, p 34: https://bit.ly/3SI1Vd6.

[58] Wales Summit Declaration, Issued by the Heads of State and Government participating in the meeting of the North Atlantic Council in Wales, 5 September 2014, NATO Press release (2014) 120, at: https://bit.ly/41pu5eU, para 17.

(i) The Principle of Distinction

The most fundamental rules of Hague Law result from the principle of distinction. This basic law-of-armed-conflict rule requires all the belligerents to 'at all times distinguish between the civilian population and combatants and between civilian objects and military objectives' and to 'direct their operations only against military objectives'. This requirement to target only combatants and other military objectives means that it is unlawful to deliberately target the civilian population, for example by shooting at individual civilians or bombing areas populated by civilians. Such an attack is a 'direct attack on civilians'. The rule also renders unlawful a military operation that does not seek to target a lawful military objective. Such an attack is 'indiscriminate'.

The rule of distinction prohibits the targeting of civilian objects. A civilian object is defined simply as an object which is not a military objective.[59] In turn, military objectives, in the language of Additional Protocol I, are objects whose 'nature, location, purpose or use make an effective contribution to military action'.[60] These rules are also of a customary nature and thus applicable in all armed conflicts.[61] An objective that is military in nature is one that is clearly military, such as an army barracks or a weapon belonging to an armed force. Hence, military aircraft, munitions, tanks, and military facilities are all lawful military objectives. So too is the Ministry of Defence's headquarters. An object may also be a military objective by virtue of its location. This includes an area of land that has strategic, tactical, or operational value to the enemy military.

An object that is ostensibly civilian in nature may also become a military objective as a consequence of its use for a military purpose. Accordingly, a home, a school, an office, or a religious building may become a military objective if it is used to store weapons, station military personnel, or to house a military communications network.[62] Where there is firm evidence – not a mere suspicion or a possibility – that a building or facility will be used in the future for a military purpose (even if this is not the case currently), it may be targeted as a lawful military objective.

While the content of the rule of distinction is unquestioned, regrettably it is still not clear under the law how accurate an attack must be to comply with its application in a situation of armed conflict. What is certain is that as a party to

[59] Art 52(1), 1977 Additional Protocol I.

[60] Art 52(2), 1977 Additional Protocol I.

[61] ICRC Customary Rule 7: 'The Principle of Distinction between Civilian Objects and Military Objectives', at: https://bit.ly/3tHhNU6; ICRC Customary Rule 8: 'Definition of Military Objectives', at: https://bit.ly/45h7lR6; and ICRC Customary Rule 9: 'Definition of Civilian Objects', at: https://bit.ly/3Mi684u.

[62] A military or civilian hospital must never be used for operational military purposes. Even if it is, in serious violation of the law of armed conflict, the enemy must still warn the other party to the armed conflict to cease and desist from such use and give it reasonable time to comply before countenancing any offensive action. Hospitals receive the highest level of protection under international humanitarian law.

any armed conflict you are not absolutely required to hit what you are aiming at in order to meet the dictates of the rule. Bombs and shells often miss their targets, but this does not mean that the law has been violated. Indeed, the judgments of international criminal tribunals indicate that, in case of long-range artillery or aerial bombardment, even missing a lawful military objective by several hundred metres may not necessarily be a breach. Naturally, however, far smaller margins of error are permissible in the case of rifles and mortars.[63]

(ii) Direct Participation in Hostilities

The protection afforded to each civilian lasts for as long as he or she does not participate directly in hostilities.[64] The precise scope of this notion is one of the most contested issues in the law of armed conflict. This is a major concern because loss of protection means that, potentially, an individual civilian who is directly participating in hostilities may be targeted and may even killed without warning.

While the notion of direct participation in hostilities certainly includes use of a weapon in combat against the enemy, other acts by a civilian, even one who is unarmed, can also lead to loss of immunity from attack. Other combat-related activities may also amount to direct participation in hostilities, such as gathering and transmission of operational intelligence or instructions; the production of weapons for proximate operational use or their delivery to the front line; and the impeding of enemy operations, for example by physically blocking roads or clearing mines in an area of hostilities. This is so, as long as the act or acts do, or are likely to, assist one party to an armed conflict in its struggle against another.

(iii) The Rule of Proportionality in Attack

Even if a military operation uses forces that is duly targeted at a lawful military objective in accordance with the rule of distinction, the decision to launch an attack[65] must also respect the rule of proportionality. This rule is codified in the 1977 Additional Protocol I[66] and is also part of customary law applicable to all armed conflict.[67] The rule of proportionality in attack is wholly distinct from the notion of proportionality under *jus ad bellum*.

Under the law of armed conflict rule, an attack against a military objective will be unlawful where it 'may be expected' to cause incidental civilian

[63] See on these issues: S Casey-Maslen with S Haines, *Hague Law Interpreted: The Conduct of Hostilities Under the Law of Armed Conflict*, Hart Publishing, Oxford, 2018, pp 157–58 and 231–32.

[64] Art 51(3), 1977 Additional Protocol I.

[65] The law of armed conflict defines the notion of an attack more broadly than our ordinary understanding of the word, as: 'acts of violence against the adversary, whether in offence *or in defence*' (emphasis added). Art 49(1), 1977 Additional Protocol I.

[66] Art 51(5)(b), 1977 Additional Protocol I.

[67] See ICRC Customary Rule 14: 'Proportionality in Attack', at: https://bit.ly/3QfqCMH.

harm that is 'excessive' compared with the projected 'concrete and direct' military advantage. Civilian harm is explicitly defined as encompassing death or injury to civilians, destruction of or damage to civilian objects, 'or a combination thereof'. Proportionality is thus not adjudged afterwards, depending, for instance, on the number of civilians harmed by an attack, but relates to the situation and the knowledge of the attacker when the attack was launched:

- What did the commander know about the risk to civilians (or what should he or she reasonably have known at the time of launching the attack)?
- Based on that knowledge, was the attack justified because of the military benefit it was likely to bring?
- Would a reasonable commander have come to a similar decision to proceed with the attack?[68]

The difficulty with proportionality is that its interpretation, and especially the notion of what is to be considered 'excessive' civilian harm, is unclear. What is accepted is that the law of armed conflict does not prohibit all incidental killing and maiming of civilians even though 'constant care' must certainly be taken to 'spare' civilians and civilian objects.[69] The question, though, remains unresolved as to how much foreseeable incidental civilian harm is legally permissible.

C. Compliance with Hague Law in the Fighting in the Donbas

From the outset of the armed conflicts in the Donbas, credible reports emerged from leading human rights organisations and bodies of widespread violations of the rules of distinction and proportionality in attack. These violations were the result of the use of force both by the Ukrainian army and by the separatist armed groups. Particular concern was expressed about indiscriminate shelling – from mortars, cannon, howitzers, tanks, and multiple launch rocket systems – meaning that the weapons were not targeting specific military objectives as the law of armed conflict demands. From around mid-July 2014, intense shelling began striking targets in Ukrainian- and separatist-held territory alike.[70] In November 2014, for instance, the Office of the United Nations High Commissioner for Human Rights (OHCHR) reported continued 'indiscriminate shelling of built-up areas' with more than 100 incidents reported in that month alone.[71]

[68] ICTY, *Prosecutor v Galić*, Judgment (Trial Chamber) (Case No IT-98-29-T), 5 December 2003, para 58.

[69] Art 57(1), 1977 Additional Protocol I.

[70] European Court of Human Rights, *Ukraine and The Netherlands v Russia*, Decision on admissibility (Grand Chamber), n 47 above, para 68.

[71] OHCHR, 'Report on the human rights situation in Ukraine', 8th Report, 15 December 2014, para 38.

Already in July, Human Rights Watch had drawn the attention of the international community to the particular problem of use of 'Grad' rockets. Grads are unguided rockets that cannot be targeted accurately, and which are often fired in salvos from multi-barrel rocket launchers to saturate a wide area. Most have a range of between 1.5 and 20 kilometres. Used at the end of this operational range, the rocket could land anywhere within a rectangle of approximately 54,000 square metres. The report by Human Rights Watch cited several specific instances where Grad rockets had hit residential buildings in Donetsk, far from the front lines or any other apparent military objective.[72]

In his mission to Ukraine in September 2015, the UN Special Rapporteur on extrajudicial, summary or arbitrary executions gave particular consideration to the indiscriminate shelling in the Donbas. In his report on the mission, Special Rapporteur Christof Heyns expressed his concern at some of the weaponry used by Ukrainian government forces in the course of hostilities:

> Some of the weapons used are inherently insufficiently precise to be used within a highly urban and civilian-populated conflict zone. In other cases, weapons with a known level of precision are being used contrary to or without regard to proper standard operating procedures for targeting.[73]

In its consolidated report on killings in Ukraine from the beginning of 2014 through to the end of May 2016, the OHCHR confirmed the dramatic impact on civilians resulting from armed hostilities. As of 31 May 2016, the OHCHR had recorded 9,404 people killed and 21,671 injured in the conflict zone of eastern Ukraine since the beginning of the armed conflict in mid-April 2014. This figure included civilians, members of Ukrainian armed forces, and members of the armed groups. It was, the OHCHR said, 'a conservative estimate based on available data'. Of the recorded total, it estimated that up to 2,000 civilians might have been killed during the armed conflict period, of whom as many as 1,800 died as a result of shelling of populated areas.[74]

III. HYBRID WARFARE BETWEEN IRAN AND ISRAEL AND THE LAW OF ARMED CONFLICT

On the morning of 7 October 2023, 50 years after the start of the Yom Kippur War in the Middle East, Hamas fighters from Gaza broke out of the enclave and attacked Israeli military personnel and civilians inside Israel. In the absence of overall control by Iran of the military operation by Hamas, a non-State armed

[72] Human Rights Watch, 'Ukraine: Unguided Rockets Killing Civilians', Report, 24 July 2014, at: https://bit.ly/40b05o8.

[73] 'Report of the Special Rapporteur on extrajudicial, summary or arbitrary executions on his mission to Ukraine', UN doc A/HRC/32/39/Add.1, 4 May 2016, para 63.

[74] OHCHR, 'Accountability for killings in Ukraine from January 2014 to May 2016', undated but 2016, paras 31 and 32.

group but the de facto authority in the Gaza Strip, the breadth and significance of the hostilities between Hamas and Israel amounted to a non-international armed conflict. In mid-October 2023, the leader of the Palestinian Authority, Mahmoud Abbas, was quoted in the official Palestinian news agency as reiterating that 'the policies and actions of Hamas do not represent the Palestinian people'. The statement was later withdrawn, however, following widespread anger among Palestinians on social media.[75]

According to official Israeli sources quoted by the UN Office for the Coordination of Humanitarian Affairs (OCHA), some 1,400 people were killed in Israel in the attacks. OCHA said that the reported fatality toll was 'over threefold the cumulative number of Israelis killed' since it began recording casualties in 2005.[76] The death toll was not disaggregated between military personnel and civilians, but it appeared that the overwhelming majority were unarmed civilians, intentionally killed by Hamas fighters. Some of the victims of the attacks were tortured before they were murdered. In addition to the war crimes of directly attacking civilians and torture, the customary law war crime of terrorising civilians appears to have been committed.[77]

The operation by Hamas included an attack on a 'rave' music festival being held at Re'im, five kilometres from the border with Gaza. More than 260 bodies of festivalgoers were found at the festival site itself, according to Israeli rescue service Zaka, but media analysis suggested that the total death toll among Israelis might be even higher. Several of those killed had fled inside bomb shelters to try and escape the ongoing massacre but had been hunted down by Hamas. In an interview with a journalist from *The Economist* on 10 October, Moussa Abu Marzouk, a senior member of the Hamas politburo and the head of its International Relations Office in Doha, claimed that the killings of the civilians at the music festival were a 'coincidence' and that they might have looked to their attackers like soldiers 'resting'. The resulting piece in *The Economist*, a publication not known for its ridiculing of interviewees,

[75] 'Palestinian Authority leader Abbas faces public anger amid Israel-Hamas war', *France24*, 22 October 2023, at: https://bit.ly/47owGtn. In late November 2023, the Rule of Law in Armed Conflict (RULAC) project at the Geneva Academy of International Humanitarian Law and Human Rights issued a classification of the hostilities between Hamas and Israel as an international armed conflict: 'Our approach in RULAC is to consider that Hamas and the Palestinian Islamic Jihad, because of their belonging to Palestine, are fighting Israel within the framework of an international armed conflict … Because the Palestinian authorities have never clearly distanced themselves from Hamas and the Palestinian Islamic Jihad, it is possible to consider them as belonging to Palestine and, thereby classifying the situation as an international armed conflict – which is what we have done'. This is unpersuasive as a matter of international law. Moreover, it appears inconsistent with the simultaneous classification by the RULAC of the fighting between Israel and Hezbollah in Lebanon as a non-international armed conflict. RULAC, 'RULAC: Update of our Entry on the Military Occupation of Palestine by Israel', 27 November 2023, at: https://bit.ly/49STaEL.

[76] 'Israel-Palestine: Gaza death toll passes 5,000 with no ceasefire in sight', *UN News*, 23 October 2023, at: https://bit.ly/3Fz9UTq.

[77] See, eg, International Criminal Tribunal for the former Yugoslavia (ICTY), *Prosecutor v Galić*, Judgment (Appeals Chamber) (Case No IT-98-29-A), 30 November 2006, paras 86–98.

duly observed that the claim 'is so risible it does more to flaunt the crime than cover up the truth'.[78]

Some of those who were not killed were abducted and taken back to Gaza to serve as hostages.[79] Hostage-taking is explicitly prohibited under the law of armed conflict[80] and is a war crime.[81] It is also prohibited, as international terrorism, under the 1979 Hostage-Taking Convention,[82] to which Iran[83] – but not Israel[84] or Palestine – is a State Party. The Convention's application is excluded in a situation of international armed conflict, but not in a non-international armed conflict.[85] Thus, Iran would be legally obligated to put on trial any responsible Hamas official found on its territory. The same would apply to Russia, which hosted Hamas officials in Moscow, including Mr Abu Marzouk, along with the Deputy Foreign Minister of the Islamic Republic of Iran on 26 October 2023.[86] The Israeli Ministry of Foreign Affairs condemned Russia's decision to invite Hamas representatives to Moscow as 'an act of support of terrorism' and called for the delegation to be expelled from Russia.[87]

The extent of the attacks by Hamas on Israeli civilians indicates the commission not only of manifold war crimes but also crimes against humanity, which are defined in international criminal law as certain predicate offences committed in the course of a widespread or systematic attack directed against a civilian population, with knowledge of the attack.[88] Indeed, it was alleged by a senior Israeli Defence Forces (IDF) commander that Hamas fighters 'came with orders to slaughter, burn citizens – not military personnel, simply citizens'. This included specific instructions to rape.[89] Palestine but not Israel is a State Party to

[78] 'A Hamas leader refuses to admit his group planned to kill civilians', *The Economist*, 11 October 2023, at: https://bit.ly/4757Yhi.

[79] E Mackintosh, G Mezzofiore, K Polglase et al, 'How a rave celebrating life turned into a frenzied massacre', CNN, 14 October 2023, at: https://bit.ly/3MgiAlx.

[80] Art 3 (non-international armed conflict) and Art 34 (international armed conflict), Convention (IV) relative to the Protection of Civilian Persons in Time of War; adopted at Geneva, 12 August 1949; entered into force, 21 October 1950 (hereafter, 1949 Geneva Convention IV).

[81] Art 147, 1949 Geneva Convention IV; and Art 8(2)(a)(viii) and (c)(iii), Rome Statute of the International Criminal Court; adopted at Rome, 17 July 1998; entered into force, 1 July 2002.

[82] International Convention Against the Taking of Hostages; adopted at New York, 17 December 1979; entered into force, 3 June 1983 (hereafter, 1979 Hostage-Taking Convention).

[83] On adhering to the Convention, however, Iran made an 'interpretative declaration' whereby it declared its 'categorical condemnation of each and every act of terrorism, including taking innocent civilians as hostages, which violates human rights and fundamental freedom of human kind, but asserted that 'fighting terrorism should not affect the legitimate struggle of peoples under colonial domination and foreign occupation in the exercise of their right of self-determination'. Text available at: https://bit.ly/3QACCcT.

[84] Israel is a signatory State but has never ratified the Convention.

[85] Art 12, 1979 Hostage-Taking Convention.

[86] G Pacchiani and L Berman, 'Moscow hosts Hamas delegation and Iran's deputy FM, prompting Israeli outrage', *The Times of Israel*, 26 October 2023, at: https://bit.ly/3FASPIR.

[87] Associated Press, 'Senior Iranian envoy met Hamas representatives in Moscow as Russia seeks to expand its clout', 27 October 2023, at: https://bit.ly/40bC2pn.

[88] Art 7(1), Rome Statute of the International Criminal Court.

[89] D Haynes, 'Israel says it has evidence of Iranian "involvement" in Hamas attack – but "cannot elaborate"', *Sky News*, 23 October 2023, at: https://bit.ly/40bBBLL.

the Rome Statute of the International Criminal Court, bringing the attacks by Hamas and the response by Israel within the material and geographical jurisdiction of the Court.[90] In May 2024, the Prosecutor of the International Criminal Court announced that he was seeking the Court's approval to issues arrest warrants for three Hamas leaders for war crimes and crimes against humanity.[91] These issues are discussed further in Chapter seven, which addresses hybrid warfare under international criminal law.

A. The Potential Role of Iran in the Hamas Attacks of 7 October 2023

Iran and Israel have been engaged in hybrid warfare for many years, with Iran refusing even to recognise Israel's right to exist. Iran and Saudi Arabia have similarly engaged in hybrid warfare, with Saudi Arabia's impending rapprochement with Israel said to be of great concern to Iran. As *The Economist* has expressed it, 'Iran's ability to cause mayhem at arm's length – through Hamas, Hezbollah, Iraq's plethora of Shia militias and Yemen's Houthis – may even give it more leverage than its conventional military capabilities, which are relatively weak'.[92]

Iran has consistently supported Hamas in Gaza with both funding and weapons.[93] Iran's support even included, according to one media report, Hamas and Islamic Jihad being sent hundreds of millions of dollars' worth of cryptocurrency in the months before the attacks.[94] According to Ismail Haniyeh, Hamas's leader, Iran funds the organisation with US$70 million a year.[95] Even if correct, however, this would not per se amount to overall control – much less effective control – as those notions are understood in international law.

Based on the available evidence, Hamas cannot be considered an agent of Iran under international law. An influential United States (US) military lawyer denied that Hamas was 'an Iranian proxy', describing it rather as 'an ally of convenience, with a shared common enemy in Israel'.[96] The relationship has ebbed and flowed over the years; it reached a nadir during the armed conflicts in Syria when Hamas supported the Syrian opposition. Moreover, as a Sunni Muslim group, Hamas differs from the usual Shi'a militias that Iran supports. 'Iran and Hamas

[90] Art 12(2), Rome Statute of the International Criminal Court.

[91] 'Statement of ICC Prosecutor Karim A. A. Khan KC: Applications for arrest warrants in the situation in the State of Palestine', News, International Criminal Court, The Hague, 20 May 2024, at: https://bit.ly/3QWdz41.

[92] 'Iran's ayatollahs play the Middle East's most dangerous game', *The Economist*, 23 October 2023, at: https://bit.ly/4789lMd.

[93] P Adams, 'Did Iran support plan for attack on Israel?', *BBC*, 9 October 2023, at: https://bit.ly/494kHm6.

[94] G Corfield, 'Hamas terrorists were sent millions in crypto before Israel attack', *The Daily Telegraph*, 11 October 2023, at: https://bit.ly/475fRmT.

[95] D Gadher, 'Iran lurks behind a massacre a year in the making', *The Times*, 29 October 2023.

[96] J Maddocks, 'Israel – Hamas 2023 Symposium – Iran's Responsibility for the Attack on Israel', Blog post, *Articles of War*, Lieber Institute for Law & Warfare at West Point, United States,

do not share a political or religious ideology'.[97] Emile Hokayem, an analyst at the International Institute of Strategic Studies specialising in the relationship between Iran and its proxies, says that Iran 'empowers, it supports, it guides, but it rarely orders'.[98]

Nonetheless, according to a number of other analysts, Iran was likely – but by no means certain – to have known of the planned attacks in advance. Thus, for instance, Karim Emile Bitar, an Associate Fellow at the Geneva Centre for Security Policy and an Associate Professor of International Relations at Lebanon's Université Saint-Joseph, 'very much doubt[ed] that Hamas alone could have prepared and decided to launch the strikes'.[99] Two days after the attacks, a senior Hamas official said that only a small number of top commanders inside Gaza knew about the plans, but claimed that allies like Iran and Hezbollah in Lebanon 'will join the battle if Gaza is subjected to a war of annihilation'.[100] Some, however, had read foreknowledge into a tweet on the social media platform 'X' (formerly known as Twitter) by Iran's Supreme Leader, Ayatollah Ali Khamenei, four days before the attacks. The tweet read simply: 'The Zionist regime is dying'. A day later, another Iranian State-run account reposted the comment adding a Palestinian flag icon.[101]

Even if it were established that Iran was aware of Hamas' intentions, under international law knowledge of the attacks is not the same as controlling, much less instructing or directing that they be perpetrated.[102] In this regard, in the aftermath of the attacks, Ayatollah Khamenei claimed that the 'supporters of the Zionist regime and some people in the usurping regime have been spreading rumours over the past two or three days, including that Islamic Iran was behind this action. They are wrong'. He did, however, also praise the military action: 'We kiss the hands of those who planned the attack on the Zionist regime'.[103] A senior US defence official said that the United States had 'no information at this time' to corroborate specific allegations of an Iranian role in the attacks.[104] But a report in *The Wall Street Journal* the day after the attacks, quoting unnamed members of Hamas and Hezbollah, claimed that not only had Iran given its approval for the operation a week before it was launched but also that

20 October 2023, at: https://bit.ly/3MgwfsP. Jenny Maddocks is an Assistant Professor in the Department of Law at the US Military Academy at West Point and the Managing Editor for *Articles of War*.

[97] Ibid.

[98] P Wintour, 'How Iran uses proxy forces across the region to strike Israel and US', *The Guardian*, 1 November 2023, at: https://bit.ly/40iRAYq.

[99] L Bullens, 'Could Hamas's attack on Israel pose a threat for the region and Saudi-Israeli normalisation?', *France24*, 8 October 2023, at: https://bit.ly/3QxS4GP.

[100] 'Biden says Hamas attacks on Israel were "sheer evil"', *France24*, 10 October 2023, at: https://bit.ly/3SiHUuW.

[101] See, eg, Gadher, 'Iran lurks behind a massacre a year in the making', n 94 above.

[102] Art 8, Draft Articles on Responsibility of States for Internationally Wrongful Acts, International Law Commission, 2001 (hereafter, 2001 Draft Articles on State Responsibility).

[103] 'Biden says Hamas attacks on Israel were "sheer evil"', *France24*, n 99 above.

[104] Adams, 'Did Iran support plan for attack on Israel?', n 92 above.

officers from the Islamic Revolutionary Guard Corps[105] had 'helped plan' the operation.[106]

Initially, Israel rebutted the suggestion that Iran had indeed helped to plan the attacks. An IDF spokesperson stated that 'Iran is a significant player, but we cannot say that it planned the operation or trained for it'.[107] But two weeks later, Major General Michael Edelstein, a retired IDF commander who was again working with its Southern Command owing to the ongoing hostilities, told journalists: 'You definitely can see evidence, we have evidence of Iranian involvement'. But he did not present any specific evidence of this involvement, nor did he elaborate on the type or form of the evidence that indicated it.[108]

B. The Hamas Attacks and *Jus ad Bellum*

The rules of the law of armed conflict apply in parallel with the rules on inter-State use of force, in particular with respect to the inherent right of States to self-defence to repel an armed attack. The supply of weapons to Hamas by Iran is sometimes characterised as an illegal use of force, following the approach taken by the International Court of Justice in its judgment on the merits in the *Nicaragua* case.[109] In fact, the parallel between the two situations is a little shaky. In the *Nicaragua* case, the allegation was that the United States was assisting a non-State armed group operating illegally in Nicaragua – the *Contras*[110] – to attack the government of Nicaragua. In the case of Palestine, Palestinians are resisting a continued, unlawful occupation by Israel of part of its territory.[111] UN Security Council Resolution 242, adopted by unanimous vote in favour in November 1967, affirmed that a 'just and lasting peace' in the Middle East required the withdrawal of Israel's armed forces from territories occupied in the 1967 conflict with Arab nations, which includes the Gaza Strip and the West Bank.[112] Of course, Hamas is a non-State actor, with the Palestinian Authority the embodiment of the State of Palestine under international law.

[105] 'Iran's Revolutionary Guards', Backgrounder, Council on Foreign Relations, Last updated 8 January 2024, at: https://bit.ly/3FUwkPr.

[106] S Said, B Faucon, and S Kalin, 'Iran Helped Plot Attack on Israel Over Several Weeks', *The Wall Street Journal*, updated 8 October 2023, at: https://bit.ly/3QAJvef.

[107] Cited in 'After Hamas attack, Biden assures Netanyahu that U.S. stands with Israel', *NPR*, 9 October 2023, at: https://bit.ly/3Sirti9.

[108] Haynes, 'Israel says it has evidence of Iranian "involvement" in Hamas attack – but "cannot elaborate"', n 89 above.

[109] Maddocks, 'Israel – Hamas 2023 Symposium – Iran's Responsibility for the Attack on Israel', n 95 above.

[110] See, eg, AE Feldmann and P Maiju, 'Reassessing the Causes of Nongovernmental Terrorism in Latin America' (July 2004) 46(2) *Latin American Politics and Society* 101–32.

[111] International Court of Justice, *Legal Consequences of the Construction of a Wall in the Occupied Palestinian Territory*, Advisory Opinion, 9 July 2004, paras 153, 159.

[112] UN Security Council Resolution 242, adopted by unanimous vote in favour on 22 November 1967, operative para 1(i). For a thoughtful discussion of whether Israel was still occupying Gaza

The question of whether force may be used to regain sovereign territory following a long-term occupation is increasingly debated under *jus ad bellum* rules. In 2020 and again in 2023, the situation with respect to the use of force by Azerbaijan to regain first partial and then total control over the breakaway region of Nagorno-Karabakh (and surrounding) territory may be instructive. Armenia had held large swathes of recognised Azerbaijani territory since 1994 following armed conflict that broke out over the status of Nagorno-Karabakh in 1988.[113] While the position taken by certain international lawyers is that force to recover territory seized a long time ago is always unlawful,[114] that would serve to reward aggression and/or to (almost) legitimise long-term, unlawful occupation, such as by Russia in Georgia, Moldova, and Ukraine. A more nuanced position to the issue was proposed by Dapo Akande and Antonios Tzanakopoulos following the first stage of Azerbaijani action in September 2020. They argued that

> a use of force in self-defence will only be lawful where it responds to an armed attack which is ongoing, is necessary, and uses force that is proportionate. In cases of occupation that result from a use of force, the armed attack has not only occurred but has not ceased. Necessity is often taken to refer both to the immediacy of the response in self-defence and to the notion that the use of force is a last resort. Since prolonged occupation arising out of force is a continuing attack, any requirement relating to immediacy is met and the question then turns to the last resort element of necessity. While passage of time may, and hopefully will, open up other means for bringing the occupation to an end, the very passage of years may itself be an indication that the last resort requirement is met.[115]

Writing in 1997, Marcelo Kohen similarly affirmed that: 'Remaining on foreign territory once an aggression has been repelled, without any other legal basis, amounts to an illegal presence'.[116] On this basis, the use of force to expel a foreign occupier, where the existence of a belligerent occupation is generally uncontested (and it is not, for example, a border dispute), would not be per se unlawful.

(as opposed to the West Bank, which is not addressed) after its pull-out of troops in 2005, see Y Shany and A Cohen, 'International Law "Made in Israel" v. International Law "Made for Israel"', Israel – Hamas 2023 Symposium, Blog post, *Articles of War*, Lieber Institute for Law & Warfare at West Point, United States, 22 November 2023, at: https://bit.ly/40SufwL.

[113] MN Schmitt and KS Coble, 'The Evolving Nagorno-Karabakh Conflict – An International Law Perspective – Part I', Blog post, *Articles of War*, Lieber Institute for Law & Warfare at West Point, United States, 27 September 2023, at: https://bit.ly/3QZbdjI.

[114] See, eg, T Ruys and F Rodríguez, 'The Nagorno-Karabakh Conflict and the Exercise of "Self-Defense" to Recover Occupied Land', Blog post, *Just Security*, 10 November 2020, at: https://bit.ly/2Vdg2JS.

[115] D Akande and A Tzanakopoulos, 'Use of Force in Self-Defence to Recover Occupied Territory: When Is It Permissible?', Blog post, *EJIL: Talk!*, 18 November 2020, at: https://bit.ly/39paQLs.

[116] MG Kohen, *Possession contestée et souveraineté territoriale*, Graduate Institute Publications Collection, Geneva, 1997, para 85. In the original French: « Rester sur un territoire étranger une fois qu'on a repoussé l'agression, sans aucune autre base juridique, constitue une présence illégale. ».

4

Hybrid Warfare and International Counterterrorism Law

THERE IS A close relationship between hybrid warfare and international terrorism. As previously noted, in 2010, the North Atlantic Treaty Organization (NATO) defined a hybrid threat as 'one posed by any current or potential adversary, including State and non-State *and terrorists*, with the ability, whether demonstrated or likely, to simultaneously employ conventional and non-conventional means adaptively, in pursuit of their objectives' (emphasis added).[1] This intertwining of distinct concepts would become more evident in Russia's forcible interventions in Ukraine, most notably in 2014 through Russian government support for, and direction of, the actions of the 'People's Militia' of the self-proclaimed Luhansk People's Republic and Donetsk People's Republic.

Frank Hoffman's own definitions have evolved over time, as the Introduction to this book detailed, but they have consistently and expressly referred to terrorism as an integral component of hybrid warfare and hybrid threats. In his 2007 paper for the Potomac Institute for Policy Studies, which did so much to popularise the term *hybrid warfare*, he was explicit that future wars would be without a 'clear-cut distinction' between 'organised violence, terror, crime and war'.[2] Then in 2014, he defined hybrid threats as: 'Any adversary that simultaneously employs a tailored mix of conventional weapons, irregular tactics, terrorism, and criminal behaviour in the same time and battlespace to obtain their political objectives'.[3] Four years later, he professed to 'update our understanding' of hybrid warfare and to 'distinguish it better from irregular warfare', reframing the notion as the 'purposeful and tailored violent application of advanced conventional military capabilities with irregular tactics, with terrorism and criminal activities … operating as part of a common design in the same battlespace'.[4]

[1] NATO, 'BI-SC Input to a New NATO Capstone Concept for the Military Contribution to Countering Hybrid Threats', 25 August 2010, at: https://bit.ly/3AikFX8, para 7.

[2] FG Hoffman, 'Conflict in the 21st Century: The Rise of Hybrid Wars', Research Paper, Potomac Institute for Policy Studies, Arlington VA, 2007, at: https://bit.ly/3R0PnuK, p 11, quoting A Dupont, 'Transformation or Stagnation? Rethinking Australia's Defence', *Australian Security in the 21st Century Lecture*, Parliament House, Canberra, 13 November 2002.

[3] FG Hoffman, 'On Not-So-New Warfare: Political Warfare Vs Hybrid Threats', *War on the Rocks*, 28 July 2014, at: https://bit.ly/3AMrZuN.

[4] FG Hoffman, 'Examining Complex Forms of Conflict: Gray Zone and Hybrid Challenges' (2018) 7(4) *Prism* 31–47, at: https://bit.ly/3QD6eH6, at p 40.

The proximity of hybrid warfare and international terrorism is to be attributed in part to the breadth of the definitions of terrorism in international law, particularly in the global sectoral treaties adopted under United Nations (UN) auspices.[5] But it is also in the nature of hybrid warfare that one State may choose to use or support a non-State armed group to employ brutal tactics in an insurgency in another State. This is on the basis that, as an element of hybrid warfare, terrorism offers the attacker State the opportunity to enjoy significant military and political advantage. In Mumford's words, 'the tactical acts of terrorism seen today in hybrid war have the collective capacity to have a strategic effect given the way it is being used in conjunction with other conventional modes of conflict'.[6]

Some measure of deniability, whether plausible or not, is of course a factor of hybrid warfare more broadly. But side-by-side with the particular benefits that accrue from harnessing terrorist groups in hybrid warfare against an international foe comes the potential for diminished accountability for the manifold breaches of international law likely to be committed. In this regard, commentators have continued to criticise the 'unexpectedly low profile' of counterterrorism in NATO's policy on hybrid threats as a response or preventive measure.[7] As a consequence, if opponents who use terrorism as part of a wider hybrid strategy are to be defeated, counter-hybrid war strategy needs 'to acknowledge the core role that acts of terrorism play in modern hybrid conflicts'.[8]

The first main section of this chapter describes the definitions of terrorism in international law – for they are multiple – and their application to situations of hybrid warfare. The issue of terrorist bombings has been chosen for this purpose. As will be discussed, a putative, albeit slightly blurred border delineates the notion of international terrorism in peacetime under international counterterrorism law from the prohibition of terrorism in armed conflict under the law of armed conflict (also termed international humanitarian law).[9] The rules governing terrorism under the law of armed conflict are markedly narrower, as they exclude from the law's proscription attacks in the context of hostilities conducted against the military targets of the enemy.

The chapter then discusses the application of the principles of international counterterrorism law to the conflicts in Ukraine since 2014 in two case studies. The first concerns the shooting down over Ukraine of Malaysian Airlines Flight MH17 in 2014 by fighters of the People's Militia of the Donetsk People's

[5] The sectoral treaties are those dedicated to particular types of prohibited action, such as hostage-taking, bombings, the financing of terrorism, or the protection of certain individuals belonging to a foreign State, notably diplomats in consulates or embassies or senior government officials on mission.

[6] A Mumford, 'The Role of Counter Terrorism in Hybrid Warfare', Report prepared for NATO's Centre of Excellence for Defence Against Terrorism (COE DAT), August 2016, at: https://bit.ly/3KS8LcC, p 17.

[7] See, eg, G Sadik, 'How Can NATO Effectively Counter Terrorism and Hybrid Threats? Analyzing the Benefits and Pitfalls of Joint Synergies' (2021) XXVI(1) *Perceptions* 54–72, at p 54.

[8] Mumford, 'The Role of Counter Terrorism in Hybrid Warfare', n 6 above, p 38.

[9] In this chapter the two most common names for the law are again used as synonyms.

Republic (DPR). The second case study concerns the sabotage of the Nord Stream pipelines in September 2022 – explosive acts which have variously been ascribed to Russian, Ukrainian, and United States (US) entities or elements. All attempts at attribution were only allegations (though of varying degrees of credibility); none had been conclusively proven at the time of writing.

I. TERRORISM DEFINED UNDER INTERNATIONAL LAW AND THE INTERPLAY WITH HYBRID WARFARE

Hybrid warfare may, its moniker notwithstanding, be wrought also outside a situation of armed conflict (as the term is understood under international humanitarian law) as well as within and in connection with an armed conflict. This necessitates review of the definitions of terrorism under international law and the implications for the international legal regulation of hybrid warfare that falls within the scope of such definitions.

As a general rule, where a State has 'effective control' of the actions of an armed group attacking a foreign enemy, that State will be responsible in international law for those acts,[10] including where they are terrorist in nature. But where a State has only 'overall control' of the actions of an armed group engaged in offensive actions against its enemy, while an international armed conflict will exist between the two States,[11] the foreign State will not be responsible under international law for terrorist acts unless it has specifically directed their perpetration.[12]

That said, no unitary or all-encompassing definition of terrorism exists under international law, and it is highly unlikely that States will ever come to agree upon one in the future.[13] In particular, States have proved unable to

[10] International Court of Justice, *Case Concerning Military and Paramilitary Activities in and against Nicaragua (Nicaragua v United States of America)*, Judgment (Merits), 27 June 1986 (hereafter, ICJ Nicaragua Merits Judgment), para 115; reaffirmed in International Court of Justice, *Case Concerning Application of the Convention on the Prevention and Punishment of the Crime of Genocide (Bosnia and Herzegovina v Yugoslavia (Serbia and Montenegro))*, Judgment, 26 February 2007, paras 399–400.

[11] International Criminal Tribunal for the former Yugoslavia (ICTY), *Prosecutor v Tadić*, Judgment (Appeals Chamber) (Case No IT-94-1-A), 15 July 1999, para 131. Overall control exists where the State 'has a role in organising, coordinating or planning the military actions of the military group, in addition to financing, training and equipping or providing operational support to that group'. International Criminal Court, *Prosecutor v Lubanga Dyilo*, Judgment (Trial Chamber I) (Case No ICC-01/04-01/06), 14 March 2012, para 541.

[12] ICJ Nicaragua Merits Judgment, n 10 above, para 115. This fragmentation of international law is potentially to the detriment of legal accountability – as the International Law Commission has remarked, fragmentation 'may occasionally create conflicts between rules and [legal] regimes in a way that might undermine their effective implementation'. 'Fragmentation of International Law: Difficulties Arising from the Diversification and Expansion of International Law', Report of the Study Group of the International Law Commission, UN doc A/CN.4/L.702, 18 July 2006, at: https://bit.ly/3Ea6RAz, para 9.

[13] K Ambos, 'Amicus Curiae brief on the question of the applicable terrorism offence in the proceedings before the Special Tribunal for Lebanon, with a particular focus on a "special" special intent and/or a special motive as additional subjective requirements', Special Tribunal for Lebanon (Re. Case No STL-11-0111), Scheduling Order of the President, 21 January 2011, p 5, para 7.

agree upon a unitary definition of 'international terrorism' outside the law of armed conflict. Furthermore, acting in some measure out of concern not to be constrained in defining terrorism offences broadly in their criminal law, States have refrained from negotiating a definition of purely 'domestic' terrorism.[14] As a consequence, such domestic terrorism is routinely and explicitly excluded from the purview of the UN sectoral treaties on terrorism.[15] This is not, however, an issue that concerns hybrid warfare, given its inherently international nature: two States are pitted directly (or more often indirectly) against each other.

For the last 25 years there has been a draft text of a UN Comprehensive Convention on International Terrorism, awaiting conclusion by States. But even though the Convention had not been adopted at the time of writing, the draft definition of the principal offence, as incorporated in the current draft text, is still significant. The core of the definition in Article 2(1) reads as follows:

> 1. Any person commits an offence within the meaning of the present Convention if that person, by any means, unlawfully and intentionally, causes:
>
> (a) Death or serious bodily injury to any person; or
>
> (b) Serious damage to public or private property, including a place of public use, a State or government facility, a public transportation system, an infrastructure facility or to the environment; or
>
> (c) Damage to property, places, facilities or systems referred to in paragraph 1 (b) of the present article resulting or likely to result in major economic loss,
>
> when the purpose of the conduct, by its nature or context, is to intimidate a population, or to compel a Government or an international organization to do or to abstain from doing any act.[16]

This definition is extremely broad, deeming an attack on either civilian or military personnel and on public or private property to be terrorist when the intent of the violence is either to coerce a change in conduct by government (or, for instance, the United Nations) or to intimidate the public at large.

The main obstacle to the adoption of the Convention, however, is not the breadth of the definition per se but specifically the situation of those involved in

[14] International human rights law is, however, relevant to such definitions. Thus, for example, the Human Rights Committee has stated that: 'The mere act of organizing or participating in a peaceful assembly cannot be criminalized under counterterrorism laws'. Human Rights Committee, General Comment No 37 (2020) on the right of peaceful assembly (Article 21), UN doc CCPR/C/GC/37, 17 September 2020, para 68. It is also true that where a terrorism offence is purely domestic in nature, the need for international cooperation and assistance that is incorporated in the sectoral terrorism treaties abates.

[15] Domestic terrorism is implicitly defined in, for instance, the 1997 Terrorist Bombings Convention as 'where the offence is committed within a single State, the alleged offender and the victims are nationals of that State, [and] the alleged offender is found in the territory of that State'. Art 3, International Convention for the Suppression of Terrorist Bombings; adopted at New York, 15 December 1997; entered into force, 23 May 2001.

[16] Art 2(1), Draft comprehensive convention against international terrorism (Consolidated text prepared by the coordinator for discussion), Appendix II to Letter dated 3 August 2005 from the Chairman of the Sixth Committee addressed to the President of the General Assembly, UN doc A/59/894, 12 August 2005.

armed struggle in support of the right of peoples to self-determination. Western nations oppose an exclusion from the Comprehensive Convention on this basis, whereas States belonging to the Non-Aligned Movement (a forum totalling 120 States), and especially those who are also members of the Organisation of Islamic Cooperation (OIC),[17] insist that individuals and groups who seek to achieve the legitimate aim of statehood for a people and who use force to do so in furtherance of that aim shall not be deemed terrorists under international law.[18] An ancillary dispute, but again one that predominantly pits the Global South against Western nations, is whether the acts of States as potential perpetrators of terrorism should be addressed in new treaty law.

The current draft text of the Convention would effectively exclude from its purview the actions of an armed group fighting on behalf of a people struggling for self-determination when the group was a party to an armed conflict (as discussed below in relation to the 1997 Terrorist Bombings Convention), but not civilians who are not members of such a group. Outside a situation of armed conflict, all those using force would be considered terrorists if they engaged in armed struggle against the territorial State. This position is legally problematic given the status of the right of peoples to self-determination as a peremptory (*jus cogens*) norm of international law.[19] It is also so even though the right to use force with a view to achieving self-determination does not enjoy customary law recognition.[20]

The OIC has proposed language to amend the draft text of the Comprehensive Convention:

> 2. The activities of the parties during an armed conflict, *including in situations of foreign occupation*, as those terms are understood under international humanitarian law, which are governed by that law, are not governed by this Convention.
>
> 3. The activities undertaken by the military forces of a State in the exercise of their official duties, *inasmuch as they are in conformity with international law*, are not governed by this Convention (emphasis added).[21]

[17] English language homepage of the OIC at: https://bit.ly/3JbGafg.

[18] The OIC Convention on Combating International Terrorism exempts from the crime of terrorism 'Peoples' struggle including armed struggle against foreign occupation, aggression, colonialism, and hegemony, aimed at liberation and self-determination in accordance with the principles of international law'. Art 2, Convention of the Organisation of the Islamic Conference on Combating International Terrorism; Annex to Resolution 59/26-P, adopted at Ouagadougou, 1 July 1999. A similar exemption was incorporated in the corresponding 1999 Organization of African Unity (OAU) Convention on Terrorism. Art 3, OAU Convention on the Prevention and Combating of Terrorism; adopted at Algiers, 1 July 1999; entered into force, 6 December 2002. At the time of writing, 43 States were party to the OAU Convention and a further 10 were signatories. Only Morocco and Zimbabwe are non-signatory States.

[19] International Law Commission, Annex to the text of the draft conclusions on peremptory norms of general international law (*jus cogens*), adopted by the Commission on first reading, in UN doc A/74/10, 2019, point (h).

[20] See, eg, S Casey-Maslen, *Jus ad Bellum: The Law on Inter-State Use of Force*, Hart Publishing, Oxford, 2020, pp 30–33.

[21] UN doc A/58/37, 11 February 2002, Annex IV, incorporated in Report of the Ad Hoc Committee established by General Assembly resolution 51/210 of 17 December 1996, UN doc A/68/37, New York, 2013, at: https://bit.ly/3Jodm39, p 18.

This is not acceptable to many Western nations. In 2005, the Coordinator of the negotiations proposed to add a preambular paragraph to the draft of the Comprehensive Convention. This additional text, which was based on an operative paragraph in a relevant General Assembly Resolution from 1991,[22] provided that the States Parties adopting the Convention were:

> *Reaffirming* that nothing in this Convention shall in any way prejudice the right to self-determination, freedom and independence, as derived from the Charter of the United Nations, of peoples forcibly deprived of that right or the right of these peoples to struggle to this end in conformity with international law.[23]

This did not suffice to break the impasse in the negotiations. The OIC has shown no signs of backing down on its demands for legislative change to the article on exclusions from the notion of who may be a terrorist. The organisation's proposed language would not amend the rules governing violations of the law of armed conflict by those engaged in the struggle for self-determination, but seeks rather to exclude from the ambit of international terrorism other acts of resistance movements that use force outside the conduct of hostilities in an armed conflict.[24] The question of 'who governs' has been part of the rhetoric surrounding the armed conflicts in Ukraine since 2014 and continues to be at the centre of the major, ongoing international armed conflict between Russia and Ukraine.

A. The 1997 Terrorist Bombings Convention

As the focus of the discussion on interplay between terrorism and hybrid warfare that follows, the issue of terrorist bombings has been chosen. This is for two main reasons. First, as is well known, the use of explosive devices against people, buildings, transportation, or infrastructure is a common terrorist tactic – indeed, it is the most common, in the view of the American terrorism expert

[22] UN General Assembly Resolution 46/51 ('Measures to eliminate international terrorism'), adopted without a vote on 9 December 1991, operative para 15: '*Considers* that nothing in the present resolution could in any way prejudice the right to self-determination, freedom and independence, as derived from the Charter of the United Nations, of peoples forcibly deprived of that right referred to in the Declaration of Principles of International Law concerning Friendly Relations and Cooperation among States in accordance with the Charter of the United Nations, particularly peoples under colonial and racist regimes or other forms of alien domination, or the right of these peoples to struggle legitimately to this end and to seek and receive support in accordance with the principles of the Charter, the above-mentioned Declaration and the relevant General Assembly resolutions, including the present resolution'.

[23] 'Report of the coordinator on the results of the informal consultations on a draft comprehensive convention on international terrorism, held from 25 to 29 July 2005', Appendix I to Letter dated 3 August 2005 from the Chairman of the Sixth Committee, pp. 3–4: https://bit.ly/49kkBqi.

[24] K Samuel, 'The legal response to terrorism of the Organization of Islamic Cooperation', ch 44 in B Saul (ed), *Research Handbook on International Law and Terrorism*, 2nd edn, Edward Elgar, Cheltenham, 2021, p 648.

Brian Michael Jenkins.[25] Second, a dedicated global treaty addresses the issue at hand – the International Convention for the Suppression of Terrorist Bombings – a UN sectoral treaty that has been very widely ratified by States.[26] Moreover, the 1997 Terrorist Bombings Convention was the first global treaty to contain the word 'terrorist' in its title.

It was negotiated at the instigation of the United States following a bombing of its air force personnel at the Khobar Towers in Dhahran, Saudi Arabia, in 1996. The resultant Convention requires the criminalisation in domestic law of the act, by 'any person', of intentionally delivering, placing, discharging, or detonating

> an explosive or other lethal device in, into or against a place of public use, a State or government facility, a public transportation system or an infrastructure facility, with the intent to cause death or serious bodily injury or to cause extensive destruction of such a place, facility or system, where such destruction results in or is likely to result in major economic loss.[27]

The use of bombings by terrorist groups fighting against the State outside the legal confines of armed conflict is systematically captured by the Convention as long as there is an international element in the attack. This may be on the basis that the offence was abetted or assisted by a foreign State (for instance, through support in the planning of the attack or the supply of relevant munitions or parts and components needed to construct a bomb), or where the bombing involves nationals of the foreign State in some other element of the offence.

States have long agreed that 'situations of internal disturbances and tensions, such as riots, isolated and sporadic acts of violence and other acts of a similar nature' are not armed conflicts.[28] Consequently, even fairly regular bombing attacks by a non-State armed group against a State will not necessarily amount to an armed conflict where the group does not engage in combat with the enemy State's armed forces.[29] This potentially allows a foreign State to cause mayhem within its adversary through the use of terrorist bombings by an ostensibly

[25] BM Jenkins, 'The 1970s and the Birth of Contemporary Terrorism', Blog entry, *The RAND Blog*, 30 July 2015, at: https://bit.ly/35OAdqe.

[26] At the time of writing, 170 of 197 States were party to the Convention and a further two States were signatories.

[27] Arts 2(1) and 4, 1997 Terrorist Bombings Convention, n 15 above. In addition to the explosive and incendiary devices its title indicates, the Convention also applies to weapons or devices that can cause serious physical harm or material damage through 'the release, dissemination or impact of toxic chemicals, biological agents or toxins or similar substances or radiation or radioactive material'. Art 1(3)(b), 1997 Terrorist Bombings Convention.

[28] Art 1(2), Protocol Additional to the Geneva Conventions of 12 August 1949, and relating to the Protection of Victims of Non-International Armed Conflicts (Protocol II); adopted at Geneva, 8 June 1977; entered into force, 7 December 1978 (hereafter, 1977 Additional Protocol II). See also Art 2(d), Rome Statute of the International Criminal Court; adopted at Rome, 17 July 1998; entered into force, 1 July 2002.

[29] JK Kleffner, 'The Legal Fog of an Illusion: Three Reflections on "Organization" and "Intensity" as Criteria for the Temporal Scope of the Law of Non-International Armed Conflict' (2019) 95 *International Legal Studies* 161–78, at p 169.

non-State armed group. Case law in the International Criminal Tribunal for the former Yugoslavia (ICTY) used the twin criteria of the intensity of the conflict and the organisation of a non-State armed group for the purpose of distinguishing an armed conflict from 'banditry, unorganized and short-lived insurrections, or terrorist activities, which are not subject to international humanitarian law'.[30]

But when a terrorist bombing does occur in an armed conflict, the legal situation under the 1997 Convention is more complex. Under the law of armed conflict, targeting military objectives using force is not just *permissible* for the parties to an armed conflict but is *mandated* by the law's peremptory principle of distinction.[31] As a consequence, an exclusion for the conduct of hostilities and for the actions of parties to armed conflict vis-à-vis persons protected under the law needed to be incorporated in the 1997 Terrorist Bombings Convention. To address this, it is stipulated in Article 19(2) that: 'The activities of armed forces during an armed conflict, as those terms are understood under international humanitarian law, which are governed by that law, are not governed by this Convention'.[32]

The notion of 'armed forces' in this exclusionary provision encompasses not only State armed forces but also organised non-State armed groups, where they are party to an armed conflict (whether this be international or non-international in character).[33] Despite contestation by a small number of commentators of this postulate,[34] this seems manifest from the wording of the

[30] ICTY, *Prosecutor v Tadić*, Judgment (Trial Chamber) (Case No IT-94-1-T), 7 May 1997, para 562; reaffirmed inter alia in ICTY, *Prosecutor v Limaj*, Judgment (Trial Chamber) (Case No IT-03-66-T), 30 November 2005, para 84. Similarly, with respect to international armed conflict, when adhering to the 1977 Additional Protocol I to the Geneva Conventions, the United Kingdom formally declared its understanding 'that the term "armed conflict" of itself and in its context denotes a situation of a kind which is not constituted by the commission of ordinary crimes including acts of terrorism whether concerted or in isolation'. Declaration of the United Kingdom upon ratification of the 1977 Additional Protocol I, 28 January 1998, text available at: https://bit.ly/44t6cVj.

[31] It is stipulated that 'the Parties to the conflict shall at all times distinguish between the civilian population and combatants and between civilian objects and military objectives and accordingly *shall direct their operations only against military objectives*' (emphasis added). Art 48, Protocol Additional to the Geneva Conventions of 12 August 1949, and relating to the Protection of Victims of International Armed Conflicts (Protocol I); adopted at Geneva, 8 June 1977; entered into force, 7 December 1978 (hereafter, 1977 Additional Protocol I).

[32] The same exclusion for the acts of armed forces *in bello* is also reflected in the draft Comprehensive Convention on International Terrorism, n 16 above. Therein, Art 20(2) provides that: 'The activities of armed forces during an armed conflict, as those terms are understood under international humanitarian law, which are governed by that law, are not governed by the present Convention'.

[33] S Witten, 'The International Convention for the Suppression of Terrorist Bombings', ch 8 in Saul (ed), *Research Handbook on International Law and Terrorism*, n 24 above, 2nd edn, p 117. See also AR Perera, 'The draft United Nations Comprehensive Convention on International Terrorism', ch 9 in ibid, p 127; and B Saul, 'From Conflict to Complementarity. Reconciling international counterterrorism law and international humanitarian law' (2021) 103(916–917) *International Review of the Red Cross* 157–202, at p 180.

[34] See, eg, M Zwanenburg, 'Foreign Terrorist Fighters in Syria: Challenges of the Sending State', (2016) 92(1) *International Legal Studies* 204–34, at: https://bit.ly/3vBEat9, at pp 216–17; and M Hmoud, 'Negotiating the Draft Comprehensive Convention on International Terrorism: Major Bones of Contention' (2006) 4(5) *Journal of International Criminal Justice* 1031, at p 1036.

paragraph, which refers first to 'armed forces' and then to the 'military forces of a State' in the same article.[35]

O'Donnell suggests that this exclusionary clause in the Convention might not apply 'to other situations in which international humanitarian law is applicable, such as occupation'.[36] This is incorrect. A situation of international armed conflict includes a situation of belligerent occupation, as the Elements of Crime for the Rome Statute of the International Criminal Court make clear.[37] Thus, Russia's actions in Ukraine since 2014, which have involved belligerent occupation, mean that terrorism by its armed forces is to be adjudged by the law of armed conflict and international criminal law (where conduct amounts to a war crime) and is not to be prosecuted in accordance with the terms of the 1997 Terrorist Bombings Convention.

There are limits to this demarcation, however. Based on the formulation in Article 19(2) of the Convention, any person who decides to engage in prohibited conduct under the Convention and who is *not* a member of any of the armed forces engaged in the conflict in Ukraine would fall outside that exclusion for armed conflict.[38] This would mean, for instance, that Ukrainian civilians who threw Molotov cocktails[39] at Russian forces in March 2022 and beyond were engaging in international terrorism as defined in the 1997 Convention. Moreover, under the terms of Article 7 of that Convention they must be prosecuted by the authorities for having done so.[40] Naturally, the same rule applies to individuals who may be sympathetic to, but who were not at the time members

[35] D Kretzmer, 'Terrorism and the International Law of Occupation', ch 15 in Saul (ed), *Research Handbook on International Law and Terrorism*, 2nd edn, n 24 above, p 216. The argument by Van Poecke, Verbruggen, and Yperman that the two terms 'operate in different legal spheres, and it seems that they should not be read in relation to one another' is unpersuasive. T Van Poecke, F Verbruggen and W Yperman, 'Terrorist offences and international humanitarian law: The armed conflict exclusion clause' (2021) 103(916–917) *International Review of the Red Cross* 295–324, at p 304. Acts of terrorism by a State in the context of a military occupation are expressly prohibited by Article 33 of the 1949 Geneva Convention IV, as discussed below.

[36] D O'Donnell, 'International treaties against terrorism and the use of terrorism during armed conflict and by armed forces' (2006) 88(864) *International Review of the Red Cross* 853–80, at p 868.

[37] Elements of Crimes under the Rome Statute of the International Criminal Court, reproduced from Official Records of the Assembly of States Parties to the Rome Statute of the International Criminal Court, First Session, New York, 3–10 September 2002, https://www.icc-cpi.int/sites/default/files/Publications/Elements-of-Crimes.pdf, Article 8(2)(a)(i), fn 34.

[38] B Saul, 'From conflict to complementarity: Reconciling international counterterrorism law and international humanitarian law', n 33 above, at p 186; and see similarly O'Donnell, 'International treaties against terrorism and the use of terrorism during armed conflict and by armed forces', n 36 above, p 869.

[39] On the legality of Molotov cocktails under the law of armed conflict more generally, see S Watts, 'Are Molotov Cocktails Lawful Weapons?', Blog post, Lieber Institute for Law & Warfare at West Point, United States, 2 March 2022, at: https://bit.ly/3vBpbze.

[40] Art 7(1) and (2), 1997 Terrorist Bombings Convention, n 15 above. In 2015, Ukraine informed the depositary of the Convention that 'from 20 February 2014 and for the period of temporary occupation by the Russian Federation of a part of the territory of Ukraine – the Autonomous Republic of Crimea and the city of Sevastopol – as a result of the armed aggression of the Russian Federation committed against Ukraine and until the complete restoration of the constitutional law and order and effective control by Ukraine over such occupied territory, as well as over certain districts of the

of, the People's Militia of the Luhansk or Donetsk People's Republics or of the Russian armed forces. If they used explosive devices against Ukrainians or Ukrainian public or private property in contravention of Article 2(1) of the Terrorist Bombings Convention, they too must be prosecuted (including by the Russian authorities).

Beyond the situation in Ukraine, the exclusion in the 1997 Terrorist Bombings Convention would, of course, not apply where resistance by a non-State armed group to occupation does not rise to the level of an armed conflict.[41] It should further be noted that, following the conclusion of the 1997 Convention, one contracting State sought to draw a distinction between criminal actions and the legitimate struggle for self-determination outside the conduct of hostilities. Thus, continuing the debate about whether national liberation movements were terrorist, Pakistan made a declaration at the time of formal adherence whereby 'nothing' in the 1997 Convention 'shall be applicable to struggles, including armed struggle, for the realization of right of self-determination launched against any alien or foreign occupation or domination, in accordance with the rules of international law'.

Predictably, many Western States objected to Pakistan's position.[42] Finland, for instance, was 'of the view that the declaration amounts to a reservation as its purpose is to unilaterally limit the scope of the Convention'. Finland further considered the declaration 'to be in contradiction with the object and purpose of the Convention, namely the suppression of terrorist bombings wherever and by whomever carried out'.[43] For its part, Russia stated in 2003 that

> the realization of the right of peoples to self-determination must not conflict with other fundamental principles of international law, such as the principle of the settlement of international disputes by peaceful means, the principle of the territorial integrity of States, and the principle of respect for human rights and fundamental freedoms.[44]

Donetsk and Luhansk oblasts of Ukraine, which are temporarily not under control of Ukraine as a result of the aggression of the Russian Federation, the application and implementation by Ukraine of the obligations under the above [Convention], as applied to the aforementioned occupied and uncontrolled territory of Ukraine, is limited and is not guaranteed'. Communication of Ukraine to the UN Secretary-General, acting in his capacity as depositary, UN Ref C.N.610.2015.TREATIES-XVIII.9 (Depositary Notification), communication received on 20 October 2015.

[41] O'Donnell, 'International treaties against terrorism and the use of terrorism during armed conflict and by armed forces', n 36 above, p 868. O'Donnell subsequently appears to equate a non-international armed conflict with the criteria related to territorial control laid down in Article 1(2) of the 1977 Additional Protocol II. Ibid, p 869. This is incorrect. No territorial control by a non-State armed group is necessary for a non-international armed conflict whose hostilities are governed by the customary rules of the law of armed conflict.

[42] Australia, Austria, Canada, Denmark, Finland, France, Germany, India, Ireland, Israel, Italy, Japan, Moldova, the Netherlands, New Zealand, Norway, Poland, Russia, Spain, Sweden, United Kingdom, and the United States.

[43] Declaration of Finland, 17 June 2003, at: http://bit.ly/2YbSI1g.

[44] Declaration of the Russian Federation, 22 September 2003, in Endnote 11 on the UN Treaty Series website entry for the 1997 Convention, available at: http://bit.ly/2YbSI1g.

B. The Definition of Terrorism in Armed Conflict

Despite the lack of agreement among States on key definitional aspects pertaining to the actors that may perpetrate terrorism under the global treaties, there is a certain, if partial, bifurcation between terrorism in peacetime and terrorism perpetrated during and in connection with armed conflict. As noted above, the need for such a differentiation is owed primarily to the fact that parties to an armed conflict are obligated under the law of armed conflict principle of distinction to 'direct their operations' in the conduct of hostilities 'only against military objectives'.[45]

The distinction between terrorism in peacetime and in armed conflict is less significant under the Geneva Law branch of the law of armed conflict. Geneva Law protects persons in the power of the enemy, in particular when they are detained or are civilians in territory occupied by a foreign State in an international armed conflict. The relevant definitions of terrorism discussed below are followed by analysis of the other branch of the law of armed conflict, Hague Law, which regulates combat between parties to an armed conflict. There, the distinction between peacetime and wartime terrorism is considerably more marked.

C. The Definition of Terrorism in Geneva Law

The prohibition on acts of terrorism against any person in detention, whether or not they had previously been engaged directly in hostilities, is today a customary rule applicable in all armed conflict. This is so, despite the surprising omission in the ICRC's detailed study of customary international humanitarian law, issued in 2005, of a discrete rule prohibiting measures or acts of terrorism against those in the power of the enemy. Such a rule assuredly exists, however.

The 1949 Geneva Convention IV concerns the protection of civilians in international armed conflict. In addition to prohibiting hostage-taking, it contains an express prohibition of 'all measures' of terrorism against civilians in occupied territories or against protected persons in the territory of a party to an armed conflict.[46] The ICRC's 1958 commentary on the provision offers little in the way of clarification of the unusual formulation, nor does it elucidate precisely what the provision envisages.[47] The commentary does, however, observe that

[45] Art 48, Additional Protocol to the Geneva Conventions of 12 August 1949, and relating to the Protection of Victims of International Armed Conflicts (Protocol I), 8 June 1977.

[46] Art 33, Convention (IV) relative to the Protection of Civilian Persons in Time of War; adopted at Geneva, 12 August 1949; entered into force, 21 October 1950.

[47] The treatment meted out by the Nazis to civilians in occupied Europe during the Second World War does, however, offer an extreme version of what was envisaged. In particular, the extermination of more than one million Jews by the *Einsatzgruppen* in Eastern Europe, first in Poland and later in the Soviet Union, is one of history's most egregious crimes. In addition to the atrocities committed by the Nazis against civilians, local puppet militia forces were also used in the Holocaust.

> in resorting to intimidatory measures to terrorise the population, the belligerents hoped to prevent hostile acts. Far from achieving the desired effect, however, such practices, by reason of their excessive severity and cruelty, kept alive and strengthened the spirit of resistance. They strike at guilty and innocent alike.[48]

The 1977 Additional Protocol I, which applies also to 'armed conflicts in which peoples are fighting against colonial domination and alien occupation and against racist régimes in the exercise of their right of self-determination',[49] does not specifically refer to measures or acts of terrorism. That said, in the fundamental guarantees that apply as a minimum standard to all who fall under the power of a party to an international armed conflict in accordance with the Protocol, many of the prohibited acts, such as murder, mutilation, torture, the taking of hostages, and collective punishments,[50] as well as arbitrary executions,[51] clearly constitute potential predicate offences for terrorism.[52]

A specific prohibition of 'acts of terrorism' is incorporated in the 1977 Additional Protocol II,[53] which is binding on parties to the non-international armed conflicts falling within its material scope.[54] The provision is broad in ambit, applying to protect '[a]ll persons who do not take a direct part or who have ceased to take part in hostilities, whether or not their liberty has been restricted'.[55] Hence, acts of terrorism may be acts committed against those who formerly participated directly in hostilities (eg by taking part in fighting) and not only against civilians.[56] Not only acts of terrorism but also threats of terrorism were punishable as war crimes under the Statute of the International Criminal Tribunal for Rwanda[57] and the Special Court for Sierra Leone.[58] The systematic,

[48] ICRC Commentary on Article 33 of 1949 Geneva Convention IV, 1958, at: https://bit.ly/2LbfkLJ, p 226.

[49] Art 1(4), 1977 Additional Protocol I.

[50] Art 75(2), 1977 Additional Protocol I.

[51] Art 75(4), 1977 Additional Protocol I.

[52] In a separate section of its commentary on other provisions in the Protocol, the ICRC describes terrorism as being 'understood to be the systematic attack on non-military objectives in order to force the military elements of the adverse Party to comply with the wishes of the attacker by means of the fear and anguish induced by such an attack'. Y Sandoz, C Swinarski and B Zimmermann (eds), *Commentary on the Additional Protocols of 8 June 1977 to the Geneva Conventions of 12 August 1949*, Martinus Nijhoff, Geneva, 1987 (hereafter, ICRC commentary on the 1977 Additional Protocols), para 1690, fn 27.

[53] Art 4(2)(d), 1977 Additional Protocol II.

[54] These are where dissident armed forces or other organised armed groups fighting State armed forces have effective control of part of that State's territory such as to enable them to carry out sustained and concerted military operations and to implement the Protocol. Art 1(1), 1977 Additional Protocol II.

[55] Art 4(1), 1977 Additional Protocol II.

[56] In the view of the ICRC, the term 'acts of terrorism' in the 1977 Additional Protocol II covers not only acts directed against people, 'but also acts directed against installations which would cause victims as a side-effect'. ICRC, Commentary on the 1977 Additional Protocols, at: http://bit.ly/2IGhscP, para 4538. Thus, for example, the deliberate destruction of civilian homes, schools, or medical facilities, where the intent or effect was to terrorise the population, would also be encapsulated by the prohibition.

[57] Art 4(d), Statute of International Tribunal for Rwanda (as amended), at: https://bit.ly/3vsollD.

[58] Art 3(d) and (h), Statute of the Special Court for Sierra Leone, at: https://bit.ly/3vByDji.

exceptionally violent treatment of prisoners – civilian and military alike – by both Russian regular forces and its militia in the ongoing Ukraine conflict is thus not only constitutive of the war crime of torture, but also of the war crime of terrorism.

When forming part of organisational policy, torture and summary execution are acts of terror. The imposition of death sentences at the conclusion of unfair trials held by the Donetsk People's courts amounted to threats of terror (given that they were not ultimately carried out). In June 2022, for instance, two British nationals and a Moroccan who were captured while fighting for Ukraine were sentenced to death by a court in the DPR. This decision was made prior to the purported annexation of the territories of the Donbas by Moscow and can be understood as falling within the concept of hybrid warfare. At the conclusion of what the United Kingdom duly labelled a sham trial, the DPR court found the three men guilty of 'mercenary activities and committing actions aimed at seizing power and overthrowing the constitutional order of the DPR'.[59] Brahim Saadoun, Aiden Aslin, and Shaun Pinner were all released in prisoner exchanges in September 2022. Aiden Aslin had been beaten, stabbed, and forced to record a series of propaganda videos prior to his trial. But after his release, he said that the worst thing he experienced during captivity was hearing a prisoner of war beaten to death in the cell next to him.[60]

D. The Definition of Terrorism in Hague Law

Within the conduct of hostilities (the law-of-armed-conflict term for combat), the use of terror tactics[61] against the civilian population is explicitly prohibited in identical terms by the two 1977 Additional Protocols to the Geneva Conventions. It is thus stipulated that: 'Acts or threats of violence the primary purpose of which is to spread terror among the civilian population are prohibited'.[62] This is also a customary rule, as the ICRC confirms, applicable to all armed conflicts.[63]

The acts proscribed by the prohibition during the conduct of hostilities constitute, the ICRC avers, a 'special type of terrorism'.[64] As its commentary on the Additional Protocols explains:

[59] Reuters, 'Two Britons, one Moroccan sentenced to death by court of Russian proxy in Ukraine', 9 June 2022, at: https://bit.ly/3KVGIsO.

[60] S Cannane and W Matteeussen, 'Aiden was beaten and tortured by his Russian captors. Then they made him a propaganda prop', *ABC News* (Australia), 20 July 2023, at: https://bit.ly/3KVDEgy.

[61] The concept of 'terror' in this context has been defined by the ICTY as 'extreme fear'. ICTY, *Prosecutor v Galić*, Judgment (Trial Chamber) (Case No IT-98-29-T), 5 December 2003 (hereafter, ICTY Galić Trial Judgment), para 135.

[62] Art 51(2), 1977 Additional Protocol I; and Art 13(2), 1977 Additional Protocol II.

[63] ICRC, Customary International Humanitarian Law (IHL) Rule 2: 'Violence Aimed at Spreading Terror among the Civilian Population', at: http://bit.ly/2ONFTT7.

[64] Ibid, para 4538.

> Air raids have often been used as a means of terrorizing the population, but these are not the only methods. For this reason the text contains a much broader expression, namely 'acts or threats of violence' so as to cover all possible circumstances.[65]

Moreover, it is true that acts of violence during conflict 'almost always give rise to some degree of terror among the population'. Hence, the Hague Law prohibition on terrorising civilians is limited to acts of violence whose *primary purpose* is to spread terror among the civilian population 'without offering substantial military advantage'.[66]

It is not prohibited to cause extreme fear in enemy soldiers, for instance by relentless bombing of lawful military targets[67] or attacks that use lawful weapons. As the ICRC has remarked: 'attacks on armed forces are purposely conducted brutally in order to intimidate the enemy soldiers and persuade them to surrender'.[68] Hence, large-scale aerial bombardments pounding military objectives and 'breaking the back of the enemy armed forces' are not unlawful even if they lead to a 'collapse of civilian morale'.[69]

Terror attacks were a central element of the Siege of Sarajevo in 1992–96 whose intent was to intimidate and humiliate the Bosnian Muslim population as much as to gain territory. General Stanislav Galić, as commander of the Bosnian Serb army around Sarajevo, was accused of having 'conducted a protracted campaign of shelling and sniping upon civilian areas of Sarajevo and upon the civilian population thereby inflicting terror and mental suffering upon its civilian population'.[70] The majority at trial in the *Galić* case were convinced by the evidence presented that civilians in government-held areas of Sarajevo were 'directly or indiscriminately attacked' from Bosnian Serb-controlled territory, and that, as a result and 'as a minimum, hundreds of civilians were killed and thousands others were injured'.[71] Starting with the decision on appeal in the case, the ICTY held consistently thereafter that terrorising civilians is also a war crime under customary law, at the least when acts rather than threats are concerned.[72] Most recently, the existence of the customary law war crime was reiterated in 2021 in the UN Residual Mechanism in judging the appeal of Ratko Mladic against, among other things, conviction for terrorising civilians in the conduct of hostilities.[73]

[65] ICRC commentary on the 1977 Additional Protocols, para 4785.

[66] Ibid, para 1940.

[67] Accordingly, in its judgment in the *Prlić* case, reversing the decision at trial, the ICTY Appeals Chamber held that the destruction of the Old Bridge at Mostar could not amount to terrorisation of the civilian population since it constituted a lawful military objective in the circumstances prevailing at the time. ICTY, *Prosecutor v Prlić*, Judgment (Appeals Chamber) (Case No IT-04-74-A), 29 November 2017, paras 411 and 425–26.

[68] ICRC commentary on the 1977 Additional Protocols, para 1940.

[69] Y Dinstein, *The Conduct of Hostilities under the Law of International Armed Conflict*, 4th edn, Cambridge University Press, Cambridge, 2022, pp 168–69, para 490.

[70] ICTY Galić Trial Judgment, n 61 above, paras 65, 66.

[71] Ibid, para 591.

[72] ICTY, *Prosecutor v Galić*, Judgment (Appeals Chamber) (Case No IT-98-29-A), 30 November 2006, paras 86–98.

[73] International Residual Mechanism for Criminal Tribunals, *Prosecutor v Ratko Mladic*, Judgment (Appeals Chamber) (Case No MICT-13-56-A), 8 June 2021, para 287.

II. THE APPLICATION OF INTERNATIONAL COUNTERTERRORISM LAW TO HYBRID WARFARE

Following the analysis of the law governing terrorism in peacetime and in armed conflict, two case studies have been chosen to consider the application of international counterterrorism law to hybrid warfare. Both case studies occurred during armed conflict in Ukraine. The first is the shooting down of Flight MH17 in July 2014 by DPR forces, an ostensible case of terrorism against a civilian aircraft. The second is the murkier sabotage of the Nord Stream pipelines in 2022, responsibility for which remained uncertain at the time of writing. It was a clear case of terrorism according to the 1997 Terrorist Bombings Convention, but the legal analysis must consider whether the exclusion for certain acts in an armed conflict applies.

A. The Shooting Down of Flight MH17 (2014)

Malaysia Airlines Flight MH17 was a scheduled passenger flight from Amsterdam to Kuala Lumpur that was shot down on 17 July 2014 while flying over eastern Ukraine by a Buk TELAR surface-to-air missile.[74] All 283 passengers and 15 crew were killed in what was one of the greatest losses of life from an act of terrorism against an airline ever recorded.[75] The missile is believed to have been fired by fighters belonging to the People's Militia of the DPR from a farm field near Pervomaiskyi in Kharkiv oblast. The field was located in separatist-controlled territory.[76]

On 21 July 2014, the UN Security Council condemned 'in the strongest terms' the downing of Flight MH17.[77] In a preambular paragraph to its Resolution 2166, the Council reaffirmed the rules of international law that prohibit acts of violence that pose a threat to the safety of international civil aviation, and emphasised the importance of holding those responsible for violations of these rules to account.[78] In July 2015, Malaysia and 12 other States[79]

[74] A Buk TELAR vehicle is fitted with radar, digital computer, missile erector and launcher, and friend-or-foe identification system. It is operated by a crew of four and carries four missiles. Radar of the Buk TELAR vehicle searches for targets, tracks them, and guides missiles on them. If required, each TELAR vehicle can operate autonomously. The radar detects aircraft flying at an altitude greater than 3 kilometres and at a distance of between 65 and 77 kilometres. *Military Today*, 'Buk: Medium-range air defense missile system', undated but accessed 25 August 2023 at: https://bit.ly/3OTkQja.

[75] The bombing of Air India Flight 182 on 23 June 1985 killed all 329 people on board. The bombing of Pan Am Flight 103 on 21 December 1988 over Scotland killed 270 people, including 11 people in the town of Lockerbie.

[76] District Court of The Hague, 'Summary of the day in court: 17 November 2022 – Judgment', at: https://bit.ly/3OGBNNq.

[77] UN Security Council Resolution 2166, adopted by unanimous vote in favour on 21 July 2014, operative para 1.

[78] Ibid, second preambular para.

[79] Australia, Belgium, Canada, France, Germany, Ireland, Israel, Italy, Lithuania, Malaysia, the Netherlands, New Zealand, Philippines, Romania, Spain, Ukraine, United Kingdom, and the United States.

proposed that the UN Security Council establish an international criminal tribunal to prosecute those responsible for the downing of the aircraft.[80]

A draft statute for the putative 'International Criminal Tribunal for Malaysia Airlines Flight MH17' was annexed to the proposed resolution, covering war crimes (under international law) and offences under the respective domestic criminal laws of Malaysia and Ukraine. The draft statute did not explicitly refer to an act of terrorism, but the salient offences in Ukraine's Criminal Code include a provision on acts of terrorism, criminalising the use of explosions in order to violate public security,[81] while the relevant Malaysian law concerned crimes against the safety of civil aviation: destroying, damaging, or endangering the safety of aircraft, as defined in section 9 of the 1984 Aviation Offences Act.[82] On 29 July 2015, the proposed resolution was supported by 11 members of the Council[83] with three others abstaining,[84] but its passage was vetoed by Russia.[85] In explanation of its vote, Russia noted that it had

> repeatedly stated that we do not support the idea of setting up a tribunal under Chapter VII of the Charter. There are no grounds for it, given that in Resolution 2166 (2014) the Security Council did not classify the Boeing tragedy as a threat to international peace and security.[86]

Instead, a national prosecution was conducted in the Netherlands where the flight had originated and whose nationals formed the majority of the victims of the bombing.[87] In November 2022, a court in the Netherlands convicted three men *in absentia* as indirect perpetrators of the murder of all those on board flight MH17[88] and for intentionally causing the crash of an aircraft.[89,90] Two of the three individuals convicted were Russian nationals while the third was

[80] Draft resolution UN doc S/2015/562, 29 July 2015, text available at: https://bit.ly/3EaTGPP, operative para 6.

[81] Art 258, Criminal Code of Ukraine, text available on the Laws on Countering Terrorism Worldwide website at: https://bit.ly/3qOmJFU.

[82] This provision implements the 1971 Montreal Convention, which pertains to an act that 'destroys an aircraft in service or causes damage to such an aircraft which renders it incapable of flight or which is likely to endanger its safety in flight'. Art 1(1), Convention for the Suppression of Unlawful Acts against the Safety of Civil Aviation; adopted and signed at Montreal, 23 September 1971; entered into force, 26 January 1973. A total of 188 States were party to the Convention at the time of writing.

[83] Chad, Chile, France, Jordan, Lithuania, Malaysia, New Zealand, Nigeria, Spain, the United Kingdom, and the United States.

[84] Angola, China, and Venezuela.

[85] Details of all vetoed resolutions are available on the UN Dag Hammarskjöld Library website at: https://bit.ly/38gGXL5.

[86] Procès-Verbal, UN doc S/PV.7498, 29 July 2015, at: https://bit.ly/45Hnf7p, p 5. The plane on flight MH17 was a Boeing 777-200ER aircraft.

[87] The Montreal Convention allocates primary responsibility to the territorial State, but a State may cede responsibility to another, as Ukraine did in this case.

[88] Art 289, Dutch Criminal Code.

[89] Art 168, Dutch Criminal Code.

[90] L Yanev, 'The MH17 Judgment: An Interesting Take on the Nature of the Armed Conflict in Eastern Ukraine', *EJIL: Talk!*, 7 December 2022, at: https://bit.ly/3E8NbwY.

a Ukrainian national. Prosecutors argued that while the men did not 'press the button themselves',[91] they were responsible for taking the BUK system from Russia and deploying it on the battlefield.[92] Leonid Kharchenko, the sole Ukrainian national on trial, commanded a combat unit in the Donetsk region in July 2014 and was accused of having helped to escort the missile after it entered Ukraine and then on its return to Russia after MH17 was shot down.[93] The finding of guilt on charges of murder under domestic law against three of the four defendants was 'not altered by the fact that the accused may not have wanted to shoot down a civil airliner, nor that 298 innocent civilians be killed as a result'.[94]

The European Court of Human Rights has held that Russia had 'effective control' over all areas in the hands of separatists from 11 May 2014 on account of its military presence in eastern Ukraine and the decisive degree of influence it enjoyed over these areas as a result of its military, political, and economic support to the DPR and the Luhansk People's Republic (LPR).[95] The hybrid nature of the armed conflicts with Ukraine was also clear from the backgrounds of the three Russian nationals on trial in the Netherlands. Igor Girkin was a Russian army veteran and former Federal Security Service officer who played a key role in the annexation of Crimea in 2014 and later the conflicts in the Donbas region, organising the militia in the DPR. At the relevant time he was serving as 'Minister of Defence' of the DPR.[96]

Sergei Dubinsky, a Major General in Russian military intelligence, allegedly served as the separatists' military intelligence chief. Dubinsky was accused of having played a key role in obtaining the missile and returning it to Russia. 'He also maintained regular contact with officials in Russia', prosecutors said.[97] Oleg Pulatov was a former member of Russia's special forces and one of Dubinsky's deputies. Mr Pulatov, the only accused who employed a lawyer to defend him at the trial in the Netherlands, was acquitted of the charges due to lack of evidence as to his role.[98] Prosecutors later decided not to appeal against his acquittal.[99]

[91] Investigators had not confirmed the identity of the crew members of the Buk TELAR at the time of writing. Netherlands Public Prosecution Service, 'JIT MH17: strong indications that Russian president decided on supplying Buk', News item, 8 February 2023, at: https://bit.ly/3YMaqGF.

[92] L Harding, 'Three Russians and one Ukrainian to face MH17 murder charges', *The Guardian*, 19 June 2019, at: https://bit.ly/45J1qEt.

[93] France24, 'MH17 verdict: who are the four suspects on trial?', 17 November 2022, at: https://bit.ly/47HHvY6.

[94] District Court of The Hague, Case ref ECLI:NL:RBDHA:2022:14036, at: https://bit.ly/44jokkt, para 6.2.6.

[95] European Court of Human Rights, *Ukraine and The Netherlands v Russia*, Decision on Admissibility (Grand Chamber), 30 November 2022, paras. 560 and 695.

[96] District Court of The Hague, Judgment in English, at: https://bit.ly/3EbiIhI.

[97] 'MH17 verdict: who are the four suspects on trial?', *France24*, 17 November 2022, at: https://bit.ly/47HHvY6.

[98] J Rankin, 'Three men found guilty of murdering 298 people in shooting down of MH17', *The Guardian*, 17 November 2022, at: https://bit.ly/47JI1F5.

[99] 'MH17: Dutch prosecutors won't appeal against acquittal of Oleg Pulatov', *NL Times*, 1 December 2022, at: https://bit.ly/3Eclrr2.

The three convicted individuals were ordered to pay 'more than €16m' in compensation to the victims[100] although – the three being tried *in absentia* – none had been arrested by the Dutch authorities at the time of writing.[101] They were deemed by the Dutch district court not to be entitled to enjoy combatant's privilege[102] as they were acting at the time as members of a non-State armed group under the effective control of Russia and not, in the case of Girkin and Dubinsky, of the regular Russian armed forces.[103] In any event, combatant's privilege only forestalls charges related to lawful acts of war and would not have prevented a prosecution for the war crime of attacking civilians. Recklessness is sufficient *mens rea* for most war crimes under customary law, including the targeting of civilians or the civilian population as such.[104]

It is at least conceivable, however, that the defendants would not have been convicted of the war crime of terror attacks given that the primary purpose of the firing of the missile was, it seems, to bring down a military aircraft belonging to Ukraine. This is a lawful military objective in an armed conflict. Since terrorisation under international criminal law is a crime of specific intent (*dolus specialis*),[105] it would have to be proven that the intent of the crew firing the missile was to spread terror among the civilian population by bringing down a civilian aircraft. It is thus likely that recklessness would not suffice to found a conviction in this case.

Ukraine has brought a case against Russia before the International Court of Justice for the shooting down of MH17 on the basis of the 1999 UN Terrorism Financing Convention,[106] whose definition of terrorism encompasses the sectoral terrorism treaties, including the 1971 Montreal Convention. In its request for provisional measures of 16 January 2017, Ukraine argued that:

> The Russian Federation has instigated and sustained an armed insurrection against the authority of the Ukrainian state, including by systematically supplying illegal

[100] District Court of The Hague, ECLI:NL:RBDHA:2022:14040, at: https://bit.ly/3spmCAT.

[101] As noted in Chapter 3 of this volume, at the time of writing, Mr Gurkin had been arrested by the Russian authorities and charged with extremism, but this was entirely unconnected to the downing of Flight MH17. A Osborn, 'Pro-war nationalist Putin critic Girkin charged with inciting extremism', *Reuters*, 22 July 2023, at: https://bit.ly/47ynd2u.

[102] See, eg, LR Blank, 'Combatant Privileges and Protections', Blog post, *Articles of War*, Lieber Institute for Law & Warfare at West Point, United States, 4 March 2022, at: https://bit.ly/44PdCTn; and JD Ohlin, 'When Does the Combatant's Privilege Apply?', Blog post, *Opinio Juris*, 1 August 2014, at: https://bit.ly/2PwKzlT.

[103] As a postscript to this case, on 23 June 2023, the European Union listed for sanctions two individuals who took an active part in Russia's military aggression against Ukraine from an early stage; these were the same two Russian nationals convicted of murder in the shooting down of flight MH17. 'Ukraine: Statement by the High Representative on behalf of the European Union on the occasion of the 9th anniversary of the downing of Malaysia Airlines Flight MH17', Council of the European Union, Brussels, 16 July 2023, at: https://bit.ly/3ONx0K7.

[104] See ICRC Customary IHL Rule 156: 'Definition of War Crimes', at: https://bit.ly/3EbGQRb.

[105] As argued by the prosecution in the *Galić* case and confirmed by the Tribunal in its judgment at trial. ICTY, *Prosecutor v Galić*, Trial Judgment, n 61 above, paras 72 and 136.

[106] International Convention for the Suppression of the Financing of Terrorism; adopted at New York, 9 December 1999; entered into force, 10 April 2002. The Convention is the most widely ratified of the global sectoral treaties, with 190 States Parties and two signatories at the time of writing.

> armed groups and associated groups and individuals, with heavy weaponry, money, personnel, training, and other support. These Russian proxies operate with no regard for civilian life, often murdering and torturing civilians. The Russian Federation knew that these illegal groups were not only engaged in combat against the Ukrainian authorities, but were routinely perpetrating acts of terrorism against Ukrainian civilians. Knowing that these groups engaged in acts of terrorism, the Russian Federation nevertheless decided to sponsor their activities, providing cash, critical weapons, and other support. With that assistance, Russian-backed illegal armed groups in Ukraine have committed a series of terrorist attacks, including … [t]he shooting down of Malaysian Airlines Flight MH17, murdering 298 civilians of numerous nationalities, including infants.[107]

In its counter-memorial, Russia observes that the wording in Article 1(1) of the 1971 Montreal Convention stipulates that any person commits an offence if he unlawfully *and intentionally* destroys an aircraft in service. Russia rejects the notion advanced by Ukraine that intent should be given a broader meaning encompassing indirect intent or recklessness, claiming that this 'is confirmed by the context'.[108] While Russia's line of argumentation, based on the law of treaties, is shaky, its fundamental conclusion may be sound.

The public hearings on the merits in the case concerning the application of the 1999 UN Terrorism Financing Convention (*Ukraine v Russian Federation*) concluded at The Hague on 14 June 2023.[109] At the time of writing, the Court was deliberating its judgment.

B. The Nord Stream Pipeline Sabotage (2022)

On 26 and 27 September 2022, a series of deep-sea explosions near the Danish island of Bornholm hit the Nord Stream and Nord Stream 2 natural gas pipelines running along the bottom of the Baltic Sea. The bombings severed three of the Nord Stream project's four underwater pipelines that had been constructed to transport natural gas from Russia to Germany[110] and on to other customers

[107] International Court of Justice, *Application of the International Convention for the Suppression of the Financing of Terrorism and of the International Convention on the Elimination of All Forms of Racial Discrimination* (*Ukraine v Russian Federation*), 'Request for the indication of provisional measures of protection submitted by Ukraine', 16 January 2017, at: https://bit.ly/3QQrLfD, para 7.

[108] International Court of Justice, *Application of the International Convention for the Suppression of the Financing of Terrorism and of the International Convention on the Elimination of All Forms of Racial Discrimination* (*Ukraine v Russian Federation*), 'Counter-Memorial on the Case Concerning Application of the International Convention for the Suppression of the Financing of Terrorism', 9 August 2021, at: https://bit.ly/3srZ4vk, para 155.

[109] International Court of Justice, *Application of the International Convention for the Suppression of the Financing of Terrorism and of the International Convention on the Elimination of All Forms of Racial Discrimination* (*Ukraine v Russian Federation*), Press release No 2023/30, 14 June 2023, at: https://bit.ly/3Pana6K.

[110] The Nord Stream 2 pipe runs for 1,230 kilometres from Russia through the Baltic Sea to Germany and had been due to carry billions of cubic feet of gas to Europe until Russia's invasion of Ukraine which led to Germany refusing to grant the pipeline's operators a licence, leaving it

in Western Europe. Owing to tensions over the war in Ukraine, none of the pipelines was delivering gas at the time of the bombing, although they did contain natural gas.[111]

Pressure in the Nord Stream 2 pipeline dropped over the course of the night of 26 September from 105 bars to 7 bars, clearly indicating a leak. Seismologists registered the equivalent of an earthquake with the magnitude of 1.8, triangulated to have occurred at almost exactly the same spot where the leak was bubbling to the surface.[112] The sites of the explosions were outside the territorial seas of Denmark and Sweden but within their exclusive economic zones.[113] By 18 November 2022, the Swedish Security Service had obtained sufficient evidence to conclude that the explosions constituted an act of 'gross sabotage'.[114] No one questions that human beings were responsible for the explosions. But to this day, no one has accepted responsibility for the bombings either, and different authorities have variously blamed alternatively Russia and Ukraine (or even the United States) for the criminal act, with perpetration laid at the door of a range of entities or groups either under or outside the effective control of one of the two States.

Attention in the West immediately focused on Russia,[115] on the basis that Russia would want to inflict economic pain on Western Europe and, in seeking to achieve this aim, would prefer to blow up its own pipeline than breach a contract with Western governments. That a State was involved in the sabotage in some manner certainly seemed highly probable. Indeed, Russia itself publicly declared that: 'Such an explosion, so powerful and at such depth, could only be conducted by experts backed by the entire potential of a State that has relevant technologies'.[116] But it also denied that it would attack its own pipeline, claiming

mothballed. Nord Stream 1 follows a similar but not identical route from Russia to Germany and had been used to transport Russian gas to Europe since 2011, until the outbreak of the Ukraine war, when it ended.

[111] C Danner, 'Who Really Blew Up the Nord Stream Pipeline? New clues keep surfacing, and the most recent appear to implicate Ukraine', Intelligencer, *New York Magazine*, updated 15 June 2023, at: https://bit.ly/45Faytw.

[112] By the beginning of October 2022, the leaks of natural gas into the Baltic Sea were largely deemed to be over. 'Kein Gasaustritt mehr aus Pipeline-Lecks?', *Frankfurter Allgemeine Zeitung*, updated 2 October 2022, at: https://bit.ly/3qGkHay.

[113] Nord Stream 2 pipe A and Nord Stream 1 pipe B were in the exclusive economic zone (EEZ) of Denmark, while separate leaks from Nord Stream 2 pipe A as well as a leak from Nord Stream 1 pipe A were within the exclusive economic zone of Sweden. According to the UN Convention on the Law of the Sea, the EEZ 'shall not extend beyond 200 nautical miles from the baselines from which the breadth of the territorial sea is measured'. Art 57, United Nations Convention on the Law of the Sea; adopted at Montego Bay, 10 December 1982; entered into force, 16 November 1994 (hereafter, UNCLOS).

[114] J Sherr, 'Pipes and Mirrors: the Nord Stream Explosions', Commentary, International Centre for Defence and Security (ICDS), Estonia, 28 April 2023, at: https://bit.ly/45vAnfI.

[115] S Harris, J Hudson, M Ryan, and M Birnbaum, 'No conclusive evidence Russia is behind Nord Stream attack', *The Washington Post*, 21 December 2022, at: https://bit.ly/3stPw2H.

[116] 'Putin rejects theory about Ukrainian role in pipeline blasts', CNBC, 14 March 2023, at: https://bit.ly/3qQ3Wtz.

that the investigation was being manipulated in order to attribute responsibility unfairly to Russia.[117]

Russia's involvement is certainly possible, but, on balance, less than probable. On 29 September 2022, President Putin called the attack on the pipeline 'an unprecedented act of international terrorism'.[118] More significantly, Biden administration officials are said to have conceded privately that no evidence conclusively points to the involvement of the Russian authorities.[119] On 17 February 2023, Russia formally submitted a proposal to the UN Security Council calling for an investigation into the Nord Stream sabotage, repeating its request on 20 February 2023.[120] This is hardly the conduct of a guilty party.

If the Russian authorities were not responsible, by far the most likely candidate is Ukraine. Indeed, the US Central Intelligence Agency (CIA) had received information from an unnamed European intelligence agency in June 2022 – later said to be that of the Netherlands[121] – that a six-person team of Ukrainian special operations forces intended to sabotage the Russia-to-Germany natural gas project. Subsequently, German law enforcement investigators uncovered evidence about the bombing that had striking similarities with what the European agency had said Ukraine was planning.[122]

In early March 2023, *The New York Times* reported that US officials had seen new intelligence suggesting that a pro-Ukraine, but not necessarily a Ukraine government-supported, group was behind the sabotage. The group was thought likely to have comprised Ukrainian and/or Russian nationals (opponents of President Putin) but there was no evidence of direct links between the saboteurs and Ukraine's leadership.[123] The divers in the group were not believed to be currently working for military or intelligence services, although they might have been trained by them in the past.[124] In November 2023, it was reported in

[117] 'Nord Stream probe "tailored" against Russia – Kremlin', *Moscow Times*, 18 October 2022, at: https://bit.ly/3P7Bi0x.

[118] RBC, 'Putin told Erdogan about the "unprecedented sabotage" at Nord Stream', 29 September 2022, at: https://bit.ly/3sq1cDN (original Russian text).

[119] Harris, Hudson, Ryan, and Birnbaum, 'No conclusive evidence Russia is behind Nord Stream attack', n 115 above.

[120] L Kelly, 'Russia urges Sweden again to share Nord Stream probe findings', *Reuters*, 21 February 2023, at: https://bit.ly/3QQBHWb.

[121] M Krever, A Marquardt, S Dean, and S Pokharel, 'Dutch intelligence warned CIA about alleged Ukrainian plot to attack Nord Stream pipelines, Netherlands' public broadcaster reports', *CNN*, 13 June 2023, at: https://bit.ly/45CO24K; B Waterfield, 'CIA warned Ukraine not to blow up Nord Stream after Dutch tip-off', *The Times*, 13 June 2023, https://bit.ly/49IjwIL (subscription required).

[122] S Harris and S Mekhennet, 'U.S. had intelligence of detailed Ukrainian plan to attack Nord Stream pipeline', *The Washington Post*, 6 June 2023, at: https://bit.ly/3YJ8miA.

[123] A Entous, JE Barnes, and A Goldman, 'Intelligence Suggests Pro-Ukrainian Group Sabotaged Pipelines, U.S. Officials Say', *The New York Times* (7 March 2023), accessed 1 May 2023. This was not, however, the view of the Swedish investigators. P Oltermann, 'State actor still main suspect behind Nord Stream sabotage, says investigator', *The Guardian*, 6 April 2023, https://bit.ly/3oYb1qL.

[124] Danner, 'Who Really Blew Up the Nord Stream Pipeline? New clues keep surfacing, and the most recent appear to implicate Ukraine', n 111 above.

the American and German press that Roman Chervinsky, a Ukrainian special forces veteran, was the mastermind of the Ukrainian diving team. He, however, claimed that the allegations were politically motivated.[125] Even before the war, Ukraine had been a vocal critic of the pipeline, which by-passed the country and cost the government revenue it had previously received from transporting Russian gas toward Western Europe.[126] Means, motive, and opportunity.

A far less likely suspect is the United States. On 7 February 2022, US President Joe Biden had pledged to 'bring an end to' Nord Stream 2 if Russia invaded Ukraine. In response to media questioning, President Biden declined to clarify how the United States would achieve this.[127] The immediate response online to the bombing by Poland's erstwhile Minister for Foreign Affairs, Radoslav Sikorski, was 'Thank you, USA!'. The post was swiftly deleted.[128] If – and it is an entirely hypothetical *if* – the United States were responsible, this would certainly have been an act of international terrorism. Article 19(2) of the 1997 Terrorist Bombings Convention stipulates that 'the activities undertaken by military forces of a State in the exercise of their official duties, inasmuch as they are governed by other rules of international law, are not governed by this Convention'.[129] But this exclusion would not pertain to the covert bombing, outside an armed conflict involving the United States as a party, of a civilian pipeline belonging, in part, to a military ally.

Bombings with purely economic impacts fall within the prohibition of terrorist bombings under Article 2(1) of the 1997 Convention. In the case of the Nord Stream pipelines, this concerns a detonation against a State infrastructure facility with the intent to cause extensive destruction likely to result in major economic loss.[130] That some of the shareholders of Nord Stream 2 AG were private companies[131] does not alter the fact that the action was primarily targeted

[125] O Moody, 'Nord Stream pipeline blast blamed on Ukrainian maverick', *The Times*, 13 November 2023.

[126] D Friedman, 'Report: Ukrainian Officer Played Key Role in Pipeline Blasts', *Mother Jones*, 11 November 2023, at: https://bit.ly/3GhnHhO.

[127] A Shalal, A Rinke, and J Mason, 'Biden pledges end to Nord Stream 2 if Russia invades Ukraine', *Reuters*, 8 February 2022, at: https://bit.ly/45vz0h4.

[128] Sherr, 'Pipes and Mirrors: the Nord Stream Explosions', n 114 above.

[129] The Convention defines the military forces of a State as 'the armed forces of a State which are organized, trained and equipped under its internal law for the primary purpose of national defence or security and persons acting in support of those armed forces who are under their formal command, control and responsibility'. Art 1(4), 1997 Terrorist Bombings Convention, n 15 above.

[130] Uniper and RWE of Germany and ENGIE of France have filed claims that will be heard by an international arbitration panel in Stockholm, arguing that they are owed damages by Gazprom, Nord Stream's majority shareholder, because of its failure to deliver contracted volumes of gas. E Crooks, 'Gas contracts central to Nord Stream pipeline mystery', *Wood Mackenzie*, 24 February 2023, at: https://bit.ly/3PbgiG9. The prices for consumers across Europe increased very substantially as a result of the bombing, and subsidies to mitigate those increased costs have come from State funds.

[131] Nord Stream is a joint project involving five major companies: Gazprom international projects North 1 LLC (Gazprom Group company), Wintershall Dea AG, PEG Infrastruktur AG (E.ON), NV Nederlandse Gasunie, and ENGIE. Nord Stream, 'Our Shareholders', https://bit.ly/3MlihGq. The State of incorporation of the Nord Stream company is Switzerland.

against States.[132] The majority shareholder of Nord Stream is Gazprom, which in turn is held by slender majority stockholding by the Russian State. Unless it turns out that the armed forces of a State that is party to an armed conflict against Russia (ie Ukraine) were responsible for the bombing, the exemption in the 1997 Terrorist Bombings Convention will not apply.

[132] Hence, the use of force was 'inconsistent with the principles of international law embodied in the Charter of the United Nations' in violation of UNCLOS and the UN Charter. Art 301, UNCLOS; and Art 2(4), Charter of the United Nations; adopted at San Francisco, 26 June 1945; entered into force, 24 October 1945.

5

Hybrid Warfare, Cognitive Warfare, and International Human Rights Law

A RANGE OF fundamental human rights are impacted by the conduct of hybrid warfare, including cognitive warfare. Affected, in particular, are the rights to life, to freedom from torture and other ill-treatment, to liberty, to private and family life, to property, and to freedom of opinion. As this chapter explores, however, their practical application to any given conduct depends on fulfilling critical jurisdictional requirements – geographical and personal, as well as material and temporal. Only then can international human rights law be used to analyse the legality of hybrid warfare and efforts to counter it.

Accordingly, this chapter first addresses the four jurisdictional bases, referring to the positions of Russia, the United States, and China where relevant. It then presents and discusses two case studies involving the application of fundamental human rights to hybrid warfare: first, the actions of Russia in Georgia beginning in 2008 and continuing through to the present day; and second, China's burgeoning cognitive warfare against the government and population of Taiwan.

I. JURISDICTION AND INTERNATIONAL HUMAN RIGHTS LAW

Ordinarily, the concept of jurisdiction in international law sets the outer limits of a State's legal competence vis-à-vis other States 'to make, apply, and enforce rules of conduct upon persons'.[1] In the particular instance of international human rights law, however, jurisdiction not only serves to determine when and where the law applies, it also acts to preclude States from performing certain acts otherwise within their sovereign competence while demanding that they engage in certain other conduct.[2]

The four jurisdictional bases cited above – geographical, personal, material, and temporal – govern the application of international human rights law to any

[1] C Staker, 'Jurisdiction', ch 11 in MD Evans (ed), *International Law*, 4th edn, Oxford University Press, Oxford, 2014, p 311.

[2] S Casey-Maslen, *The Right to Life under International Law*, Cambridge University Press, Cambridge, 2021, para 3.02.

given scenario. These equate, respectively, to *where* human rights law applies; *to whom* it applies (as both duty bearer and beneficiary); *to which acts, omissions, and situations* it applies (and what conduct it requires of the duty bearer); and *when* it applies (with a starting point in time and potentially also an end point). These jurisdictional bases are considered in turn.

A. Geographical Jurisdiction (*Ratione Loci*)

International human rights law is geographically circumscribed. Its primary focus concerns the treatment by States of all persons living or present on sovereign territory as well as on overseas territories for whose international relations the State is responsible, whether that territory be metropolitan or non-metropolitan. This territorial application is made explicit in Article 2(1) of the 1966 International Covenant on Civil and Political Rights, according to which each State Party 'undertakes to respect and to ensure to all individuals within its territory' the rights recognised therein.[3] A total of 174 of the 197 States recognised by the Secretary-General of the United Nations (UN) are party to the Covenant. The list of States Parties contains both Russia and the United States, but not China, which is only a signatory.

But the geographical application of international human rights law is not confined to a State's own territory. Extraterritorially, the law also governs conduct in areas the State effectively controls by virtue of the presence of its armed forces or a proxy armed group. This is so irrespective of whether that presence is based on the valid consent of the territorial State, the result of aggression, and/or if it constitutes an unlawful belligerent occupation bringing into play the law of armed conflict.[4] Thus, for instance, in 2018 the UN Committee against Torture affirmed that the 1984 Convention against Torture and Other Cruel, Inhuman or Degrading Treatment or Punishment[5] applied to the conduct of Russia in Crimea:

> Without prejudice to the legal status of Crimea under international law, and emphasizing the fundamental importance of the principle of territorial integrity of all States Members of the United Nations, the Committee notes that Crimea is under the effective control of the Russian Federation and that the Russian Federation has the obligation to implement the Convention in Crimea.[6]

[3] Art 2(1), International Covenant on Civil and Political Rights; adopted at New York, 16 December 1966; entered into force, 23 March 1976.

[4] European Court of Human Rights, *Catan and others v Moldova and Russia*, Judgment (Grand Chamber), 19 October 2012, para 106.

[5] Convention against Torture and Other Cruel, Inhuman or Degrading Treatment or Punishment; adopted at New York, 10 December 1984; entered into force, 26 June 1987. China, Russia, and the United States all figure among the 174 States Parties to the 1984 Convention against Torture.

[6] Committee against Torture, Concluding Observations on the Sixth Periodic Report of the Russian Federation, UN doc CAT/C/RUS/CO/6, 28 August 2018, para 48.

In 2019, in its eighth periodic report under the International Covenant on Civil and Political Rights, the Russian Federation declared that its Constitution, Russian legislation, and 'other laws and regulations' were

> fully applicable in the territory of the Republic of Crimea and the city of Sevastopol, as constituent entities of the Russian Federation, as are the international treaties to which the Russian Federation is a party, *including human rights instruments* (emphasis added).[7]

Thus, if a State claims territory as its own it has human rights obligations towards those living or otherwise present on it without prejudice to whether the territorial claim is legitimate under international law.

Human rights jurisdiction also pertains to conduct on board a State's nationally flagged or registered ships or aircraft, whether they be military or civilian in nature, and irrespective of where in the world they are located. In this regard, the 1984 Convention against Torture requires that each State Party take effective measures to prevent acts of torture not only in its sovereign territory but also in 'any territory under its jurisdiction'.[8] The Committee against Torture has recognised that this notion of any territory encompasses 'all areas where the State Party exercises, directly or indirectly, in whole or in part, de jure or de facto effective control, in accordance with international law'. This includes prohibited acts committed 'on board a ship or aircraft registered by a State Party'.[9] A similar position is taken by the UN Human Rights Committee with regard to the implementation of the right to life under the 1966 Covenant on Civil and Political Rights: 'States parties are also required to respect and protect the lives of all individuals located on marine vessels and aircraft registered by them or flying their flag'.[10]

In the view of the Human Rights Committee, at least the right to life protected under the Covenant further governs acts with respect to persons over whom a foreign State exercises 'effective control' in any other place outside their territory. This is so where their right to life is 'affected' by the State's 'military or other activities in a direct and reasonably foreseeable manner'.[11] An obvious example of such jurisdiction would occur through targeted killings, including by the use of remotely piloted combat aircraft (more commonly referred to as armed drones). Peremptory (*jus cogens*) norms apply to acts by States perpetrated anywhere in the world.[12] A peremptory norm of general international law

[7] Eighth Periodic Report of the Russian Federation under the Covenant on Civil and Political Rights, UN doc CCPR/C/RUS/8, 17 May 2019, paras 8, 9.

[8] Art 2(1), 1984 Convention against Torture.

[9] Committee against Torture, General Comment No 2: Implementation of Article 2 by States Parties, UN doc CAT/C/GC/2, 24 January 2008, para 16.

[10] Human Rights Committee, General Comment No 36 – Article 6: Right to Life, UN doc. CCPR/C/GC/36, 3 September 2019, para. 63.

[11] Ibid.

[12] Casey-Maslen, *The Right to Life under International Law*, n 2 above, para 3.9.

> is a norm accepted and recognized by the international community of States as a whole as a norm from which no derogation is permitted and which can be modified only by a subsequent norm of general international law having the same character.[13]

Examples of such norms are given below.

The United States, however, rejects all extraterritorial application of the 1966 Covenant on Civil and Political Rights. In its fifth periodic report on the implementation of the Covenant, submitted in 2021, it declared that it 'has not changed its position that Article 2(1) creates obligations for a State Party only with respect to individuals who are both within the territory of the State Party and within that State Party's jurisdiction'.[14] To do so, it relies on a literal reading of the jurisdictional provision of the Covenant cited, in part, above. The provision applies the rights recognised in the Covenant to all individuals within a State Party's territory '*and subject to its jurisdiction*'. In contradistinction to the view of the United States (a view shared only by Israel) the 'and' in the clause is generally construed not as a conjunctive but as disjunctive, meaning 'within its territory *or otherwise subject to its jurisdiction*'.[15] This broader understanding of the Covenant's application, which arguably reflects general State practice, has been endorsed by the International Court of Justice.[16]

China is not a State Party to the Covenant on Civil and Political Rights although its implementation in the Special Administrative Region of Hong Kong[17] occurs consonant with a 1984 agreement between China and the United Kingdom.[18] China is, however, a State Party to the 1984 Convention against Torture. In the Committee against Torture's formal review of China's latest periodic report on its implementation of the Convention against Torture, the issue of Taiwan was not raised.[19] Given China's unrestricted view that Taiwan falls within its sovereign jurisdiction, however, both the Convention against Torture and customary international human rights law apply to China's actions with respect to the island. Such customary rights certainly include the rights to life, to private and family life, and to liberty, as well as to freedom from torture

[13] Draft Conclusion 2, Fifth report on peremptory norms of general international law (*jus cogens*) by Dire Tladi, Special Rapporteur, International Law Commission, UN doc A/CN.4/747, 24 January 2022.

[14] Fifth Periodic Report of the United States under the Covenant on Civil and Political Rights, UN doc CPR/C/USA/5, 19 January 2021, para 14.

[15] Casey-Maslen, *The Right to Life under International Law*, n 2 above, para 3.07.

[16] International Court of Justice, *Legal Consequences of the Construction of a Wall in the Occupied Palestinian Territory*, Advisory Opinion, 9 July 2004, paras 109, 111.

[17] For a brief discussion of the thorny nature of the Covenant's application to Hong Kong as a matter of international treaty law, see, eg, E Hoffberger-Pippan and S Casey-Maslen, 'The EU's Role in Addressing Human Rights Violations in Hong Kong: Realistic Expectations or Pie in the Sky?', *European Yearbook on Human Rights 2022*, 178–201, at p 183, fn 32.

[18] Joint Declaration of the Government of the United Kingdom of Great Britain and Northern Ireland and the Government of the People's Republic of China on the Question of Hong Kong; signed at Beijing, 19 December 1984; entered into force, 27 May 1985.

[19] Committee against Torture, Concluding Observations on the Fifth Periodic Report of China, UN doc CAT/C/CHN/CO/5, 3 February 2016.

and other ill-treatment. At the time of writing, China had not yet submitted its sixth periodic report under the Convention against Torture, which fell due on 9 December 2019.

B. Personal Jurisdiction (*Ratione Personae*)

Personal jurisdiction pertains both to those who benefit from the protection of human rights and to those who are obligated under international law to provide that protection. Only States – and, in certain circumstances, also international organisations[20] – become party to human rights treaties, meaning that non-State armed groups do not. That said, in an exceptional number of cases, what might be considered a non-State actor, particularly by the United Nations, may be accepted as a party to a regional human rights treaty. For example, the Sahrawi Arab Democratic Republic (SADR) is an African Union Member State whose sovereignty is proclaimed over Western Sahara, and is also a party to the 1981 African Charter on Human and Peoples' Rights.[21] Morocco, though, firmly rejects the SADR's jurisdiction over that territory.

A possible future example of a non-State political entity is Kosovo. In February 2018, the European Commission published an expansion plan that included the possibility of Kosovo's accession to membership of the European Union (EU) at some unspecified point in time after 2025. The Commission did cite the prerequisite of a 'comprehensive, legally-binding normalisation agreement' being in place between Serbia and Kosovo 'so that they can advance on their respective European paths'.[22] Kosovo formally submitted an application for EU membership in December 2022. At the time of writing, however, among EU Member States, Cyprus, Greece, Spain, Romania, and Slovakia did not recognise Kosovo's statehood.[23] In the meantime, the Constitutional Framework for Provisional Self-Government in Kosovo, established pursuant to UN Security Council Resolution 1244 (1999), requires those provisional institutions of self-government to observe and ensure internationally recognised human rights and fundamental freedoms, including those contained in the 1950 European Convention on Human Rights and the 1966 International Covenant on Civil and Political Rights.[24]

[20] The European Union has been a party to the UN Convention on the Rights of Persons with Disabilities since its formal confirmation of adherence in 2010. This adherence is in accordance with the possibility to do so that is granted to regional integration organisations. Art 44(1), Convention on the Rights of Persons with Disabilities; adopted at New York, 13 December 2006; entered into force, 3 May 2008.

[21] African Charter on Human and Peoples' Rights; adopted at Nairobi, 27 June 1981; entered into force, 21 October 1986. The SADR ratified the African Charter in May 1986.

[22] European Commission, 'Strategy for the Western Balkans: EU sets out new flagship initiatives and support for the reform-driven region', Press release, Strasbourg, February 2018.

[23] Associated Press, 'Kosovo Leaders Sign Application Request to Join EU', *Voice of America*, 14 December 2022, at: https://bit.ly/462sXR2.

[24] European Commission for Democracy Through Law (Venice Commission), 'The Human Rights Situation in Kosovo', Opinion No 280/2004, Strasbourg, 4 June 2004, at: https://bit.ly/462tnXC.

Where a State exercises effective control over a non-State actor, it will be generally responsible under international human rights law for the conduct of that non-State actor. This notion of effective control was set by the International Court of Justice in the *Nicaragua* case as the standard under international law with respect to US control over the *Contras*.[25] In reaffirming the standard two decades later, the Court declared that: 'It must … be shown that this "effective control" was exercised, or that the State's instructions were given, in respect of each operation in which the alleged violations occurred'.[26] Thus, in its 'list of issues' for Russia in relation to its eighth periodic report under the International Covenant on Civil and Political Rights, the Human Rights Committee called on the Russian Federation to

> outline any measures taken to ensure the application of the Covenant in situations of armed conflict involving foreign Governments, armed groups and proclaimed authorities over which the State party exercises considerable influence, to the extent that such influence amounts to effective control over their activities.[27]

As will be seen, however, the European Court of Human Rights has adopted a nuanced approach to the interpretation of 'effective control' that focuses on control of territory as well as (or even rather than) control of any given non-State actor.

If a foreign State does not exercise the requisite level of control over an armed group or other non-State actor, it will not normally be responsible for the acts or omissions of that group or actor that breach human rights. Whether the non-State actor itself is directly responsible for a violation of international human rights law remains unresolved. Under the classical view of human rights, it would not be so answerable, but the trend in international law is firmly towards holding non-State actors legally responsible for a violation, not merely finding that they have 'abused' human rights when they act in a manner inconsistent with those rights.[28] The basis on which international legal responsibility is founded typically follows two paths: either the specific norms being infringed have the status of *jus cogens* – ie they are of a peremptory nature; or the non-State actor is a de facto authority with control over certain territory. Examples of the latter scenario are the Somaliland government in Somalia or Hamas in Gaza, as well as the Polisario Front and the Kosovo government.

[25] International Court of Justice, *Case Concerning Military and Paramilitary Activities in and against Nicaragua (Nicaragua v United States)*, Judgment (Merits), 27 June 1986, paras 115–16 (hereafter ICJ Nicaragua Merits Judgment).

[26] International Court of Justice, *Case Concerning Application of the Convention on the Prevention and Punishment of the Crime of Genocide (Bosnia and Herzegovina v Yugoslavia (Serbia and Montenegro))*, Judgment (Merits), 26 February 2007, para 400.

[27] Human Rights Committee, List of issues in relation to the eighth periodic report of the Russian Federation, UN doc CCPR/C/RUS/Q/8, 14 August 2020, para 2.

[28] This specific language is used to denote an actor that is not directly bound by international human rights law.

Certain missions of the United Nations have endorsed the approach to binding non-State actors to such peremptory norms in a number of instances. In 2012, the Independent International Commission of Inquiry on the Syrian Arab Republic affirmed that: 'At a minimum, human rights obligations constituting peremptory international law (*ius cogens*) bind States, individuals and non-State collective entities, including armed groups'.[29] Two years later, the UN Mission in South Sudan (UNMISS) declared that: 'The most basic human rights obligations, in particular those emanating from peremptory international law (*ius cogens*) bind both the State and armed opposition groups in times of peace and during armed conflict'.[30]

Such peremptory norms would include, at a minimum, the prohibition on arbitrary deprivation of life, the prohibition of torture, and the prohibition of enforced disappearance. Customary norms that have not attained peremptory status would include the duty to protect life and the prohibition of ill-treatment not amounting to torture as well as the prohibition of arbitrary deprivation of liberty. The right to a private and family life is also a customary norm, but it is unlikely that the right to property has attained customary law status as a fundamental human right.

The alternative means by which non-State actors are held responsible for human rights violations is when they serve as *de facto authorities* holding sway over certain territory. Thus, the approach of the United Nations' system in Afghanistan before the Taliban takeover in August 2021 was that: 'Non-state actors are increasingly deemed to be bound by certain international human rights obligations, particularly those actors exercising *de facto* control over some areas, such as the Taliban'.[31] At the time of writing, the United Nations was continuing to regard the Taliban as the de facto not de jure authorities in Afghanistan.[32] As a matter of international law, however, their exercise of effective control of the territory and organs of Afghanistan[33] means that they are its government and the legal embodiment of the State of Afghanistan. They are thus directly responsible for compliance with international human rights treaties and observance of customary law. As Ben Saul has written: 'To pretend that a government does not exist where a political entity is obviously exercising authority would mean that the entity is not bound by the State's international obligations or responsible for breaches of them'.[34]

[29] Report of the Independent International Commission of Inquiry on the Syrian Arab Republic, UN doc A/HRC/19/69, 22 February 2012, para 106.

[30] UNMISS, 'Conflict in South Sudan: A Human Rights Report', 8 May 2014, at http://bit.ly/3lpLYqi, para 18.

[31] UN Assistance Mission in Afghanistan (UNAMA), *2019 Annual Report on the Protection of Civilians in Armed Conflict in Afghanistan*, Kabul, February 2020, at http://bit.ly/34GCBg6, p 81.

[32] See, eg, S Zaman, 'UN Conference on Afghanistan Begins Without Taliban', *Voice of America*, 18 February 2024, at https://bit.ly/42OHYWr.

[33] H Kelsen, *General Theory of Law and State*, trans. A Wedberg, Lawbook Exchange, Clark, NJ, 2011 edn [1945], pp 220–21.

[34] B Saul, '"Recognition" and the Taliban's International Legal Status', International Centre for Counter-Terrorism, 15 December 2021, at: https://bit.ly/3QPvGZK.

C. Material Jurisdiction (*Ratione Materiae*)

Material jurisdiction concerns the subject matter of an international legal obligation. In the context of international human rights law, this is of course first and foremost the rights that are protected and the respect and protection that they require from the State. Most often these rights are set forth in global or regional treaties. As noted above, however, even though China is not a State Party to the Covenant on Civil and Political Rights, it is still bound by customary human rights norms, including the rights to life and liberty. Thus, if China arbitrarily deprives any person under its personal and geographical jurisdiction of their life or liberty it bears responsibility under international law for this internationally wrongful act.[35]

Material jurisdiction also pertains to the ambient context, such as the existence of an armed conflict or the occurrence of a natural disaster. With respect to the former, as the International Court of Justice has confirmed, the protection of the 1966 Covenant on Civil and Political Rights

> does not cease in times of war, except by operation of Article 4 of the Covenant whereby certain provisions may be derogated from in a time of national emergency. Respect for the right to life is not, however, such a provision. In principle, the right not arbitrarily to be deprived of one's life applies also in hostilities. The test of what is an arbitrary deprivation of life, however, then falls to be determined by … the law applicable in armed conflict which is designed to regulate the conduct of hostilities.[36]

In addition to the right to life, the right to freedom from torture and other ill-treatment is also non-derogable under the 1966 Covenant (and under the Convention Against Torture). The right to liberty is derogable in 'time of public emergency which threatens the life of the nation and the existence of which is officially proclaimed', but only to the extent 'strictly required by the exigencies of the situation' and as long as the measures taken by States 'are not inconsistent with their other obligations under international law and do not involve discrimination solely on the ground of race, colour, sex, language, religion or social origin'.[37] Thus, armed groups in the Donbas, operating under Russia's effective control, who had detained a person solely on the basis of their speaking Ukrainian or supporting the authorities in Kyiv would be engaging Russia's responsibility under international law. This would be so, even were Russia to derogate from the right to liberty under the Covenant.

The right to private and family life, which is set forth in global and regional human rights treaties, is also a fundamental human right recognised in

[35] Articles 1 and 2, Draft Articles on Responsibility of States for Internationally Wrongful Acts, International Law Commission, UN doc A/56/10, 2001. See Chapter 8 of this volume on the issue of State responsibility for unlawful acts in hybrid warfare.

[36] International Court of Justice, *Legality of the Threat or Use of Nuclear Weapons*, Advisory Opinion, 8 July 1996, para 25.

[37] Art 4(1), 1966 International Covenant on Civil and Political Rights.

customary law. Article 17 of the International Covenant on Civil and Political Rights provides that:

> 1. No one shall be subjected to arbitrary or unlawful interference with his privacy, family, home or correspondence, nor to unlawful attacks on his honour and reputation.
> 2. Everyone has the right to the protection of the law against such interference or attacks.

In the view of the Human Rights Committee, the right must be guaranteed

> against all such interferences and attacks whether they emanate from State authorities or from natural or legal persons. The obligations imposed by this article require the State to adopt legislative and other measures to give effect to the prohibition against such interferences and attacks as well as to the protection of this right.[38]

The right to property has had a rather chequered existence in modern international human rights law.[39] The 1948 Universal Declaration of Human Rights stipulated that: 'Everyone has the right to own property alone as well as in association with others' and further that: 'No one shall be arbitrarily deprived of his property'.[40] But the right was not subsequently incorporated in either the International Covenant on Civil and Political Rights or the International Covenant on Economic, Social and Cultural Rights, global human rights treaties that were adopted on the same day by the UN General Assembly.[41]

At regional treaty level, the right was not set forth in the 1950 European Convention on Human Rights,[42] although it was subsequently included in the first Protocol to the Convention that was concluded and adopted in 1952.[43] The right is, however, found in both the 1969 American Convention on Human Rights[44] and the 1981 African Charter on Human and Peoples' Rights.[45] In the case of the American and European Conventions, the right is potentially subject to derogation (the African Charter not providing for derogation from any of its articles). But in accordance with the terms of any derogation, the rules of

[38] Human Rights Committee, General Comment No 16, 1988, para 1.

[39] See, eg, J Mchangama, 'The Right to Property in Global Human Rights Law', Policy Report, Cato Institute, May/ June 2011, at: https://bit.ly/3dUJTzG.

[40] Art 17, Universal Declaration of Human Rights; adopted at New York, 10 December 1948.

[41] International Covenant on Economic, Social and Cultural Rights; adopted at New York, 16 December 1966; entered into force, 3 January 1976. At the time of writing, 171 States were party to the Covenant, including China and Russia but not the United States, which is only a signatory.

[42] Convention for the Protection of Human Rights and Fundamental Freedoms; adopted at Rome, 4 November 1950; entered into force, 3 September 1953.

[43] 'Every natural or legal person is entitled to the peaceful enjoyment of his possessions. No one shall be deprived of his possessions except in the public interest and subject to the conditions provided for by law and by the general principles of international law'. Art 1, Protocol to the Convention for the Protection of Human Rights and Fundamental Freedoms; opened for signature at Paris, 20 March 1952; entered into force, 18 May 1954. At the time of writing, 44 States were party to the Protocol while Monaco and Switzerland were signatories.

[44] Art 21, American Convention on Human Rights; adopted at San José, 22 November 1969; entered into force, 18 July 1978.

[45] Art 14, African Charter on Human and Peoples' Rights.

international humanitarian law will apply in an armed conflict and therefore acts such as wanton destruction of property or pillage would still engage the responsibility of the State for a violation of international human rights law.[46]

D. Temporal Jurisdiction (*Ratione Temporis*)

Temporal jurisdiction concerns whether a given act falls within the jurisdiction of a particular court or tribunal based on *when* it occurred. This is particularly an issue with respect to the date on which a State became party to a particular treaty. As a consequence, events that took place prior to a State becoming party to a human rights treaty and which involved a potentially unlawful killing may well not be subject to adjudication in relation to the substantive component of the right to life. That said, the procedural component of that right – the duty to investigate suspicious death – may persist for many years, including after a State becomes party to the salient human rights treaty, thereby according to a court jurisdiction that it would otherwise not have in a particular case.[47]

The *Mocanu* case, adjudged before the European Court of Human Rights in 2014, involved allegations by the applicants that they had been victims of the violent crackdown on anti-government demonstrations in Bucharest in June 1990, but that no effective investigation had been carried out into those events.[48] Romania only adhered to the European Convention on Human Rights in 1994, and therefore an allegation before the Court of a substantive violation of the right to life would fail *ratione temporis*.

It was indicated that investigations conducted over approximately 19 years by the civilian prosecutor's offices and, subsequently, by the military prosecuting authorities, had not made it possible to establish the identity of the perpetrators or the degree of involvement of the security forces.[49] The Court observed that the majority of the proceedings and the most important procedural measures were carried out after the date on which Romania adhered to the Convention.[50] Consequently, the Court held that it had 'jurisdiction *ratione temporis* to examine the complaints raised' by the applicants under the procedural aspect of the right to life and the right to freedom from torture and other ill-treatment under the Convention 'in so far as those complaints relate to the criminal investigation conducted in the present case after the entry into force of the Convention in respect of Romania'.[51]

[46] This is because measures taken in derogation must not be inconsistent with the State's other obligations under international law. See Art 15(1), European Convention on Human Rights; Art 27(1), American Convention on Human Rights.

[47] Casey-Maslen, *The Right to Life under International Law*, n 2 above, para 3.15.

[48] European Court of Human Rights, *Mocanu and others v Romania*, Judgment (Grand Chamber), 17 September 2014, para 3.

[49] Ibid, para 155.

[50] Ibid, para 210.

[51] Ibid, para 211.

The application of temporal jurisdiction is also especially common in the case of enforced disappearances. These are where State agents arrest or detain an individual and then maintain him or her incommunicado. The individual is often tortured and may then be either released or killed. The Inter-American Court of Human Rights, among others, has interpreted enforced disappearance as an unlawful act that continues until the person who is alleged to have been subject to such disappearance is accounted for.[52] Similarly, according to the Human Rights Committee, deprivation of liberty followed by a refusal to acknowledge that deprivation of liberty, or by concealment of the fate of the disappeared person, results in a violation of the right to life as well as other rights recognised in the Covenant. These are, in particular, the prohibition of torture or other ill-treatment (Article 7), the rights to liberty and security of person (Article 9), and the right to recognition as a person before the law (Article 16 of the Covenant).[53]

Temporal jurisdiction may also, though, be brought to an end with respect to a human rights treaty. In the aftermath of its invasion of Ukraine in February 2022, Russia was first suspended and then ejected from the Council of Europe.[54] In March, the European Court of Human Rights adopted a resolution on the consequences of Russia's cessation of membership of the Council of Europe, decreeing that Russia would cease to be a State Party to the Convention on 16 September 2022.[55] But notwithstanding the fact that it is no longer party to the Convention, Article 58, paragraphs 2 and 3 of the European Convention accords the European Court of Human Rights temporal jurisdiction to examine claims against Russia committed until the date of its departure.[56] This jurisdiction pertains to acts and omissions not only of the Russian authorities but also of non-State actors which were on territory under its effective control. As of 16 September 2022, 17,450 applications directed against the Russian Federation were pending before the Court.[57]

In March 2023, Volker Türk, the UN High Commissioner for Human Rights, told the 52nd Session of the UN Human Rights Council that his office had documented 621 cases of enforced disappearance and arbitrary detention

[52] Inter-American Court of Human Rights, *Blake v Guatemala*, Judgment (Merits), 24 January 1998, para 67.

[53] Human Rights Committee, General Comment No 36, para 58.

[54] Resolution CM/Res(2022)2 on the cessation of the membership of the Russian Federation to the Council of Europe, adopted by the Committee of Ministers on 16 March 2022, at: https://bit.ly/3MyttPw.

[55] European Court of Human Rights, 'The Russian Federation ceases to be a Party to the European Convention on Human Rights', Press release ECHR 286 (2022), 16 September 2022, at: https://bit.ly/49E9A3G.

[56] See, eg, R Spano, P Plumptre, and T Tyrrell, 'Russia in the European Court of Human Rights – Recent Decisions May Impact Rights of Investors', *Gibson Dunn*, 30 May 2023, at: https://bit.ly/474M3HA.

[57] European Court of Human Rights, 'The Russian Federation ceases to be a Party to the European Convention on Human Rights', n 55 above.

in occupied areas of Ukraine both by Russia's military forces and its affiliated armed groups, including the Wagner Group.[58]

II. THE APPLICATION OF FUNDAMENTAL HUMAN RIGHTS TO HYBRID WARFARE AND HYBRID THREATS

This part of the chapter assesses the application of fundamental human rights to hybrid warfare and hybrid threats. It looks first at the conduct of Russian and South Ossetian forces in Georgia in 2008 and subsequently and then at the conduct of China with respect to its use of cognitive warfare in Taiwan. Each of these cases offers specific jurisdictional challenges.

A. The Conduct of Russian and South Ossetian Forces in Georgia Since 2008

In August 2008, the five-day-long international armed conflict between Russia and Georgia and the surrounding events represented an early instance of modern hybrid warfare. The situation involved cyberattacks and the use of non-State armed groups by, or on behalf of, the Russian Federation. But as the report of the Independent International Fact-Finding Mission on the Conflict in Georgia, established by the EU, observed, the shelling of Tskhinvali (in South Ossetia) by the Georgian armed forces during the night of 7 to 8 August 2008, which initiated major hostilities, was only 'the culminating point of a long period of increasing tensions, provocations and incidents'.[59]

Prior to the outbreak of major conflict, however, Russia had been supporting armed groups in both South Ossetia and Abkhazia in classic hybrid warfare style. As the EU-mandated Fact-Finding Mission noted:

> there are a number of reports and publications, including of Russian origin, indicating the provision by the Russian side of training and military equipment to South Ossetian and Abkhaz forces prior to the August 2008 conflict. Additionally there seems to have been an influx of volunteers or mercenaries from the territory of the Russian Federation to South Ossetia through the Roki tunnel and over the Caucasus range in early August, as well as the presence of some Russian forces in South Ossetia.[60]

The conflict itself was one of the first instances in which cyberspace superiority had an effect on conventional military operations. Hybrid operations engaged

[58] Office of the UN High Commissioner for Human Rights, 'On Ukraine, High Commissioner Türk details severe violations and calls for a just peace', Geneva, 31 March 2023, at: https://bit.ly/46bSyXE.

[59] Report of the Independent International Fact-Finding Mission on the Conflict in Georgia, Vol I, September 2009, at: https://bit.ly/3QOdrne, p 11.

[60] Ibid, p 20.

a cyberspace campaign in support of a conventional, kinetic ground attack,[61] with 'patriotic hackers', seemingly operating under the direction of Russian authorities, executing the cyberattacks in support of Russian armed forces.[62] Evidence to support the widespread belief that the Russian State was responsible for the cyberattacks included their timing and the precision with which they were perpetrated. These indicated, in Bryant's words, 'extensive' prior reconnaissance and preparation. At the tactical level, the ability of Georgian military forces to communicate was disrupted, resulting in mobile phones, landlines, and email all being rendered unavailable at times during the international armed conflict between the two States.[63] This disruption had a significant effect on the ability of the Georgian armed forces to resist the Russian invasion.[64]

The conflict saw Russia establish full control over both Abkhazia and South Ossetia, which together constitute one-fifth of Georgian territory, and which they control to this day. Hostilities followed the Bucharest Summit of the North Atlantic Treaty Organization (NATO), where a commitment had been made by the North Atlantic Council to admitting Georgia (and Ukraine) as NATO members in the future.[65]

(i) The Approach of the European Court of Human Rights to Jurisdiction Over Armed Conflict in Georgia v Russia (II)

In the human rights jurisprudence that resulted from the August 2008 conflict, jurisdictional issues were at the forefront. In its judgment on the merits in *Georgia v Russia (II)*, the Court used its earlier reasoning in the landmark case of *Catan v Moldova and Russia* to assess whether Russia exercised jurisdiction over South Ossetian forces.[66] Its analysis pertained primarily to control over *territory* rather than purely to control over specific *actors*, although the latter issue was also in the mix. Thus, the Court had explained that:

> It is a question of fact whether a Contracting State exercises effective control over an area outside its own territory. In determining whether effective control exists, the Court will primarily have reference to the strength of the State's military presence in the area … Other indicators may also be relevant, such as the extent to which its military, economic and political support for the local subordinate administration provides it with influence and control over the region.[67]

[61] The two principal weapons used in the cyberattacks were directed denial-of-service (DDoS) attacks and identified software flaws.

[62] WD Bryant, *International Conflict and Cyberspace Superiority: Theory and Practice*, 1st edn, Routledge, London, 2017, pp 142, 143.

[63] Ibid, p 144.

[64] Ibid, pp 173, 199.

[65] Bucharest Summit Declaration, Issued by the Heads of State and Government participating in the meeting of the North Atlantic Council in Bucharest on 3 April 2008, Press release (2008) 049, 3 April 2008, at: https://bit.ly/3SzpBBN, para 23.

[66] European Court of Human Rights, *Catan and others v Moldova and Russia*, Judgment (Grand Chamber), 19 October 2012, paras 106, 107.

[67] Ibid, para 107.

Applying to the situation in Georgia this mixed analytical approach – territorial control and, as a subsidiary issue, support of local actors – the Court considered that the Russian Federation exercised effective control 'within the meaning of the Court's case-law' over South Ossetia, Abkhazia and the 'buffer zone'. This extended out from South Ossetia from 12 August to 10 October 2008, the date of the official withdrawal of the Russian troops. But even after that period, 'the strong Russian presence' and the dependency on the Russian Federation of South Ossetian and Abkhazian authorities 'on whom their survival depends' indicated that there was 'continued "effective control" over South Ossetia and Abkhazia'.[68] The Court therefore concluded that the events which occurred after the cessation of hostilities (from the date of the ceasefire agreement signed on 12 August 2008) fell within the jurisdiction of the Russian Federation for the purposes of Article 1 of the European Convention, and dismissed Russia's jurisdictional objections in this regard.[69]

With geographical jurisdiction established, it then had to be determined, on an examination of the merits, whether there had been a violation of the rights protected by the Convention capable of engaging the responsibility of the Russian Federation. Georgia claimed multiple violations of the rights to life, to freedom from torture and other ill-treatment, to private and family life, and to property. Before analysing the details of each alleged violation, the Court decided to distinguish two temporal and material situations: the 'active phase of hostilities' from 8 to 12 August 2008 and the 'occupation phase' after the cessation of hostilities following the ceasefire agreement between Russia and Georgia of 12 August 2008.[70]

(ii) Jurisdiction Over Extraterritorial Hostilities in International Armed Conflict

In relation to the hostilities, the European Court's reasoning followed, to a certain extent, the argument advanced by Russia in its pleadings, whereby

> it is one thing to say that the Convention applies, and that IHL [international humanitarian law] can be used to modify Convention rights in a situation of detention, or in relation to soldiers performing a policing role in an area where they have effective control. It is quite another to suggest that the Convention applies in armed conflict and the chaos that follows.[71]

Thus, the Court held that:

> [I]n the event of military operations – including, for example, armed attacks, bombing or shelling – carried out during an international armed conflict, one cannot

[68] European Court of Human Rights, *Georgia v Russia (II)*, Judgment (Grand Chamber), 21 January 2021, para 174.
[69] Ibid, para 175.
[70] Ibid, para 83.
[71] Ibid, para 86.

> generally speak of 'effective control' over an area. The very reality of armed confrontation and fighting between enemy military forces seeking to establish control over an area in a context of chaos means that there is no control over an area. This is also true in the present case, given that the majority of the fighting took place in areas which were previously under Georgian control.[72]

The Court declared itself 'sensitive' to the fact that such a narrow interpretation of the notion of jurisdiction 'may seem unsatisfactory to the alleged victims of acts and omissions' by a State Party to the European Convention during active hostilities in an international armed conflict outside its territory 'as well as to the State in whose territory the active hostilities take place'.[73] But owing to the large number of alleged victims and contested incidents, the difficulty in establishing the circumstances, and the fact that such situations are 'predominantly' regulated by international humanitarian law/the law of armed conflict, the Court declared that it would not effectively overrule the decision it had made on jurisdiction in the *Banković* case in 2001.[74]

The Court's approach to jurisdiction is not good law.[75] In adjudicating *Georgia v Russia (II)*, it would have been relatively straightforward to have distinguished the *Banković* case since that pertained to events during the 1999 conflict over Kosovo with Yugoslavia, which was not a party to the European Convention. In rejecting jurisdiction, the Grand Chamber in *Banković* had stated that the Convention is a multilateral treaty operating 'in an essentially regional context and notably in the legal space (*espace juridique*) of the Contracting States'. The Convention, it had added, 'was not designed to be applied throughout the world, even in respect of the conduct of Contracting States'.[76] In contrast, Georgia in 2008 was a State Party to the European Convention on Human Rights, as was, at the salient time, Russia.

But the Court went further in its analysis in *Georgia v Russia (II)*, declaring that:

> If, as in the present case, the Court is to be entrusted with the task of assessing acts of war and active hostilities in the context of an international armed conflict outside the territory of a respondent State, it must be for the Contracting Parties to provide the necessary legal basis for such a task.[77]

[72] Ibid, para 126 and *cf* also para 137.

[73] Ibid, para 140.

[74] European Court of Human Rights, *Banković and others v Belgium and others*, Decision on Admissibility (Grand Chamber), 12 December 2001.

[75] A more coherent approach was advocated by Judge Chanturia in his partly dissenting opinion to the decision of the Court's Grand Chamber in *Georgia v Russia (II)*, n 68 above. He states plainly that *Banković* was wrongly decided; that the Court can apply the law of armed conflict/international humanitarian law accurately and reliably; and that where there are many victims, it is possible to select a number of representative incidents, just as the Court has done in the earlier inter-State case of *Cyprus v Turkey*. In short, as he concludes, the decision of the majority in *Georgia v Russia (II)* is an 'unsage precedent'.

[76] European Court of Human Rights, *Banković and others v Belgium and others*, Decision on Admissibility (Grand Chamber), n 74 above, para 80.

[77] European Court of Human Rights, *Georgia v Russia (II)*, Judgment (Grand Chamber), n 68 above, para 142.

With all due respect to the Court, this affirmation lacks legal foundation. The European Convention manifestly pertains both to international and to non-international armed conflict and the Court has found jurisdiction in both instances in both situations in multiple cases. Article 2 of the Convention (on the right to life) refers to 'the use of force which is no more than absolutely necessary' in 'action lawfully taken for the purpose of quelling [an] insurrection'.[78] An insurrection (or insurgency) is a non-international armed conflict. With respect to international armed conflict, it is expressly open to States to derogate from full observance of the right to life for 'deaths resulting from lawful acts of war'.[79] A war is an international armed conflict.

These wordings are clearly the 'necessary legal basis' for the application of the Convention. Indeed, in its earlier decision in *Hassan*, cited by the Court in *Georgia v Russia (II)*, it had been stipulated that formal derogation from the right to life was not even necessary – the Court would interpret rights by reference to the law of armed conflict as and where relevant.[80] Nonetheless, the Grand Chamber concluded in its judgment on the merits in *Georgia v Russia (II)* that the events which occurred during the active phase of the hostilities (namely, on 8–12 August 2008) did not fall within the jurisdiction of the Russian Federation for the purposes of Article 1 of the European Convention and therefore ruled all claims of substantive violation of rights that occurred during that period inadmissible.[81]

(iii) Jurisdiction and Violations of Fundamental Human Rights During the 'Occupation Phase'

In contrast, in the so-called occupation phase that followed the cessation of hostilities, the Court held that Russia's actions *did* fall within the material jurisdiction of the European Convention. It noted that a substantial Russian military presence remained after hostilities had ceased in South Ossetia.[82] Moreover, Russia itself provided 'numerous indications showing the extent of the economic and financial support' it had provided 'and continued to provide' to South Ossetia.[83] Without the chaos of conflict, the Court decided that the Russian Federation exercised effective control over South Ossetia both from 12 August to 10 October 2008 (the date of the official withdrawal of Russian troops) and beyond. It therefore concluded that the events which occurred *after* the cessation of hostilities fell within the jurisdiction of the Russian Federation for the purposes of Article 1 of the Convention.[84]

[78] Art 2(2)(c), European Convention on Human Rights.
[79] Art 15(2), European Convention on Human Rights.
[80] European Court of Human Rights, *Hassan v United Kingdom*, Judgment (Grand Chamber), 16 September 2014, para 107.
[81] European Court of Human Rights, *Georgia v Russia (II)*, Judgment (Grand Chamber), n 68 above, para 144.
[82] Ibid, para 164.
[83] Ibid, para 166.
[84] Ibid, para 174–75.

The responsibility of the Russian Federation for acts of violence against Georgian civilians was complicated by the fact that most were perpetrated in a systematic campaign of burning and looting of homes in Georgian villages in South Ossetia by South Ossetian militias, not Russian troops. Based on reports by Human Rights Watch and Amnesty International, the EU Fact-Finding Mission concluded that, after the Russian attacks, 'South Ossetians in uniform as well as Ossetian civilians who followed the Russian forces' advance undertook a systematic campaign of arson against homes and other civilian buildings in villages populated predominantly by ethnic Georgians'. Interviews confirmed that, with a few exceptions, Russian forces did not participate directly in the destruction of villages (apart from a brief period in the middle of August), 'but nor did they intervene to stop it'.[85]

The Court found an 'administrative practice' of unlawful acts by Russia in Georgia. Such a practice is defined by the repeated occurrence of human rights violations combined with official tolerance of that illegality. Despite indications that, at certain times, Russian troops *did* intervene to stop acts of violence being committed against civilians and their property, in many cases they were 'passively present' during scenes of looting.[86] The measures taken by the Russian authorities to prevent the alleged violations proved to be insufficient and indeed, such violations were even officially tolerated, 'as is also shown by the fact that the latter did not carry out effective investigations into the alleged violations'.[87]

As a consequence, the Court found sufficient evidence to conclude beyond reasonable doubt that there was an administrative practice of the killing of civilians and the torching and looting of houses in Georgian villages in South Ossetia (and elsewhere). This breached the rights to life, to a private and family life, and to property. The seriousness of the abuses amounted to inhuman and degrading treatment 'owing to the feelings of anguish and distress suffered by the victims, who, furthermore, were targeted as an ethnic group', and thus also breached Article 3 of the European Convention.[88]

(iv) Borderisation and the Georgia v Russia (IV) *Case*

On 26 August 2008, Russia recognised both South Ossetia and Abkhazia as independent States, a decision without basis in international law and which has been generally ignored by the international community ever since. But starting in 2009, and especially in recent years, it has been implementing a so-called 'borderisation' policy within Georgia, which Seskuria characterises as a 'silent war' against the authorities in Tbilisi. The approach involves

[85] Report of the Independent International Fact-Finding Mission on the Conflict in Georgia, Vol I, n 59 above, p 368.

[86] European Court of Human Rights, *Georgia v Russia (II)*, Judgment (Grand Chamber), n 68 above, paras 216–17.

[87] Ibid, paras 218–19.

[88] Ibid, paras 220, 222.

> the installation of barbed wire, border markers, and illegal fencing and, most importantly, the seizing of the Georgian land. This further divides families and harms the humanitarian situation on the ground by consistently violating human rights … As additional leverage, Kremlin-backed forces have systematically kidnapped and illegally detained Georgian citizens. In 2020, about 64 citizens were illegally detained for crossing the so-called Administrative Border Line or for just being in close proximity to it. Although most of the 'detained' citizens are released in exchange for paying a fine, there are incidents of ill-treatment and violence in detention and, in worst-case scenarios, death. Such malign actions constantly threaten the local population and increase tensions.[89]

The policy of borderisation is the subject of a further inter-State case between Georgia and Russia before the European Court of Human Rights. *Georgia v Russia (IV)* had not been adjudged on the merits at the time of writing, but in March 2023, the Court decided that it could proceed to this stage, with the application by Georgia having overcome the various jurisdictional barriers.[90] With respect to temporal jurisdiction, the Court noted that Georgia complained, in essence, about various human rights consequences from the process of borderisation which started in 2009. This will be the starting point for consideration of alleged violations of human rights in the case. Given that Russia ceased to be a Party to the Convention on 16 September 2022, this will be the end point for jurisdiction of the complaints by Georgia.[91]

Russia had objected to the exercise of jurisdiction by the European Court of Human Rights on the basis that it could not be held responsible for the conduct of the Abkhazian and South Ossetian authorities. It submitted an argument based on the case law of the International Court of Justice, namely the *Nicaragua* judgment and the judgment in the *Bosnian Genocide* case as referred to above. Russia concluded that the Court had no jurisdiction *ratione loci* to hear the case.[92] In respect of Abkhazia and South Ossetia, however, the Court referred to its decision in *Georgia v Russia (II)* that the strong Russian presence and the dependency of the de facto Abkhazian and South Ossetian authorities on the Russian Federation, on whom their survival depended, indicated that there had been continued 'effective control' over those two breakaway regions (as it understands that notion for the purpose of jurisdiction *ratione loci* of the European Convention) at least until 23 May 2018. 'Given the absence of any relevant new information to the contrary, the Court considers that this conclusion continues to be valid'.[93]

[89] N Seskuria, 'Russia's "Hybrid Aggression" against Georgia: The Use of Local and External Tools', Center for Strategic and International Studies, 21 September 2021, at: https://bit.ly/47FfWOD.

[90] European Court of Human Rights, *Georgia v Russia (IV)*, Decision (Second Section), 28 March 2023.

[91] Ibid, paras 22 and 23.

[92] Ibid, paras 33 and 34. ICJ Nicaragua Merits Judgment, n 25 above. ICJ Bosnia Genocide Merits Judgment, n 26 above.

[93] European Court of Human Rights, *Georgia v Russia (IV)*, Decision, n 90 above, para 44.

Based on the weight of evidence presented by Georgia, the Court decided that it would proceed to a judgment on the merits of the alleged violations of the following rights:

- the right to life in its substantive and procedural limbs (meaning unlawful killings and a failure to investigate suspicious death) (Article 2 of the European Convention);
- the right to freedom from torture and other ill-treatment in its substantive and procedural limbs (Article 3);
- the right to liberty and security of person (Article 5(1));
- the right to a private and family life (Article 8);
- the right to an effective remedy (Article 13);
- the prohibition of discrimination (Article 14);
- the prohibition of unlawful restrictions on the enjoyment of rights (Article 18 of the Convention);
- the right to property (Article 1 of Protocol No 1);
- the right to education (Article 2 of Protocol No 1); and
- the right to freedom of movement (Article 2 of Protocol No 4).[94]

B. China's Cognitive Warfare against the Population of Taiwan

(i) *The Notion of Cognitive Warfare*

There is increasing discussion in strategic military and hybrid warfare circles of the possibility of China using 'cognitive warfare' to help bring Taiwan under its active control, as well as to destabilise potential foes, such as the United States. Two Chinese National Defense University academics explained in an article in 2023 in the *People's Liberation Army (PLA) Daily* that what are termed 'confrontational actions' – comprising 'Information Disturbance', 'Discourse Competition', 'Public Opinion Blackout', and 'Block Information' – combine to achieve an 'invisible manipulation' and 'invisible embedding' of information in order to 'shape the target audience's macro framework for recognising, defining, and understanding events'.[95]

As with hybrid warfare and hybrid threats, cognitive warfare is not the subject of an internationally agreed definition, although several elements are common to commentators' understandings of the notion. Key features include the following:

[94] Ibid, para 69.

[95] J Baughman and PW Singer, 'China's social-media attacks are part of a larger "cognitive warfare" campaign', *Defense One*, 17 October 2023, at: https://bit.ly/3Mz7XKM, citing Duan Wenling and Liu Jiali, professors of the Military Propaganda Teaching and Research Department of the School of Political Science at the university, in the *PLA Daily*.

- the targeting of entire populations;
- the focus on changing behaviour by changing an entire population's way of thinking (rather than merely by providing discrete items of false information);
- reliance on increasingly sophisticated psychological techniques of manipulation (and, potentially, neurophysiological techniques); and
- destabilising news media organisations as a means to destabilise governments and other institutions.[96]

The oft-cited definition by Bernal and others characterises cognitive warfare succinctly as 'the weaponization of public opinion, by an external entity, for the purpose of 1) influencing public and governmental policy and 2) destabilizing public institutions'.[97]

Typically comprehended as a subset of hybrid warfare or a form of hybrid threat, cognitive warfare nonetheless has a demarcator: it is 'waged on the battlefield of the human mind', making it, in the view of certain authorities, the 'sixth domain of operations'.[98] For Rickli and others, what is integral to cognitive warfare is that it targets a nation's 'entire human capital' meaning that 'humans – and their cognitive space – become the contested domain'.[99] Described by NATO as 'the most advanced form of human mental manipulation … to date', cognitive warfare is

> the art of deceiving the brain or making it doubt what it thinks it knows. Its playground is the domain of the limits, constraints, and stereotypes of human thought, of false theories and of the culture of error in which it leads the opponent.[100]

But while cognitive warfare uses misinformation and disinformation to achieve its goals of modifying collective behaviour, it is considerably more sophisticated than are those longstanding notions of warfare. For sure, it operates through the medium of cyberwarfare and information warfare but as its moniker indicates, cognitive warfare also engages another fast-evolving domain – the cognitive neurosciences.[101] Pappalardo thus describes cognitive warfare as 'a multidisciplinary approach combining social sciences and new technologies to directly

[96] S Miller, 'Cognitive warfare: an ethical analysis' (2023) 25 *Ethics and Information Technology* [46], at: https://bit.ly/3u1VVmx, p 1.

[97] A Bernal, C Carter, I Singh, K Cao, and O Madreperla, *Cognitive Warfare: An Attack on Truth and Thought*, NATO and Johns Hopkins University, Baltimore MD, 2020, at: https://bit.ly/3MARhTb, p 3.

[98] B Claverie, B Prébot, N Buchler, and F Du Cluzel (eds), *Cognitive Warfare: The Future of Cognitive Dominance*, NATO, March 2022, at: https://bit.ly/49CVC26, pp S-1 and 3-1. The other five domains are land, sea, air, outer space, and cyberspace.

[99] J-M Rickli, F Mantellassi, and G Glasser, *Peace of Mind: Cognitive Warfare and the Governance of Subversion in the 21st Century*, Geneva Centre for Security Policy (GCSP) Policy Brief No 9, Geneva, August 2023, at: https://bit.ly/3QQVSTR, p 7.

[100] B Claverie, 'What is Cognition? And How to Make it One of the Ways of the War', ch 4 in Claverie et al (eds), *Cognitive Warfare: The Future of Cognitive Dominance*, n 98 above, p 4–15.

[101] Claverie et al (eds), *Cognitive Warfare: The Future of Cognitive Dominance*, n 98 above, p x.

alter the mechanisms of understanding and decision-making in order to destabilize or paralyze an adversary'.[102]

The temporal aspect of cognitive warfare is, however, said to be variable. In this regard, according to a piece from May 2021 jointly authored by Johns Hopkins University and Imperial College London, its aims

> can be limited, with short time horizons. Or they can be strategic, with campaigns launched over the course of decades. A single campaign could focus on the limited aim of preventing a military manoeuvre from taking place as planned, or to force the alteration of a specific public policy. Several successive campaigns could be launched with the long-term objective of disrupting entire societies or alliances, by seeding doubts about governance, subverting democratic processes, triggering civil disturbances, or instigating separatist movements.[103]

NATO's first scientific meeting on cognitive warfare was convened only relatively recently: in June 2021. The resultant publication, *The Future of Cognitive Dominance*, makes bold claims for cognitive warfare: 'Pursued to the fullest, cognitive warfare has the potential to destabilize societies, military organizations, and fracture alliances'.[104] The chapter on China in the report, authored by two Belgian academics, asserts simply, and without caveat, that: 'The Chinese will overtake the West in cognitive warfare'.[105] One of their arguments is that polarisation within democracies – said to be 'a blessing for Beijing' – facilitates Chinese disinformation and malign influence.[106] Another is that the Chinese approach to influencing others is more nuanced than in the West. Chinese strategy is 'more people-centric, less techno-centric, based on relative wins and subversion and deception'. As Orinx and Struye de Swielande aver metaphorically, 'China plays Go, the West chess'.[107]

(ii) China's Involvement in Cognitive Warfare

It is certainly the case that China is significantly engaged in developing cognitive warfare, particularly (but not only) with Taiwan in mind. Moreover, with the development of artificial intelligence (AI), neuroscience, and social media, senior officers and strategists in the PLA are said to believe that, in the future, it will be possible to influence an adversary's brain to affect human cognition directly.[108]

[102] D Pappalardo, '"Win the War Before the War?": A French Perspective on Cognitive Warfare', Commentary, *War on the Rocks*, 1 August 2022, at: https://bit.ly/3u6ge2q.

[103] Johns Hopkins University and Imperial College London, 'Countering cognitive warfare: awareness and resilience', *NATO Review*, 20 May 2021, at: https://bit.ly/3SvLsKi.

[104] Claverie et al (eds), *Cognitive Warfare: The Future of Cognitive Dominance*, n 98 above, p S-1.

[105] K Orinx and T Struye de Swielande, 'China and Cognitive Warfare: Why is The West Losing?', ch 8 in Claverie et al (eds), *Cognitive Warfare: The Future of Cognitive Dominance*, n 98 above, pp 8-1 to 8-6, at p 8-1.

[106] Ibid, p 8-3.

[107] Ibid, p 8-4.

[108] K Takagi, 'The Future of China's Cognitive Warfare: Lessons from the War in Ukraine', *War on the Rocks*, 22 July 2022, at: https://bit.ly/3FO5vMH.

Indeed, Rickli argues that in particular generative AI and neurotechnologies are already enabling 'highly accessible and efficient subversion within the cognitive domain of warfare'.[109]

According to NATO, China already achieves cognitive bias domestically by leveraging official and party-aligned influence to manipulate and control the information environment. But a secondary effect also results:

> [O]ther nations' citizens also develop cognitive biases towards Chinese mainland citizens and their collective disconnect with external information, which produces two fundamentally opposed perceptions of reality. This form of 'us vs. them' polarization can lead to increasing marginalization and exclusion of populations, as well as emotional exploitation, which contributes to China's Cognitive Warfare strategy.[110]

Chinese strategists argue that directly interfering with or subconsciously controlling the enemy's brain can induce mental damage, confusion, and hallucinations in the enemy, forcing them to lay down their arms and surrender. Beijing could use social media and other means to spread disinformation, including via 'deep fakes', and thereby manipulate public opinion in Taiwan. It could also try to discredit US efforts to support Taiwan.[111] But Takagi also urges caution in this regard: 'Cognitive warfare alone cannot win wars. Western analysts should similarly be careful not to assume China will rely on cognitive or other non-physical measures to subdue Taiwan'.[112]

Nevertheless, in the view of a number of commentators, a range of forms of cognitive warfare are already underway against Taiwan, at the least with a view to influencing public opinion there. Hung and Hung thus affirm that the expectation that Taiwanese independence means war with China has been ingrained in the Taiwanese psyche and affects people's attitude toward de jure independence. They recall that, in 2017, according to the Taiwan National Security Survey polls, only 41.3 per cent of Taiwanese citizens believed that China would attack if Taiwan declared independence on its own. But by the end of 2020, almost 62 per cent did so. The main reason for this increase, they believe, 'is that the PLA has ramped up its military intimidation since 2019 in response to the stagnation of cross-Strait relations and changes in US–China relations'.[113]

[109] J-M Rickli, 'Neurotechnologies and Future Warfares', S. Rajaratnam School of International Studies (RSIS), Nanyang Technological University, 7 December 2020, at: https://bit.ly/40yhyY6. Generative AI is artificial intelligence capable of generating text, images or other data using generative models. Neurotechnology refers to any technology that provides greater insight into brain or nervous system activity, or affects brain or nervous system function.

[110] NATO Allied Command Transformation, 'Cognitive Warfare: Strengthening and Defending the Mind', 5 April 2023, at: https://bit.ly/3QtzrT6.

[111] G Dominguez, 'Winning without fighting? Why China is exploring "cognitive warfare"', *The Japan Times*, 26 May 2023, at: https://bit.ly/40u8p2t.

[112] Takagi, 'The Future of China's Cognitive Warfare: Lessons from the War in Ukraine', n 108 above.

[113] TC Hung and TW Hung, 'How China's Cognitive Warfare Works: A Frontline Perspective of Taiwan's Anti-Disinformation Wars' (2022) 7(4) *Journal of Global Security Studies*, at: https://bit.ly/3T3vya0, p 5.

Meanwhile, 'disinformation and content farms on the Internet are another battlefield'. For example, the KKnews (*meiri toutiao*) and read01 (*yidu*) websites are popular among traditional Chinese users with their offer of reliable information on consumer products, medicine and health, entertainment news, cultural and historical stories, and technology and science. But PRC-approved ideology – including carefully selected narratives about how the United States betrays its allies – are embedded in this content and become Taiwanese internet users' key knowledge sources when Googling in Mandarin. This creates a China-friendly information space that affects Taiwan's readers largely without their being conscious of it. Many articles of KKnews and read01 use the term 'our country' when mentioning laws, the government, social customs, and scientific innovations.[114]

Other approaches involve denigrating Taiwanese institutions and individuals. For example, during the management of COVID-19 in May 2021, fake news was circulated that the disinfectant used by Taiwan's 'chemical warfare' troops in public places was highly toxic.[115] In 2018, China effectively ascribed a Taiwanese diplomat's death to the 'incompetence' of the Tsai administration, leading to a substantial defeat for the Democratic Progressive Party (DPP) in that year's Taiwanese local elections. More than half of all voters cast their votes while still believing the false campaign news.[116]

Stirring negative emotions in Taiwanese people against their government has been found to be more effective than inspiring positive emotions toward China as a way of altering perception and cognition. Moreover, behavioural studies suggest that political conservatives are more sensitive to negative stimuli, both physical and mental, and tend to use more psychological resources dealing with them, such as by forwarding fake news.[117] Hung and Hung fear that in the future, to maximise the effects, China might customise cognitive warfare with AI technologies to deliver 'the right information' to 'the right individual'.[118]

(iii) The Regulation of Cognitive Warfare under International Human Rights Law

Pappalardo acknowledges that offensive warfare in the cognitive domain raises 'ethical questions that should not be evaded'.[119] Miller even claims that

[114] Ibid, p 6.

[115] Ibid, p 7.

[116] Ibid, citing E Keoni, 'Beijing-Based PTT Users Spread Fake Osaka Airport Bus Story', 17 September 2018, at: https://bit.ly/3QNP09G.

[117] Hung and Hung, 'How China's Cognitive Warfare Works: A Frontline Perspective of Taiwan's Anti-Disinformation Wars', n 113 above, p 11, citing JR Hibbing, KB Smith, and JR Alford, 'Differences in Negativity Bias Underlie Variations in Political Ideology' (2014) 37(3) *Behavioral and Brain Sciences* 297–307.

[118] Hung and Hung, 'How China's Cognitive Warfare Works: A Frontline Perspective of Taiwan's Anti-Disinformation Wars', n 112 above, p 12.

[119] Pappalardo, '"Win the War Before the War?": A French Perspective on Cognitive Warfare', n 102 above.

'covert cognitive warfare is (more or less) by definition unlawful (at least in the nation-state against which it is directed)' and that hence 'there is a strong moral presumption against its use'.[120] In fact, neither argument is robust as a matter of international law. Rickli and others refer to the law of armed conflict and arms control as the traditional ways of reducing the likelihood of war and lessening the suffering in the event of its occurrence. But, they aver, these ways of conceptualising 'aggression', which pertain to the use of physical force, territoriality, and 'recognisable effects' in the physical domain such as injuries or destruction, 'cannot be transposed to the realities of cognitive warfare'.[121] They call upon the international community to work to devise an international governance framework for 'subversion control'.[122]

Part of this international legal response can certainly involve international human rights law. The human rights analysis of cognitive warfare is founded on the fundamental right of everyone to freedom of opinion, a right that is an 'indispensable' condition for 'the full development of the person'.[123] Thus, the 1966 International Covenant on Civil and Political Rights confirms simply that: 'Everyone shall have the right to hold opinions without interference'.[124] Although not formally free from derogation, the right is one that, in the view of the Human Rights Committee, 'cannot be made subject to lawful derogation' since it can never become necessary to derogate from it during a state of emergency'.[125] The right is also of a customary nature, and is thereby applicable to all States.

But the challenge of avoiding ever-more targeted disinformation through the medium of AI is potentially a huge one. According to one commentator, Nita A Farahany, writing in an article in June 2023 entitled '"Cognitive Liberty" Is the Human Right We Need to Talk About': 'We stand at a fork in the road – where rapid advances in AI and neurotechnology could change our lives for the better or lead us to a more dystopian future where even our brains are hacked and tracked'.[126]

She explains that US technology giants such as Meta, Snap, Microsoft, and Apple are investing heavily in technology that can track and decode our brains and mental experiences. She quotes a former Apple employee and neurotechnology prototyping researcher, who described how AI is used to analyse data 'to predict if you are feeling curious, mind wandering, scared, paying attention, remembering a past experience, or some other cognitive state'. In China,

[120] Miller, 'Cognitive warfare: an ethical analysis', n 96 above, p 5.

[121] Rickli et al, *Peace of Mind: Cognitive Warfare and the Governance of Subversion in the 21st Century*, n 99 above, p 10.

[122] Ibid, p 12.

[123] Human Rights Committee, General Comment No 34 – Article 19: Freedoms of opinion and expression, UN doc. CCPR/C/GC/34, 12 September 2011, para 2.

[124] Art 19(1), Covenant on Civil and Political Rights.

[125] Human Rights Committee, General Comment No 34, n 123 above, para 5.

[126] NA Farahany, '"Cognitive Liberty" Is the Human Right We Need to Talk About', *Time*, 26 June 2023, at: https://bit.ly/3so0VSf.

Hangzhou Enter Electronic Technology (Enter-tech) has a suite of consumer and enterprise neurotechnology devices with applications for education, psychological health, virtual reality, and the military.[127] The data such sensors generate 'are at risk of being commodified just as the rest of our personal data that has been before. A fear that is already materializing', Farahany concludes.[128] One should expect cognitive warfare to grow exponentially in every data-rich society.

[127] Ibid.
[128] Ibid.

6

Hybrid Warfare and Disarmament Law

Disarmament law is the body of international law that addresses the elimination of weapons.[1] The North Atlantic Treaty Organization (NATO), for instance, describes disarmament as 'the act of eliminating or abolishing weapons (particularly offensive arms) either unilaterally or reciprocally'.[2] NATO considers that disarmament refers both to reductions in the number of arms (sometimes termed arms control) and to the elimination of entire categories of weapons.[3] But while the destruction, without replenishment, of stockpiles of weapons is central to disarmament action, disarmament law also encompasses the prohibition of weapons development, production, transfer, and use. With respect to the latter notion, there is an obvious interrelationship with the law of armed conflict, which specifically regulates the legality of the use of particular weapons in armed conflict.

Always to be borne in mind are the dicta of the International Court of Justice whereby 'in international law there are no rules, other than such rules as may be accepted by the State concerned, by treaty or otherwise, whereby the level of armaments of a sovereign State can be limited'.[4] This principle of voluntary assumption of disarmament obligations pertains to 'all States without exception',[5] although it is also subject to the power of the United Nations (UN) Security Council to impose such obligations on a State that threatens or breaches international peace and security.[6] Thus, for example, under its Resolution 687 adopted in April 1991, the Security Council decided that Iraq 'shall unconditionally accept the destruction, removal, or rendering harmless,

[1] S Casey-Maslen and T Vestner, *A Guide to International Disarmament Law*, Routledge, Abingdon, 2019, para 0.1.

[2] NATO, 'Arms Control, Disarmament and Non-Proliferation in NATO', last updated 27 February 2023, at: https://bit.ly/2ND8I41.

[3] Ibid.

[4] International Court of Justice, *Case Concerning Military and Paramilitary Activities In and Against Nicaragua* (*Nicaragua v United States*), Judgment (Merits), 27 June 1986 (hereafter, ICJ Nicaragua Merits Judgment), para 269.

[5] Ibid.

[6] Arts 39 and 41, Charter of the United Nations; adopted at San Francisco, 26 June 1945; entered into force, 24 October 1945.

under international supervision' of all chemical and biological weapons and agents, and all related research, development, and manufacturing facilities, as well as of all ballistic missiles with a range greater than 150 kilometres.[7] At the time of the resolution's adoption in 1991, Iraq was not yet a State Party to the 1971 Biological Weapons Convention;[8] the Chemical Weapons Convention had not yet even been adopted;[9] and, as is still the case today, no multilateral treaty banned intermediate and long-range ballistic missiles.

Under the law of State responsibility as delineated by the International Law Commission in its 2001 Draft Articles, the application of disarmament obligations to a State pertains first and foremost to the conduct of its organs – most obviously the armed forces, the police, and other security forces that form part of the Executive. But under Article 8 of the 2001 Draft Articles, a State is also responsible for the conduct of a 'person or group of persons' which is 'in fact' acting on its instructions or under its direction or control in carrying out that conduct.[10] In his commentary on the draft article, James Crawford, the Commission's Special Rapporteur for the issue of State responsibility, duly recalled that as 'a general principle, the conduct of private persons or entities is not attributable to the State under international law'.[11] But in his following observations he omitted to address the particularities of disarmament law. The notion of the prohibited conduct of a State Party to a disarmament treaty purposively includes all private companies or other non-State actors within the jurisdiction of that State, as well as any non-State actor which a State supports extraterritorially, irrespective of whether it effectively controls their actions. To assert otherwise is to negate entirely the efficacy of disarmament. This application of disarmament law is consistent with the understanding of the use of force under *jus ad bellum*.[12]

The remainder of this chapter is divided into two main sections. The first considers disarmament and non-proliferation[13] of weapons of mass destruction

[7] UN Security Council Resolution 687, adopted on 3 April 1991 by 12 votes to 1 (Cuba), with 2 abstentions (Ecuador and Yemen), operative para. 8(a) and (b).

[8] Convention on the Prohibition of the Development, Production and Stockpiling of Bacteriological (Biological) and Toxin Weapons and on Their Destruction; adopted at Geneva, 28 September 1971; opened for signature at London, Moscow, and Washington, DC, 10 April 1972; entered into force, 26 March 1975 (hereafter, 1971 Biological Weapons Convention).

[9] Convention on the Prohibition of the Development, Production, Stockpiling and Use of Chemical Weapons and on Their Destruction; adopted at Geneva, 3 September 1992; entered into force, 29 April 1997 (hereafter, 1992 Chemical Weapons Convention).

[10] Art 8, Draft Articles on the Responsibility of States for Internationally Wrongful Acts, International Law Commission, UN doc A/56/10, 2001 (hereafter, 2001 Draft Articles on State Responsibility).

[11] Commentary para 1 on Art 8, 2001 Draft Articles on State Responsibility: https://legal.un.org/ilc/texts/instruments/english/commentaries/9_6_2001.pdf.

[12] ICJ Nicaragua Merits Judgment, n 4 above, para 228.

[13] Non-proliferation or 'non-armament' is to be understood in a slightly distinct manner from disarmament as it does not involve taking away weapons. It is, though, akin to a prohibition on transfer. For NATO, 'non-proliferation refers to all efforts to prevent proliferation from occurring, or should it occur, to reverse it by any other means than the use of military force. Non-proliferation applies to both WMD and to conventional capabilities 'such as missiles and small arms'. NATO, 'Arms Control, Disarmament and Non-Proliferation in NATO', n 2 above.

(WMD) in the context of hybrid warfare. WMD is a collective term generally interpreted to cover nuclear weapons, radiological weapons, biological weapons, and chemical weapons, at the least when they are likely to cause mass casualties.[14] The second section of the chapter concerns the disarmament of conventional weapons, ordinarily defined as all weapons other than WMD.[15] Disarmament treaties adopted in 1997 and 2008, respectively, comprehensively prohibit two specific conventional weapons: anti-personnel mines and cluster munitions. In addition, the 2013 UN Arms Trade Treaty prohibits the export of conventional weapons either where they undermine peace and security, or where they would be used to commit or facilitate a serious violation of international humanitarian law or international human rights law, an act of terrorism, or transnational organised crime.[16]

I. HYBRID WARFARE AND WMD DISARMAMENT AND NON-PROLIFERATION

It is far from inconceivable that hybrid warfare could involve some form of WMD use. The most likely candidates are chemical weapons and potentially also radiological weapons (radioactive substances disseminated by means of conventional explosives). In 2018, a toxic chemical, Novichok, was used in Salisbury by agents of the Russian government with a view to killing a Russian defector living in the United Kingdom.[17] Two years earlier, a New Yorker was sentenced to 30 years' imprisonment for a plot to kill Muslims using a radiological dispersion device. Glendon Scott Crawford, a 52-year-old man from Galway, a town in New York state, was sentenced for conspiracy to kill Muslims with a weapon of mass destruction. His goal was to acquire and modify an industrial-grade X-ray radiation device and use it to cause death or injury by exposing people to lethal doses of ionising radiation. Mr Crawford, a self-professed member of

[14] Thus, riot-control agents such as tear gas may be considered conventional weapons and not WMD. See Arts I(5) and II(9)(d), 1992 Chemical Weapons Convention; and European Court of Human Rights, *Finogenov and others v Russia*, Judgment (First Section), 20 December 2011 (as rendered final on 6 March 2012), para 229. Earlier interpretation by the US Department of Defense (DoD) considers WMD to be those weapons 'that are capable of a high order of destruction and/or of being used in such a manner as to destroy large numbers of people'. This includes certain high-explosive conventional munitions but would seemingly exclude chemical riot-control agents such as tear gas. US DoD, *Department of Defense Dictionary of Military and Associated Terms*, Joint Publication 1-02, Washington DC, 12 April 2001 (as amended up to 17 October 2007), p 584.

[15] UN Office for Disarmament Affairs (UNODA), 'Conventional Arms', undated but accessed 13 February 2024 at: https://bit.ly/3rCvzH7. The 1980 Convention on Prohibitions or Restrictions on the Use of Certain Conventional Weapons Which May Be Deemed to Be Excessively Injurious or to Have Indiscriminate Effects uses the term in its title but does not formally define the scope of the notion.

[16] Art 7, Arms Trade Treaty; adopted at New York, 2 April 2013; entered into force, 24 December 2014.

[17] 'Salisbury Incident', Statement by the United Kingdom Prime Minister (Mrs Theresa May), in *Hansard*, HC Vol 637, 14 March 2018, at: https://bit.ly/3ddI6ta.

the Ku Klux Klan, was the first person in the United States to be found guilty of attempting to acquire and use a radiological dispersal device.[18] Dedicated provisions on radiological devices are contained in the US Criminal Code.[19]

In addition, although similarly not part of hybrid warfare, non-State actors engaged in a number of chemical warfare attacks in the course of the armed conflicts in Syria that began in 2011.[20] In this regard, in its Resolution 2118 (2013), the UN Security Council demanded that non-State actors not 'develop, acquire, manufacture, possess, transport, transfer or use nuclear, chemical or biological weapons and their means of delivery', and called upon all Member States, in particular those neighbouring Syria, to report any actions inconsistent with the demand to the UN Security Council 'immediately'.[21]

A. Nuclear Weapons and Nuclear Material

A nuclear explosive device is one that is capable of producing an explosion and massive damage and destruction by the sudden release of energy instantaneously emitted from self-sustaining nuclear fission and/or fusion.[22] A nuclear weapon is a nuclear explosive device that has been weaponised – typically where the device has been miniaturised and then incorporated in a bomb or missile for delivery. This is so, even though the 1968 Treaty on the Non-Proliferation of Nuclear Weapons (NPT),[23] the cornerstone of the nuclear non-proliferation regime, does not explicitly define either term.

The NPT was intended to stem the spread of nuclear weapons beyond the five nuclear-weapon States designated under the treaty: China, France, the Soviet Union (with Russia as successor State following the dismantling of the USSR in 1991), the United Kingdom, and the United States.[24] It has been largely successful in this endeavour, with only four others currently developing such weapons: India, Israel, the Democratic People's Republic of Korea (North Korea), and Pakistan. Subsequent to the NPT's entry into force in 1970, three other States

[18] US Department of Justice, 'New York Man Sentenced to 30 Years for Plot to Kill Muslims', Press release No 16-1497, Washington DC, 19 December 2016, at: https://bit.ly/45nWvrU.

[19] 18 US Code § 832(c): 'Participation in nuclear and weapons of mass destruction threats to the United States', at: https://bit.ly/3F6RgSR.

[20] The UN Joint Investigative Mechanism (JIM), established in August 2015, attributed responsibility for use of chemical weapons to both the Syrian government and non-State actors before its mandate ended on 16 November 2017. This concerned the use of munitions containing sulphur mustard by non-State actors at Marea on 21 August 2015 and at Umm Hawsh on 16 September 2016. See J Hart, 'Allegations of use of chemical weapons in Syria', ch 8, section 1, *SIPRI Yearbook 2018: Armaments, Disarmament and International Security*, Stockholm International Peace Research Institute, Stockholm, 2018, 349–61, at pp 349, 350.

[21] UN Security Council Resolution 2118, adopted by unanimous vote in favour on 27 September 2013, operative para 19.

[22] P5 Working Group on the Glossary of Key Nuclear Terms, *P5 Glossary of Key Nuclear Terms*, 1st edn, China Atomic Energy Press, Beijing, 2015, at https://bit.ly/36I801R, p 6, para 1.3.5.

[23] Treaty on the Non-Proliferation of Nuclear Weapons; opened for signature at London, Moscow, and Washington, DC, 1 July 1968; entered into force, 5 March 1970.

[24] Art IX(3), NPT.

at some time or other possessed nuclear weapons (Belarus, Kazakhstan, and Ukraine, each of which inherited stockpiles from the Soviet Union upon its demise) while a fourth, South Africa, developed nuclear explosive devices that had not been weaponised,[25] but all four States voluntarily renounced them. Of the current possessor States, only North Korea was a party to the NPT but then chose to withdraw and produce nuclear weapons.

The first article of the treaty stipulates that each of the five nuclear-weapon States will not 'transfer *to any recipient whatsoever* nuclear weapons or other nuclear explosive devices or control over such weapons or explosive devices *directly, or indirectly*' (emphasis added). This broad formulation clearly precludes the provision of access to nuclear weapons or other nuclear explosive devices to any non-State armed group, including in the course of hybrid warfare. In the aftermath of the 9/11 attacks against the United States, there was concern that al-Qaeda was seeking to procure weapons of mass destruction. This led to the adoption in 2004 by the UN Security Council of Resolution 1540, in which it decided that 'all States shall refrain from providing any form of support to non-State actors that attempt to develop, acquire, manufacture, possess, transport, transfer or use nuclear, chemical or biological weapons and their means of delivery'.[26]

To date, no unauthorised non-State actor has been able to seize control of a nuclear explosive device. In November 1995, however, nuclear material was found in a Moscow park, in conduct seemingly linked to the conflict in Chechnya. Members of an unknown Chechen armed group contacted a Russian television station declaring they *could* construct a radiological explosive device (commonly known as a dirty bomb), which is not a nuclear explosive device. The callers told the station that they had buried radiological materials in Moscow's Ismailovsky park. The authorities found a partially buried container of caesium at the claimed location.[27] No one was ever arrested, much less convicted for the act. Several years later, Khalid Sheikh Mohammed, al-Qaeda's former Head of Propaganda, is reported to have suggested to Osama bin Laden that one of the aircraft to be hijacked in the attacks against the United States on 11 September 2001 should be dive-bombed into a nuclear energy plant.[28] In testimony before the Select Committee on Intelligence in the US Senate in February 2005, then FBI director, Robert S Mueller, stated:

> Another area we consider vulnerable and target rich is the energy sector, particularly nuclear power plants. Al-Qa'ida planner Khalid Sheikh Mohammed had nuclear power plants as part of his target set and we have no reason to believe that Al-Qa'ida has reconsidered.[29]

[25] South Africa, which had not weaponised the five nuclear explosive devices it had developed.

[26] UN Security Council Resolution 1540, adopted by unanimous vote in favour on 28 April 2004, operative para 1.

[27] L Krock and R Deusser, 'Dirty Bomb: Chronology of Events', PBS NOVA, February 2003, at: https://bit.ly/46yZ4se.

[28] *The 9/11 Commission Report*, at: https://bit.ly/3LbEJRt, p 245 fn 148.

[29] Cited in MH Saier and JT Trevors, 'Is Nuclear Energy the Solution?' (2010) 208(1) *Water, Air, and Soil Pollution* 1–3, at: https://bit.ly/3F1n7nO.

The most recent global counterterrorism treaty is the Nuclear Terrorism Convention whose elaboration was concluded by States in 2005.[30] Its negotiation had begun in 1998 with a draft proffered by Russia,[31] which declared that the proposed convention would be the first international counterterrorism treaty specially designed as a 'pre-emptive instrument'.[32] The Convention proscribes the unlawful and intentional possession of radioactive material and the production or possession of a related device with the intent either to cause death, serious bodily injury, or substantial damage to property or to the environment.[33] It also calls for the criminalisation of the unlawful and intentional use of radioactive material or a device or damage to a nuclear facility in a manner that either releases, or risks the release of, radioactive material. This is the case where the intent exists to cause death or serious bodily injury or to inflict substantial damage on property or the environment, or to compel conduct by a natural or legal person, an international organisation, or a State.[34]

The 2005 Nuclear Terrorism Convention excludes from its purview the acts of armed forces that are governed by the law of armed conflict.[35] This designation encompasses a non-State armed group that is a party to an armed conflict, irrespective of whether it is supported by a State engaged in hybrid warfare.

B. Biological Weapons

Biological and toxin weapons are micro-organisms such as viruses, bacteria, or fungi, or toxic substances produced by living organisms that are released deliberately to cause disease and death in humans, animals, or plants. Biological agents such as anthrax, botulinum toxin, and plague can cause large numbers of deaths in a short amount of time. Biological agents capable of secondary transmission can lead to epidemics.[36]

The use of biological weapons in warfare was first prohibited in 1925. The so-called Geneva Protocol, adopted under the auspices of the League of Nations, declared that the prohibition on use in war of asphyxiating, poisonous or other gases, and of all analogous liquids materials or devices, first introduced in 1899 had become part of customary international law, and agreed to extend the prohibition 'to the use of bacteriological methods of

[30] International Convention for the Suppression of Acts of Nuclear Terrorism; adopted at New York, 13 April 2005; entered into force, 7 July 2007 (2005 Nuclear Terrorism Convention). At the time of writing, 123 States were party to the Convention.

[31] J Boulden, 'The United Nations General Assembly and Terrorism', ch 34 in B Saul (ed), *Research Handbook on International Law and Terrorism*, 2nd edn, Edward Elgar, Cheltenham, 2020, p 499.

[32] Nuclear Threat Initiative (NTI), 'International Convention on the Suppression of Acts of Nuclear Terrorism', last reviewed 29 April 2020, at: https://bit.ly/3gusq2Y.

[33] Art 2(1)(a), 2005 Nuclear Terrorism Convention.

[34] Art 2(1)(b), 2005 Nuclear Terrorism Convention.

[35] Art 4(2), 2005 Nuclear Terrorism Convention.

[36] World Health Organization (WHO), 'Biological weapons', 2023, at: https://bit.ly/3LNSIwY.

warfare'.[37] The 1971 Biological Weapons Convention added prohibitions on the development, production, stockpiling, and transfer of biological and toxin weapons to the existing prohibition on their use. The Biological Weapons Convention was the first multilateral disarmament treaty banning an entire category of WMD.[38]

As was the case with the NPT and similarly with later disarmament treaties, the Biological Weapons Convention binds its States Parties (numbering 185 at the time of writing)[39] and any actors under its jurisdiction as well as any armed groups under its effective control. Although the number of attacks by non-State armed groups using biological agents is relatively small, several have occurred. Most notable of these involved Aum Shinrikyo, which used anthrax and botulinum toxin in a series of attacks in Japan in 1990–95, although they did not succeed in causing mass casualties.[40] Aum Shinrikyo was not supported in its terror attacks by any State.

But the risk of 'bioterrorism' – the use or threatened use of biological agents against civilian targets with the intent of causing injury or harm for political, religious, or ideological objectives[41] – has not disappeared. Only a few years ago, when at the summit of its territorial control in Iraq and Syria, Islamic State showed interest in acquiring biological capabilities.[42] Since then, the risk of bioweapons being generated synthetically has increased significantly. A 2018 report by the US National Academy of Sciences concluded that advances in the field of synthetic biology have led to the capabilities to recreate dangerous viruses from scratch in the laboratory; to render harmful bacteria more deadly; and to modify common microbes so that they disseminate lethal toxins once they enter the body.[43]

In June 2022, NATO issued a new policy on chemical, biological, radiological, and nuclear (CBRN) weapons that gave greater prominence to hybrid

[37] Protocol for the Prohibition of the Use of Asphyxiating, Poisonous or Other Gases, and of Bacteriological Methods of Warfare; adopted at Geneva, 17 June 1925; entered into force, 8 February 1928.

[38] UN Office for Disarmament Affairs (UNODA), 'Biological Weapons Convention', undated but accessed on 1 October 2023, at: https://bit.ly/3F5RlGi.

[39] The 12 States not party are the following: Chad, Comoros, Djibouti, Egypt (a signatory), Eritrea, Haiti (a signatory), Israel, Kiribati, Micronesia, Somalia (a signatory), Syria (a signatory), and Tuvalu.

[40] R Danzig, M Sageman, T Leighton, L Hough, H Yuki, R Kotani, and ZM Hosford, *Aum Shinrikyo: Insights Into How Terrorists Develop Biological and Chemical Weapons*, Center for a New American Security, July 2011, at: https://bit.ly/46wKq4s, pp 16–26.

[41] Nuclear Threat Initiative (NTI), 'Bioterrorism', undated but accessed 1 October 2023 at: https://bit.ly/3rK5Mwv.

[42] D McElroy, 'Islamic State Seeks to Use Bubonic Plague as a Weapon of War', *Daily Telegraph*, 29 August 2014, at: https://bit.ly/3LNHGba; and SE Meulenbelt and MS Nieuwenhuizen, 'Non-State actors' pursuit of CBRN weapons: From motivation to potential humanitarian consequences' (2015) 97(899) *International Review of the Red Cross* 831–58, at p 850.

[43] I Sample, 'Synthetic biology raises risk of new bioweapons, US report warns', *The Guardian*, 19 June 2018, at: https://bit.ly/3RNmaqP.

threats and meeting attacks across multiple domains.[44] NATO believes that 'the development of new CBRN materials, including those that are more difficult to detect, trace, or investigate, and novel means of targeting and delivery, may generate new opportunities for CBRN use alongside hybrid techniques'.[45] At a National Academy of Sciences workshop held the following month, the specific risk of a biological attack in Ukraine envisaged Russia conducting a biological attack to avoid using nuclear weapons.[46]

More recently, the risk of non-State actors using artificial intelligence to create bioweapons has been raised by the United Kingdom (UK) government. 'Frontier AI' is the term used to refer to the most advanced AI models that could be dangerous enough to pose a risk to human life, such as through the creation of bioweapons or toxic chemical agents. In 2022, an AI tool took just six hours to suggest 40,000 different potentially lethal molecules, some of which were similar to VX, the most potent chemical nerve agent yet developed.[47]

C. Chemical Weapons

The threat from the development and use of chemical weapons by non-State actors has been illustrated above. The 1992 Chemical Weapons Convention is clearer than its nuclear and biological antecedents that it is not only State organs that are bound by a disarmament treaty. In this regard, the duty of domestic incorporation of the treaty upon each State Party stipulates as follows:

> Each State Party shall, in accordance with its constitutional processes, adopt the necessary measures to implement its obligations under this Convention. In particular, it shall:
>
> (a) Prohibit natural and legal persons anywhere on its territory or in any other place under its jurisdiction as recognized by international law from undertaking any activity prohibited to a State Party under this Convention, including enacting penal legislation with respect to such activity;[48]

This reflects the reality that private enterprises (legal persons) and private individuals (natural persons) may be involved in the production, supply, or use of chemical weapons.

The Convention further obligates each State Party to never under any circumstances 'assist, encourage or induce, in any way, anyone to engage in any activity

[44] NATO, 'NATO's Chemical, Biological, Radiological and Nuclear (CBRN) Defence Policy', 14 June 2022 (last updated 5 July 2022), at: https://bit.ly/3Q5OaVw (hereafter, NATO 2022 CBRN Policy).

[45] Ibid, para 25.

[46] National Academies of Sciences, Engineering, and Medicine, *Assessing and Improving Strategies for Preventing, Countering, and Responding to Weapons of Mass Destruction Terrorism: Biological Threats: Proceedings of a Workshop in Brief*, The National Academies Press, Washington, DC, 2023, at: https://bit.ly/3ZHz3Ve, p 5.

[47] K Stacey and D Milmo, 'No 10 worried AI could be used to create advanced weapons that escape human control', *The Guardian*, 25 September 2023, at: https://bit.ly/3ti9rCq.

[48] Art VII(1), 1992 Chemical Weapons Convention.

prohibited to a State Party' under its provisions.[49] This clearly precludes supporting non-State actors to engage in unlawful use of chemical agents. NATO's revised CBRN defence policy of 2022 warned that non-State actors 'are known to both seek access to more sophisticated CBRN materials and WMD, as well as to attempt to weaponise toxic industrial chemicals and other materials that may be easier to acquire'. As the Alliance further cautions, 'scientific and technological innovation continues to reduce the barriers to acquiring or developing advanced and diverse CBRN materials and means of delivery. Consequently, the risk of CBRN use or proliferation by non-state actors is likely to continue to grow'.[50] The policy stated that the Alliance also had 'grave concerns that Russia is considering the use of chemical or biological weapons in the future'.[51]

II. HYBRID WARFARE AND THE DISARMAMENT AND NON-PROLIFERATION OF CONVENTIONAL WEAPONS

Far more prevalent than the actual or potential use of WMD in hybrid warfare, however, is the use of conventional weapons. Only two such weapons are comprehensively prohibited by disarmament treaty: anti-personnel mines and cluster munitions. Anti-personnel mines can be manually emplaced by a single person, but in many cases they are remotely delivered, particularly by artillery. Also capable of delivery by light weapons – weapons that can be fired by a crew of two or three persons[52] – are cluster munitions. This makes these weapons readily usable in hybrid warfare, as the relevant logistical requirements are far less onerous than those integral to the deployment and supply with ammunition of heavy weapons.

A. Anti-Personnel Mines

The 1997 Anti-Personnel Mine Ban Convention (APMBC) entered into force on 1 March 1999.[53] To date, it has attracted 164 States Parties. The core obligations, and in particular the prohibitions on development, production, stockpiling, and

[49] Art I(1)(d), 1992 Chemical Weapons Convention.

[50] NATO 2022 CBRN Defence Policy, https://www.nato.int/cps/en/natohq/official_texts_197768.htm, para 15.

[51] Ibid, para 13.

[52] Although not defined by treaty, the 2005 International Tracing Instrument explains that '"Light weapons" are, broadly speaking, weapons designed for use by two or three persons serving as a crew, although some may be carried and used by a single person. They include, inter alia, heavy machine guns, hand-held under-barrel and mounted grenade launchers, portable anti-aircraft guns, portable anti-tank guns, recoilless rifles, portable launchers of anti-tank missile and rocket systems, portable launchers of anti-aircraft missile systems, and mortars of a calibre of less than 100 millimetres'. Art II(4)(b), 2005 International Instrument to Enable States to Identify and Trace, in a Timely and Reliable Manner, Illicit Small Arms and Light Weapons, available at: https://bit.ly/3ZQldQv.

[53] Convention on the Prohibition of the Use, Stockpiling, Production and Transfer of Anti-Personnel Mines and on Their Destruction; adopted at Oslo, 18 September 1997; entered into force, 1 March 1999 (APMBC).

transfer, mirror those in the Chemical Weapons Convention on which the 1997 Convention was modelled. There was, however, one significant difference of circumstance. As noted above, the Chemical Weapons Convention reflected a longstanding prohibition, under the law of armed conflict, on the use of chemical weapons in a situation of international armed conflict. This prohibition was first instituted in the Hague Convention of 1899 and was then formalised as customary law in 1925. In contrast, the APMBC had no prior ban on the use of anti-personnel mines in international law on which to build.

The 1980 Convention on Certain Conventional Weapons had a protocol annexed to it on landmines (covering anti-vehicle as well as anti-personnel mines) but this did little more than require compliance with the law-of-armed-conflict principle of distinction applicable to all weapons.[54] The protocol (Protocol II) was revised by States in the 1990s and an Amended Protocol II concluded in May 1996.[55] But while specific prohibitions were instituted on anti-personnel mines designed to be detonated by mine detectors and on remotely delivered anti-personnel mines that did not meet specified requirements for self-destruction and self-deactivation, the new protocol fell far short of the total ban on the weapons an increasing number of States were seeking.

The limited prohibitions and restrictions on use of anti-personnel mines under the law of armed conflict within the UN framework justified the decision to negotiate the APMBC in a stand-alone diplomatic process and at a diplomatic conference convened outside UN auspices. The lack of a prior ban also explains the formulation of the title and the first article of the Convention, both of which privilege the prohibition on *use*.[56] But despite the widespread adherence to the Convention, the prohibition on use of anti-personnel mines is not yet of a customary international law nature.[57]

The explicit framing of a disarmament treaty in terms of the actions of a State Party – 'Each State Party undertakes never under any circumstances …' – means that unless an armed group is under its jurisdiction or its effective control, conduct by that group contrary to the terms of the APMBC will not engage the international responsibility of the State. In this, a disarmament treaty differs from certain international humanitarian law treaties which apply also to a non-State armed group that is a party to an armed conflict.[58]

[54] Protocol on prohibitions or restrictions on the use of mines, booby-traps and other devices (Protocol II), annexed to the Convention on Prohibitions or Restrictions on the Use of Certain Conventional Weapons Which May Be Deemed to Be Excessively Injurious or to Have Indiscriminate Effects; adopted at Geneva, 10 October 1980; entered into force, 2 December 1983.

[55] Protocol on Prohibitions or Restrictions on the Use of Mines, Booby-Traps and Other Devices as amended on 3 May 1996 (Amended Protocol II); adopted at Geneva, 3 May 1996; entered into force, 3 December 1998.

[56] The wording of the APMBC differs from that of the Chemical Weapons Convention by beginning with the prohibition on use of the weapon. In Article 1(1) of the APMBC, the prohibition on use of anti-personnel mines is set forth in subparagraph (a).

[57] For a discussion of this issue, see S Casey-Maslen, *The Anti-Personnel Mine Ban Convention: A Commentary*, 3rd edn, Oxford University Press, Oxford, 2023, paras 0.123, 1.40.

[58] This is particularly the case with Article 3 common to the four 1949 Geneva Conventions, which stipulates that: 'In the case of armed conflict not of an international character occurring in the terri-

The Wagner Group is a private military company headquartered in Russia. It has operated widely in the conflict in Ukraine (until the rebellion notoriously launched by the Group within Russia in June 2023)[59] as well as in a number of African States, including the Central African Republic (CAR), Libya, Mali, Mozambique, and Sudan. Its weaponry comes from the Russian Ministry of Defence.[60] In a number of instances, Wagner fighters have emplaced anti-personnel mines. In Libya, for example, Human Rights Watch said that between April 2019 and June 2020, the Wagner Group laid landmines in Tripoli's southern districts. Some devices were hidden inside homes and were often activated by tripwire.[61] The US Embassy in Tripoli said that a demining team near the capital had deactivated 34 mines in May–June 2020, including MON-50 and POM-2 Russian-made AP mines, adding that the mines were emplaced by the Wagner Group in residential areas.[62]

This potentially involves the State responsibility of Russia for an indiscriminate attack or even an attack directed against civilians. This responsibility is the result of the level of control exerted by the Kremlin over the actions of the Group, at least in many instances (and the provision of the weapons they employed). There is also the possible individual responsibility of the Wagner Group fighters themselves for war crimes.[63] The situation in Libya was referred to the International Criminal Court in 2011. On 26 February, UN Security Council Resolution 1970 granted the Court jurisdiction over war crimes and other international crimes committed in Libya since 15 February 2011.[64] At the time of writing, the Office of the Prosecutor (OTP) was investigating alleged crimes against humanity and war crimes committed in Libya since that date.[65] On 9 November 2022, Prosecutor Karim Khan briefed the UN Security Council on the OTP investigation into the situation in Libya and announced that he had submitted applications for further warrants of arrest to the Pre-Trial Chamber of the Court. As the warrants are submitted under seal, the OTP stated in December 2022 that it 'cannot expand upon the number or names of the suspects; nor can it detail the alleged crimes included in the applications'.[66]

tory of one of the High Contracting Parties, each Party to the conflict shall be bound to apply, as a minimum, the following provisions …'.

[59] See, eg, J Yaffa, 'Inside the Wagner Group's Armed Uprising', *New Yorker Magazine*, 31 July 2023, at: https://bit.ly/3tq7pAg.

[60] UK House of Commons Foreign Affairs Committee, 'Guns for gold: the Wagner Network exposed', Seventh Report of Session 2022–23, 26 July 2023, at: https://bit.ly/3ZLD0rT, para 8.

[61] Human Rights Watch, 'Libya: Russia's Wagner Group Set Landmines Near Tripoli', 31 May 2022, at: https://bit.ly/3xRfzQy.

[62] Embassy of the United States in Libya website, post on 21 July 2022, at: https://bit.ly/3DJZX4G.

[63] Human Rights Watch, 'Libya: Russia's Wagner Group Set Landmines Near Tripoli', n 61 above.

[64] UN Security Council Resolution 1970, adopted by unanimous vote in favour on 26 February 2011, operative para 4.

[65] ICC OTP, 'Libya: Situation in Libya' ICC Ref ICC-01/11, accessed 1 October 2023, at: https://bit.ly/3PIKQhx.

[66] ICC OTP, *Towards a More Just World Every Day*, Annual Report of the Office of the Prosecutor – 2022, The Hague, 1 December 2022, at: https://bit.ly/3th2C3L, p 75.

There is another important difference between the APMBC and the Chemical Weapons Convention. The APMBC incorporates a duty to clear anti-personnel mines that have been remotely delivered or manually emplaced on the territory under the jurisdiction of a State Party or on territory which it controls abroad.[67] No such duty with respect to used chemical weapons was incorporated in the Chemical Weapons Convention. But a State Party to the APMBC which exercises effective control over an armed group operating in a third country that produces or emplaces anti-personnel mines is obligated to clear (ie remove from the ground) and destroy those mines.[68] It is irrelevant for the purpose of this obligation whether the mines were supplied by that State.

Thus, for example, although it is not an instance of hybrid warfare, Türkiye has effective control over the conduct of the self-proclaimed Turkish Republic of Northern Cyprus – recognised only by Türkiye – and is therefore required to clear all anti-personnel mines originally laid by its own armed forces following the 1974 invasion as well as any laid since then by the authorities in the north.[69] The UN Security Council, most recently (at the time of writing) in its Resolution 2674 adopted at the end of January 2023, once again urged both the Republic of Cyprus and the authorities in the north to 'agree and continue a plan of work to achieve a mine-free Cyprus' so as 'to make expeditious progress towards clearing the 29 remaining suspected hazardous areas on the island'.[70]

B. Cluster Munitions

Cluster munitions are weapons containing multiple explosive submunitions. Formally defined in the 2008 Convention on Cluster Munitions (CCM) as 'a conventional munition that is designed to disperse or release explosive submunitions each weighing less than 20 kilograms, and includes those explosive submunitions',[71] cluster munitions are dropped from aircraft or fired from the ground or sea, with the canister or dispenser opening in mid-air to release tens or even several hundred submunitions. These submunitions (also sometimes called bomblets) can saturate an area up to the size of several football fields.[72]

[67] 'Each State Party undertakes to destroy or ensure the destruction of all anti-personnel mines in mined areas under its jurisdiction or control, as soon as possible but not later than ten years after the entry into force of this Convention for that State Party'. Art 5(1), APMBC, n 53 above.

[68] Casey-Maslen, *The Anti-Personnel Mine Ban Convention: A Commentary*, 3rd edn, n 57 above, para 0.80.

[69] Country report on Türkiye in Mine Action Review, *Clearing the Mines 2023*, Norwegian People's Aid, London, 2023, available at: https://www.mineactionreview.org/.

[70] UN Security Council Resolution 2674 (2023), adopted by unanimous vote in favour on 30 January 2023, operative para 16.

[71] Art 2(2), Convention on Cluster Munitions; adopted at Dublin, 30 May 2008; entered into force, 1 August 2010.

[72] Cluster Munition Coalition, 'What is a cluster bomb?', 2023, at: https://bit.ly/3F3Fx7o.

The CCM, the second (and at the time of writing the only other) comprehensive disarmament treaty governing a conventional weapon, largely follows the precedent set by the APMBC. Again, no prior prohibition in the law of armed conflict of the use of cluster munitions had been agreed upon by States. Thus, under Article 1(1)(a) of the CCM, each State Party undertakes never under any circumstances to use cluster munitions. At the time of writing, this concerned 112 States.[73]

There has been use of cluster munitions by non-State armed groups in the past, including those supported by foreign States. For instance, in Croatia the forces of the Serb Krajina, led by Milan Martić, which had previously received support from the Yugoslav National Army (the JNA), fired cluster munitions at the Croatian capital, Zagreb, in early May 1995. This led to the conviction of Mr Martić for crimes against humanity (inhumane acts) and war crimes (direct attacked on civilians) before the International Criminal Tribunal for the former Yugoslavia (ICTY) in 2007.[74] His conviction for these and multiple other international crimes resulted in a sentence of 35 years' imprisonment. Both the conviction and the sentence were confirmed on appeal the following year.[75]

In the hybrid warfare in Ukraine that began in 2014, Russian-backed separatist forces used cluster munitions in the east of the country in February 2015, according to Human Rights Watch.[76] This involved the use of Smerch ('Tornado') cluster munition rockets, which deliver anti-personnel fragmentation submunitions, in Kramatorsk and Hrodivka on 10 February and in Artemivsk three days later. The attacks, which appear to have been launched by both the People's Militia of the Donetsk People's Republic and People's Militia of the Luhansk People's Republic, resulted in multiple civilian casualties.[77] While the weapons may have been looted from government stockpiles, it is also probable that Russia supplied both armed groups with the weapons. Ukraine has also been a major user of cluster munitions in the armed conflicts on its territory since 2014, despite formal denials of use at that time. Neither Russia nor Ukraine is a State Party to the CCM. In 2023, the United States supplied an unreported quantity of cluster munitions to Ukraine, potentially amounting to hundreds of thousands of submunitions.[78] The United States is also not party to the CCM.

[73] A further 12 States were signatories.

[74] ICTY, *Prosecutor v Milan Martić*, Judgment (Trial Chamber) (Case No IT-95-11-T), 12 June 2007, paras 461–63 and 471.

[75] ICTY, *Prosecutor v Milan Martić*, Judgment (Appeals Chamber) (Case No IT-95-11-A), 8 October 2008, paras 247–62 and 354.

[76] Human Rights Watch, 'Ukraine: More Civilians Killed in Cluster Munition Attacks', 19 March 2015, at: https://bit.ly/46uEaKK.

[77] Ibid.

[78] SM Zeigler, 'Why Biden Was Justified to Send Cluster Munitions to Ukraine', Commentary, *The RAND Corporation*, 14 August 2023, at: https://bit.ly/49WtEyf.

C. The Arms Trade Treaty

The UN Arms Trade Treaty regulates the transfer of most conventional weapons.[79] Adopted in 2013 and entering into force in 2014, 113 States were party to the Arms Trade Treaty and another 28 were signatories at the time of writing.[80] Despite repeated calls from several States during the negotiations for an explicit prohibition on transfers of weapons to armed non-State actors, none is included. (Such transfers to armed non-State actors fighting the regime in another State is still a breach of international law, just not specifically under the Arms Trade Treaty.)[81] The inclusion of such a provision was resisted most overtly by the United States. But its omission was one of the main reasons put forward by several States that abstained from or voted against the adoption of the Treaty in the UN General Assembly in April 2013 for their decision to do so.[82]

Instead, transfers[83] to any end user are governed by reference to the end use. Article 6 of the Arms Trade Treaty concerns core 'prohibitions'. Thus, States Parties must not authorise any transfer of conventional arms covered by the treaty if:

- this would breach an arms embargo adopted by the UN Security Council acting under Chapter VII of the UN Charter;[84] or
- this would violate their relevant international obligations under treaties to which they are party, 'in particular those relating to the transfer of, or illicit trafficking in, conventional arms';[85] or

[79] The treaty applies to 'all conventional arms within the following categories: battle tanks; armoured combat vehicles; large-calibre artillery systems; combat aircraft; attack helicopters; warships; missiles and missile launchers; and small arms and light weapons' as well as munitions. Each State Party must 'establish and maintain a national control system to regulate the export of ammunition/munitions fired, launched or delivered by' those weapons. Arts 2(1) and 3, Arms Trade Treaty, n 16 above: https://bit.ly/3I5ToM4.

[80] One of the signatories is the United States. In a communication received on 18 July 2019, the US government informed the depositary (the UN Secretary-General) that the United States 'does not intend to become a party to the treaty. Accordingly, the United States has no legal obligations arising from its signature on September 25, 2013'. Text available on the UN Treaty Series website at: https://bit.ly/3EZ0652.

[81] See Chapter 1 of this volume for a discussion of this issue.

[82] S Casey-Maslen, A Clapham, G Giacca, and S Parker, *The Arms Trade Treaty: A Commentary*, Oxford University Press, Oxford, 2016, para 1.11. States criticising the failure to prohibit all transfers to non-State actors at the time of the passage of the resolution before the General Assembly were Angola, Belarus, Bolivia, Brazil, Côte d'Ivoire, Cuba, India, Indonesia, Nicaragua, North Korea, Russia, and Syria. UN Department of Public Information, 'Overwhelming Majority of States in General Assembly Say "Yes" to Arms Trade Treaty to Stave off Irresponsible Transfers that Perpetuate Conflict, Human Suffering', Press release, UN doc GA/11354, New York, 2 April 2013, at: https://bit.ly/46CJb3N.

[83] The term transfer is defined under Article 2(2) of the Arms Trade Treaty as comprising 'export, import, transit, trans-shipment and brokering'.

[84] Art 6(1), Arms Trade Treaty.

[85] Art 6(2), Arms Trade Treaty.

- they had knowledge at the time of authorisation that the weapons would be used in the commission of genocide, crimes against humanity, or certain war crimes.[86]

If a transfer is not prohibited under Article 6, the export of conventional weapons (and not also other forms of transfer) may be rendered unlawful by the terms of Article 7. If a proposed transfer would, on the basis of an objective and non-discriminatory assessment by the exporting State, undermine peace and security, it must not be authorised.[87] In other circumstances, the proposed export must not be authorised if there is an 'overriding risk' that the arms would be used to commit or facilitate: a serious violation of international humanitarian law; a serious violation of international human rights law; an act constituting an offence under treaties relating to terrorism to which the exporting State is a Party; or an act constituting an offence under treaties relating to transnational organised crime to which the exporting State is a Party.[88]

Given the breadth of the offences instituted under the 1997 Terrorist Bombings Convention,[89] it is hard to envisage a transfer of explosive munitions to an unauthorised non-State actor which would not breach its provisions, unless of course that were to concern a recipient that is a party to an ongoing armed conflict.[90] A total of 170 of 197 States are party to the Terrorist Bombings Convention. An exception to the definition of transfer, however, stipulates that the Arms Trade Treaty 'shall not apply to the international movement of conventional arms by, or on behalf of, a State Party for its use provided that the conventional arms remain under that State Party's ownership'.[91] This could be read as excluding from the ambit of the treaty the transfer of weapons by Russia to its militia forces in the Donbas (now incorporated into the Russian armed forces under domestic law in Russia). At the time of writing, however, Russia was not a State Party to the Arms Trade Treaty and was unlikely to adhere.

[86] Art 6(3), Arms Trade Treaty.

[87] Art 7(1)(a), Arms Trade Treaty.

[88] Art 7(1)(b)(i) to (iv) and Art 7(3), Arms Trade Treaty.

[89] International Convention for the Suppression of Terrorist Bombings; adopted at New York, 15 December 1997; entered into force, 23 May 2001.

[90] Article 19(2) of the Convention stipulates that: 'The activities of armed forces during an armed conflict, as those terms are understood under international humanitarian law, which are governed by that law, are not governed by this Convention'. See on this issue Chapter 4 of this volume.

[91] Art 2(3), Arms Trade Treaty.

7

Hybrid Warfare and International Criminal Law

IN THE WORDS of the International Military Tribunal at Nuremburg, 'Crimes against international law are committed by men, not by abstract entities, and only by punishing individuals who commit such crimes can the provisions of international law be enforced'.[1] This axiom is no different in the case of international crimes committed during hybrid warfare. This chapter addresses the four 'core' international crimes that may occur in hybrid warfare and hybrid threats: war crimes (the most common), crimes against humanity, genocide, and aggression. A brief overview of international criminal law is offered before moving to consider the specificities of the four different crimes in turn, along with examples of their commission in hybrid warfare over the past decade.

I. AN OVERVIEW OF INTERNATIONAL CRIMINAL LAW

Just as is the case with a crime under domestic law, there are two elements to any international crime that must be successfully established for a conviction to be secured. There must be a culpable act (often known by its Latin name, *actus reus*) and an associated culpable state of mind (the *mens rea*).[2] This simple statement does, however, need a little nuancing.

First, while the *actus reus* is normally a positive act, it also applies to an *omission* where there is a duty of care. So, for instance, the wilful failure to feed a prisoner held in connection with an armed conflict so that he or she starves to death still amounts to murder as a war crime even though no physical violence has been inflicted on the prisoner. Second, the *mens rea* for an international crime does not always demand an intention that certain consequences will occur as a result of one's actions – in certain instances, recklessness as to whether they

[1] *Trial of the Major War Criminals before the International Military Tribunal*, Vol I, Nuremberg, 1947, p 223.

[2] Thus, for example, under the law in force in England and Wales, the crime of murder is where one person kills another unlawfully (the *actus reus* element) with the intention to cause either death or serious physical injury (the *mens rea* element).

occur will suffice for a conviction. There are also specific *mens rea* elements that pertain to each of the four classifications of international crime. These are discussed under each of the four crimes.

The official status of the perpetrator is almost always irrelevant, with the notable exception of the crime of aggression, which is committed only by a senior military or political official of a culpable State.[3] The responsibility of a State for 'internationally wrongful acts' (a technical term for violations of international law), which is considered in the next chapter, exists separately and often in parallel to individual criminal responsibility. Thus, as the Rome Statute of the International Criminal Court confirms, none of its provisions relating to individual criminal responsibility 'shall affect the responsibility of States under international law'.[4]

II. WAR CRIMES

War crimes are serious violations of the law of armed conflict (also called international humanitarian law) whose commission in the context of an armed conflict is criminalised. In order to amount to a war crime a violation of the law of armed conflict 'must be serious, that is to say, it must constitute a breach of a rule protecting important values, and the breach must involve grave consequences for the victim'.[5] The relevant conduct (again, act or omission) must be directly linked to an armed conflict, which is a contextual nexus requirement. War crimes may be committed by members of State armed forces and by members of organised armed groups. They may also be committed by individual civilians who do not belong to any armed force or armed group.

Deliberately attacking civilians during combat (during 'the conduct of hostilities', in law-of-armed-conflict terminology) is one of a number of war crimes that may be perpetrated against the general population. The International Committee of the Red Cross (ICRC), which has undertaken a detailed study of customary international humanitarian law rules, identified a number of customary law war crimes that exist irrespective of whether a given State has joined the relevant treaty and even if no treaty has codified them.[6] With respect to those that concern the targeting of individual civilians or which affect the civilian population more broadly, war crimes include the following:

[3] R Cryer, D Robinson, and S Vasiliev, *An Introduction to International Criminal Law and Procedure*, 4th edn, Cambridge University Press, Cambridge, 2019, p 7.

[4] Art 25(4), Rome Statute of the International Criminal Court; adopted at Rome, 17 July 1998; entered into force, 1 July 2002 (hereafter, ICC Statute). At the time of writing, 124 States were party to the ICC Statute.

[5] International Committee of the Red Cross (ICRC), 'War Crimes', How Does Law Protect in War?, at: http://bit.ly/39ay33m.

[6] ICRC, Customary International Humanitarian Law (IHL) Rule 156: 'Definition of War Crimes', at: http://bit.ly/32HjZb2.

- 'making the civilian population or individual civilians, not taking a direct part in hostilities, the object of attack';
- 'making civilian objects, that is, objects that are not military objectives, the object of attack'; and
- 'launching an indiscriminate attack that results in loss of life or injury to civilians'.

These war crimes, the ICRC confirms, are applicable in all armed conflict.[7]

Acts of murder, torture, rape, or other sexual violence against civilians, particularly when they are in the power of the enemy, are also war crimes under customary law in all armed conflict. They are materially subject to the jurisdiction of the International Criminal Court in both international and non-international armed conflict.[8]

The attacks by Hamas against Israelis on 7 October 2023 are believed to have involved a very great number of war crimes against civilians and civilian objects. For instance, a month later, Reuters reconstructed the attack on Kibbutz Be'eri, a main target in the Hamas assault, where firing continued for over 24 hours. The kibbutz is a largely secular, left-wing community, with the ideal of creating a collective, egalitarian farming community. Be'eri was established in 1946 close to Gaza by the Israel Working Youth Movement, a Zionist group.[9] By the end of the attacks, more than 80 residents of Be'eri – almost one in 10 members of the kibbutz – had been killed by Hamas fighters and at least 30 others were missing.[10] Each of the killings of unarmed civilians is almost certain to constitute the war crime of murder.[11]

Among the survivors captured by Hamas, children as young as three years old were led away by the group's fighters.[12] The taking of a hostage in armed conflict of any age is a war crime.[13] A number of houses were set on fire with unarmed Israelis inside. This is the war crime of violence to life and person[14] as well as the customary law war crime of making civilian objects the object of attack.[15]

Palestine, but not Israel, is a State Party to the Rome Statute of the International Criminal Court, which brings the attacks against Israelis on Israeli soil within the

[7] See ibid.

[8] Art 8(2)(a)(i), (ii), and (iii); (2)(b)(xxii); (2)(c)(i); and (2)(d)(vi), ICC Statute.

[9] S Grey, M Lubell, and R McNeill, 'Hunted by Hamas: 27 hours of slaughter and survival inside Israel's Kibbutz Be'eri', Special Report, *Reuters*, 3 November 2023, at: https://bit.ly/3R5IJq9.

[10] Ibid. A separate investigation by Sky News identified 118 of a total of 130 it said were killed during the attacks. 'Murder, Kidnap, Survival: Kibbutz Be'eri Attack', *Sky News*, 15 November 2023, at: https://bit.ly/3QXSA0R.

[11] Of course, every person accused of a war crime is innocent until proven guilty, but *a priori* the facts of the attacks indicate the commission of multiple war crimes by members of the attacking Hamas forces.

[12] 'Murder, Kidnap, Survival: Kibbutz Be'eri Attack', *Sky News*; and Grey, Lubell, and McNeill, 'Hunted by Hamas: 27 hours of slaughter and survival inside Israel's Kibbutz Be'eri', n 9 above.

[13] Art 8(2)(c)(iii), ICC Statute.

[14] Art 8(2)(c)(i), ICC Statute.

[15] ICRC, Customary IHL Rule 156: 'Definition of War Crimes'.

material and geographical jurisdiction of the Court.[16] For each of the war crimes under the jurisdiction of the Court, there is an associated set of 'elements', which define the *actus reus* and *mens rea* of the offence. For the war crime of murder of a civilian in a non-international armed conflict, five such elements must be proven against an accused beyond reasonable doubt.[17] The *actus reus* is (i) that the perpetrator killed one or more persons and (ii) that such person or persons were civilian who were taking no active part in the hostilities at the time. The *mens rea* elements are that the perpetrator was aware (iii) of the factual circumstances that established the victim's civilian status and (iv) of the factual circumstances that established the existence of an armed conflict.[18] There is also a contextual element (v) that the criminal conduct took place in the context of and was associated with an armed conflict not of an international character. On 20 May 2024, the Prosecutor of the International Criminal Court announced that he was seeking the Court's approval to issue arrest warrants for three Hamas leaders for the war crimes of murder, the taking of hostages, rape and other sexual violence, torture, and cruel treatment and outrages upon personal dignity.[19]

Starvation of the civilian population is also a war crime under the jurisdiction of the Court, in all armed conflict. Thereunder the war crime involves intentionally using starvation of civilians as a method of warfare by depriving them of objects indispensable to their survival, including wilfully impeding relief supplies.[20] It is also a war crime under customary law in all armed conflict, according to the ICRC.[21] In October 2023, strong – and mounting – evidence indicated that Israel's refusal to allow sufficient quantities of relief supplies into Gaza during its military response to the Hamas attacks amounted to

[16] On 1 January 2015, the Government of Palestine lodged a declaration under Article 12(3) of the ICC Statute accepting the jurisdiction of the International Criminal Court over alleged crimes committed 'in the occupied Palestinian territory, including East Jerusalem, since June 13, 2014'. On 2 January 2015, Palestine acceded to the Statute, becoming a State Party on 1 April 2015. On 20 December 2019, the Prosecutor announced that following a thorough, independent and objective assessment of the reliable information available to her Office, the preliminary examination into this Situation had concluded with the determination that all the statutory criteria under the Rome Statute for the opening of an investigation had been met. However, given the complex legal and factual issues attaching to this situation, she announced that she would be making a request to Pre-Trial Chamber I for a ruling to clarify the territorial scope of the Court's jurisdiction in this Situation. On 5 February 2021, Pre-Trial Chamber I decided that the Court could exercise its criminal jurisdiction in the Situation and, by majority, that the territorial scope of this jurisdiction extends to Gaza and the West Bank, including East Jerusalem. ICC, 'State of Palestine: Situation in the State of Palestine', ICC doc ICC-01/18, accessed on 17 November 2023, at: https://bit.ly/3sCz9RY.

[17] Elements of crime for Art 8(2)(c)(i)-1, ICC Statute: https://bit.ly/3UEwnY6.

[18] Thus, it is not required that the perpetrator be a legal expert who understands the classification of armed conflict under IHL.

[19] 'Statement of ICC Prosecutor Karim A. A. Khan KC: Applications for arrest warrants in the situation in the State of Palestine', News, International Criminal Court, The Hague, 20 May 2024, at: https://bit.ly/3QWdz41.

[20] Art 8(2)(b)(xxv) and (e)(xix), ICC Statute.

[21] ICRC, Customary IHL Rule 156: 'Definition of War Crimes': https://ihl-databases.icrc.org/en/customary-ihl/v1/rule156.

the starvation of civilians as a method of warfare.[22] Speaking publicly on 29 October 2023, the Prosecutor of the International Criminal Court, Karim Khan, declared that:

> We've heard a lot from the Secretary General of the United Nations, from the head of the Office for the Coordination of Humanitarian Affairs, Martin Griffiths, and from the World Health Organization regarding the dire humanitarian situation in Gaza. Impeding relief supplies as provided by the Geneva Conventions may constitute a crime within the Court's jurisdiction. I want to underline clearly to Israel that there must be discernible efforts, without further delay, to make sure civilians receive basic food, medicine, anaesthetics, morphine. We hear reports of operations taking place without these basic medicines, as if we're in the Middle Ages. Civilians must receive basic food and water and the desperately needed medical supplies.
>
> This morning, I saw trucks full of goods, full of humanitarian assistance stuck where nobody needs them, stuck in Egypt, stuck on Rafah and away from the hungry mouths or the bleeding wounds. These supplies must get to the civilians of Gaza without delay. And in the same way, I underline to Hamas and anybody who has control in Gaza, that when Inshallah, such aid reaches Gaza, it's imperative that the assistance gets to the civilian population, and is not misused or diverted away from them.[23]

The *actus reus* element of the war crime under the jurisdiction of the International Criminal Court is simply that the perpetrator deprived civilians of objects indispensable to their survival. The *mens rea* requirements are that the perpetrator intended to starve civilians as a method of warfare and further that the perpetrator was aware of factual circumstances that established the existence of an armed conflict. The contextual element is that the conduct took place in the context of, and was associated with, an international armed conflict.

This latter jurisdictional element may prove tricky. The Statute of the International Criminal Court was amended in 2019 to cover non-international armed conflict,[24] with the amendment entering into force in October 2021. But Palestine did not figure among the 13 States Parties to the Statute that had ratified the amendment at the time of writing,[25] suggesting that there would not be material jurisdiction for the Court over the possible war crime. If, however, the Office of the Prosecutor believed that intentional starvation formed part of an international armed conflict between Israel and Palestine occurring through the belligerent occupation by Israel of part of the Gaza Strip, the war crime could potentially be charged against senior commanders in the Israeli Defence Forces (IDF).[26] In fact, on 20 May 2024, the Prosecutor announced that he was seeking

[22] 'Impeding relief aid to Gaza may be a crime under ICC jurisdiction, prosecutor says', *Reuters*, 29 October 2023, at: https://bit.ly/47cF8Mo.

[23] ICC, 'Statement of ICC Prosecutor Karim A.A. Khan KC from Cairo on the situation in the State of Palestine and Israel', 30 October 2023, at: https://bit.ly/3G7NDfS.

[24] Amendment to Article 8 of the Rome Statute of the International Criminal Court (Intentionally using starvation of civilians); adopted at The Hague, 6 December 2019; entered into force, 14 October 2021.

[25] See the updated list on the UN Treaty Series website, at: https://bit.ly/3k8WSl8.

[26] Art 8(2)(b)(xxv), ICC Statute.

the issuance of arrest warrants against Benjamin Netanyahu, the Prime Minister of Israel, and Yoav Gallant, the Minister of Defence of Israel. Among other crimes, this included the starvation of civilians as a method of warfare as a war crime contrary to Article 8(2)(b)(xxv) of the Rome Statute, that is to say, in an international armed conflict.[27]

War crimes may also be committed against 'combatants' (or, in the course of a non-international armed conflict, fighters). During the fighting, using an unlawful weapon, such as a toxic chemical, would be a war crime.[28] So too would 'denial of quarter' where one side informs the other that they will not accept any surrender or take prisoners.[29] Once in the power of the enemy, an enemy combatant must be treated humanely. Thus, punishable as war crimes are the following: wilful killing; torture or inhuman treatment, including biological experiments; wilfully causing great suffering or serious injury to body or health; compelling a prisoner of war to serve in the forces of a hostile Power; and wilfully depriving a prisoner of war of the rights of fair and regular trial.[30]

With respect to the war crime of compelling a prisoner of war to serve in the forces of a hostile Power, in November 2023, Russia announced that it was sending Ukrainian prisoners of war to fight on Moscow's side in the war. Video from State media outlet RIA Novosti showed the Ukrainians swearing allegiance to Russia to fight in a battalion named after medieval nobleman Bogdan Khmelnitsky, seen as a national hero in Russia for bringing parts of Ukraine under Moscow's control in the fifteenth century. The Associated Press, which reported the story in the West, could not confirm the authenticity of the report or of videos released by the Russian news agency, nor whether the prisoners had been coerced in some manner.[31]

The elements of crime under the International Criminal Court for the war crime of compelling service in hostile forces[32] are that the perpetrator coerced, by act or threat, one or more persons who were protected under the 1949 Geneva Conventions to take part in military operations against their own country or forces (*actus reus*). The *mens rea* elements are that the perpetrator was aware of the factual circumstances that established that protected status as well as of the factual circumstances that established the existence of an armed conflict. The contextual element is that the conduct took place in the context of and was associated with an international armed conflict.

There is a general duty to prosecute (or to hand over to another State or international court for prosecution) all those reasonably suspected to have

[27] Statement of ICC Prosecutor Karim A. A. Khan KC: Applications for arrest warrants in the situation in the State of Palestine', News, International Criminal Court, The Hague, 20 May 2024, at: https://bit.ly/3QWdz41.

[28] Art 8(2)(b)(xviii) and (e)(xiv), ICC Statute.

[29] Art 8(2)(b)(xii) and (e)(x), ICC Statute.

[30] Art 8(2)(a) (i), (ii), (iii), (v), and (vi), ICC Statute.

[31] Associated Press, 'Ukrainian PoWs being sent to fight their own army, Russian news claims', *The Guardian*, 8 November 2023, at: https://bit.ly/479A6QO.

[32] Art 8(2)(a)(v), ICC Statute.

committed war crimes, whether they acted as perpetrators or under other modes of liability (such as ordering the crime to be committed, or aiding and abetting its commission).[33] In international armed conflict, the law obligates States to search for and either prosecute or extradite for prosecution every individual alleged to have committed 'grave breaches' of the 1949 Geneva Conventions and 1977 Additional Protocol I anywhere in the world and regardless of the alleged war criminals' nationality.[34] This is known as compulsory universal jurisdiction. For the purpose of the application of the law, it does not matter whether an individual benefits from so-called 'combatant's privilege' in the course of an armed conflict. No one enjoys immunity from prosecution for their involved in international crimes perpetrated in an armed conflict.

For war crimes that do not amount to grave breaches of the Geneva Conventions, as they are committed in non-international armed conflict, States have the obligation under customary law to investigate and prosecute them when the crimes have been committed by their own nationals, by members of their armed forces, or have been perpetrated on their territory.[35] The prerogative to also seek to punish other war crimes, when committed by other armed forces abroad in non-international armed conflict, is known as permissive universal jurisdiction. But as the preamble to the Rome Statute of the International Criminal Court cited above indicates, a customary duty always to prosecute suspected war criminals including non-nationals whose conduct occurred abroad, is at the least *de lege ferenda* – that is to say, in the course of crystallising as international law.

III. CRIMES AGAINST HUMANITY

Crimes against humanity are acts of violence perpetrated 'as part of a widespread or systematic attack directed against any civilian population, with knowledge of the attack'.[36] The essence of a crime against humanity is therefore an attack against civilians where the civilian population is the 'primary object' of the attack rather than 'an incidental object'.[37] Crimes against humanity may

[33] Thus, the preamble to the ICC Statute both affirms 'that the most serious crimes of concern to the international community as a whole must not go unpunished and that their effective prosecution must be ensured by taking measures at the national level and by enhancing international cooperation' and recalls 'that it is the duty of every State to exercise its criminal jurisdiction over those responsible for international crimes'. ICC Statute, preambular paras 4 and 6.

[34] Art 49, 1949 Geneva Convention I; Art 50, Geneva Convention II; Art 129, Geneva Convention III; and Art 146, Geneva Convention IV.

[35] ICRC, Customary IHL Rule 158: 'Prosecution of War Crimes', at: http://bit.ly/37FdYin.

[36] Art 7, ICC Statute. The core elements of 'a widespread or systematic attack directed against any civilian population, with knowledge of the attack' and the associated crimes are part of customary law but, in distinction to war crimes and genocide, there is no specific treaty that exists to prevent and repress crimes against humanity.

[37] ICC, *Prosecutor v Bemba Gombo*, Decision Pursuant to Article 61(7)(a) and (b) of the Rome Statute on the Charges (Case No ICC-01/05–01/08), 15 June 2009, para 76; and ICC, *Prosecutor v Katanga and Chui*, Decision on the Confirmation of Charges (Case No ICC-01/04–01/07–717), 13 October 2008, para 399.

be committed either in a situation of armed conflict or during peacetime.[38] When a crime against humanity is committed during an armed conflict, the same conduct may also amount to a war crime.

An attack is widespread if it is conducted on a large scale and results in many victims,[39] although there is no specific numerical threshold.[40] More specifically, 'widespread' implies either an attack conducted over a large geographical area or an attack in a small geographical area but directed against a large number of civilians. This does not mean, however, that a single act cannot qualify as a crime against humanity, but it implies that the overall conduct of the perpetrators 'is intended to generate a certain quantum of harm'.[41] The International Criminal Tribunal for the former Yugoslavia (ICTY) has defined 'systematic' as 'the organised nature of the acts of violence and the improbability of their random occurrence',[42] and found that evidence of a pattern or a methodical plan establishes that an attack was systematic.[43] The perpetrator of crimes against humanity may be a State official or a member of an armed group, where there is either a governmental or organisational policy to commit such an attack.

An array of acts may be prosecuted as crimes against humanity. These include murder, enslavement, unlawful deprivation of liberty, torture, rape or sexual slavery, enforced disappearance, and other inhumane acts intentionally causing great suffering or serious bodily injury.[44] These underlying offences must be linked to the attack; that is, they must be committed in furtherance of the attack considering the 'nature, aims and consequences of such act'.[45]

The crime against humanity of rape, under the jurisdiction of the International Criminal Court,[46] requires proof of a detailed set of elements of crime. These are as follows:

1. The perpetrator invaded[1] the body of a person by conduct resulting in penetration, however slight, of any part of the body of the victim or of the perpetrator with a sexual organ, or of the anal or genital opening of the victim with any object or any other part of the body.

[38] International Law Commission, 'Draft articles on Prevention and Punishment of Crimes Against Humanity, with commentaries', in UN doc A/74/10, 2019, at: https://bit.ly/3odgLXD, para 45, commentary para 1.

[39] ICTY, *Prosecutor v Blaškić*, Judgment (Trial Chamber) (Case No IT-95–14-T), 3 March 2000, para 206.

[40] C Stahn, *A Critical Introduction to International Criminal Law*, Cambridge University Press, Cambridge, 2019, p 57.

[41] R Dubler and M Kalyk, *Crimes against Humanity in the 21st Century*, Brill, Boston MA, 2018, p 316.

[42] ICTY, *Prosecutor v Mrkšić*, Judgment (Trial Chamber) (Case No IT95-13/1-T), 27 September 2007, para 437.

[43] ICTY, *Prosecutor v Kunarac*, Judgment (Appeals Chamber) (Case Nos IT-96–23 & IT-96–23/1-A), 12 June 2002, para 94. This approach was confirmed by the ICC. See ICC, *Prosecutor v Katanga and Chui*, Decision on the Confirmation of Charges, para 397.

[44] See generally Art 7(1)(a) to (k), ICC Statute.

[45] See ICC, *Prosecutor v Katanga and Chui*, Decision on the Confirmation of Charges, para 400; ICC, *Prosecutor v Bemba Gombo*, Decision Pursuant to Article 61(7)(a) and (b) of the ICC Statute on the Charges, paras 84, 86.

[46] Art 7(1)(g)-1, ICC Statute.

2. The invasion was committed by force, or by threat of force or coercion, such as that caused by fear of violence, duress, detention, psychological oppression or abuse of power, against such person or another person, or by taking advantage of a coercive environment, or the invasion was committed against a person incapable of giving genuine consent.[2]
3. The conduct was committed as part of a widespread or systematic attack directed against a civilian population.
4. The perpetrator knew that the conduct was part of or intended the conduct to be part of a widespread or systematic attack directed against a civilian population.[47]

> [1] The concept of 'invasion' is intended to be broad enough to be gender-neutral.
> [2] It is understood that a person may be incapable of giving genuine consent if affected by natural, induced or age-related incapacity.

As noted in Chapter three, the extent of the attacks by Hamas on Israeli civilians on 7–8 October 2023 indicate the commission not only of manifold war crimes[48] but also of crimes against humanity.[49] A senior IDF commander alleged that Hamas fighters 'came with orders to slaughter, burn citizens – not military personnel, simply citizens'. This included specific instructions to rape.[50] If confirmed, this is strong evidence not only of a general policy of attacking civilians but also of a specific intent to commit rape. The attacks by Hamas were certainly widespread.

In the report of the attack on the Kibbutz Be'eri by Reuters, a number of the murdered Israeli women were reportedly found without clothing or with their trousers pulled down by their ankles.[51] At the time of writing, Israeli police were undertaking their largest ever investigation into sexual violence and crimes against women. 'It's clear now that sexual crimes were part of the planning and the purpose was to terrify and humiliate people', Shelly Harush, the police commander leading the investigation, told a senior journalist at *The Times*.[52] Ruth Halperin-Kaddari, a member of the UN Committee on the Elimination of Discrimination against Women from 2006 to 2018, told the BBC that the concentration of cases in one day and in several locations left her in 'no doubt' that there was a 'premeditation to use sexual violence as a weapon of war'.[53] On 20 May 2024, the Prosecutor of the International Criminal Court announced that he was seeking the Court's approval to issue arrest warrants for three

[47] Elements of the crime against humanity of rape with the original footnotes.

[48] N Quénivet, 'Israel – Hamas 2023 Symposium – Sexual Violence on October 7', Blog post, *Articles of War*, Lieber Institute for Law & Warfare at West Point, United States, 19 December 2023, at: https://bit.ly/3v87E3I.

[49] Art 7(1), ICC Statute.

[50] D Haynes, 'Israel says it has evidence of Iranian "involvement" in Hamas attack – but "cannot elaborate"', *Sky News*, 23 October 2023, at: https://bit.ly/40bBBLL.

[51] Grey, Lubell, and McNeill, 'Hunted by Hamas: 27 hours of slaughter and survival inside Israel's Kibbutz Be'eri', n 9 above.

[52] See further in this regard C Lamb, 'First Hamas fighters raped her. Then they shot her in the head', *The Times*, 2 December 2023.

[53] M Moloney, 'Hamas planned sexual violence as weapon of war – Israeli campaigner', *BBC News*, 4 December 2023, at: https://bit.ly/3Rp2bOx.

Hamas leaders for the crimes against humanity of extermination, murder, rape and other sexual violence, torture, and other inhumane acts.[54]

IV. GENOCIDE

The first United Nations General Assembly in 1946 described genocide as 'a denial of the right of existence of entire human groups, as homicide is the denial of the right to live of individual human beings' and affirmed that it is 'a crime under international law which the civilized world condemns'.[55] Genocide, termed the 'crime of crimes' by the International Criminal Tribunal for Rwanda (ICTR) in 1998,[56] was formally outlawed by the 1948 Genocide Convention. Its definition under the Convention remains the basis for that international crime today:

> any of the following acts committed with intent to destroy, in whole or in part, a national, ethnical, racial or religious group, as such:
>
> (a) Killing members of the group;
> (b) Causing serious bodily or mental harm to members of the group;
> (c) Deliberately inflicting on the group conditions of life calculated to bring about its physical destruction in whole or in part;
> (d) Imposing measures intended to prevent births within the group;
> (e) Forcibly transferring children of the group to another group.[57]

Thus, genocide is the act of killing or seriously injuring or starving members of another nationality or an ethnic minority group, or a religious or racial group, where the act is committed 'with intent to destroy, in whole or in part' that group.[58] That 'special' intent to destroy a defined nationality or minority, religious, or racial group (*dolus specialis* to use the Latin term) is what primarily distinguishes crimes against humanity from genocide. (Additional, separate intent to commit one of the underlying genocidal crimes is also needed.) The requisite intent for genocide is a particularly challenging element of the crime to prove, as is, on occasion, a victim's membership of one of the protected groups. Indeed, Cryer and others suggest that almost 'every word' of the legal definition 'has raised difficulties of interpretation'.[59]

As is the case with crimes against humanity, however, genocide may be committed not only in a situation of armed conflict but also in peacetime.[60] In

[54] Statement of ICC Prosecutor Karim A. A. Khan KC: Applications for arrest warrants in the situation in the State of Palestine', News, International Criminal Court, The Hague, 20 May 2024, at: https://bit.ly/3QWdz41.

[55] UN General Assembly Resolution 96 (I), adopted on 11 December 1946, first preambular para and first operative para, respectively.

[56] ICTR, *Prosecutor v Kambanda*, Judgment (Trial Chamber) (Case No ICTR 97-23-S), 4 September 1998, para 16.

[57] Art II, Convention on the Prevention and Punishment of the Crime of Genocide; adopted at Paris, 9 December 1948; entered into force, 12 January 1951 (hereinafter, 1948 Genocide Convention).

[58] Art 6, ICC Statute.

[59] Cryer, Robinson, and Vasiliev, *An Introduction to International Criminal Law and Procedure*, 4th edn, n 3 above, p 207.

[60] Art I, 1948 Genocide Convention.

the case of Rwanda, however, the mandate of the ICTR was limited to genocide that occurred in the course of an armed conflict. On 2 September 1998, Jean-Paul Akayesu, the mayor of Taba and a former teacher and politician, became the first person to be convicted of genocide before an international criminal tribunal.[61] Reflecting customary law, however, genocide is punishable in either situation as an international crime before the International Criminal Court.[62] It may be perpetrated by a government or a non-State armed group, irrespective of whether or not the group receives support from a State. It may also be committed by a 'rank-and-file' *génocidiaire*, provided he or she has the requisite intent.[63] Where an individual assisting in acts of genocide does not himself possess the requisite intent, he may be held liable as an accessory where he was aware of the nature of those acts.[64]

The list of protected groups is 'a closed one'.[65] Efforts by some States during the drafting of the Genocide Convention to include also social or political groups did not succeed.[66] So-called cultural genocide is also not part of the international crime, although acts of ethnic cleansing, and attacks on cultural property, may be considered significant evidence towards establishing the intent to destroy a protected group.[67] The ICTR in its *Akayesu* judgment sought to explain the four categories as follows:

- A *national group* is defined as a collection of people who are perceived to share a legal bond based on common citizenship, coupled with reciprocity of rights and duties.
- An *ethnic group* is generally defined as a group whose members share a common language or culture.
- The conventional definition of *racial group* is based on the hereditary physical traits often identified with a geographical region, irrespective of linguistic, cultural, national or religious factors.
- A *religious group* is one whose members share the same religion, denomination or mode of worship.[68]

While perhaps useful as a guide, if applied rigorously this series of definitions would lead to practical problems. What is the situation, for instance, if a person is of mixed heritage? In its judgment in the *Ndindabahizi* case, the ICTR had to decide whether the victim, who was characterised in varying ways by different

[61] ICTR, *Prosecutor v Akayesu*, Judgment (Trial Chamber) (Case No ICTR-96-4), 2 September 1998.
[62] Art 6, ICC Statute.
[63] Cryer, Robinson, and Vasiliev, *An Introduction to International Criminal Law and Procedure*, 4th edn, n 3 above, p 220.
[64] ICTY, *Prosecutor v Krstić*, Judgment (Appeals Chamber) (Case No IT-98–33-A), 19 April 2004, para 140.
[65] Cryer, Robinson, and Vasiliev, *An Introduction to International Criminal Law and Procedure*, 4th edn, n 3 above, p 210.
[66] Ibid.
[67] Ibid, p 223.
[68] ICTR, *Prosecutor v Akayesu*, Judgment (Trial Chamber), n 59 above, paras 512–15.

witnesses, was protected under the Convention. One close relative explained that his father was German and his mother Rwandan, without further defining her ethnicity as Hutu or Tutsi. Another testified that the attackers wanted to kill him because he was white, or Belgian. Other witnesses described the man as a 'half-caste', and said that he had the physical traits of a Tutsi, suggesting that he was perceived to be part-Tutsi.[69] The Trial Chamber found that the man was targeted because he was understood to be, at least in part, Tutsi. This was on the basis that he was perceived to be, at least in part, of Tutsi ethnicity. As he had 'the physical appearance of a Tutsi, he would have been understood to be Tutsi'. Moreover, the 'presence of additional motives for the killing' (such as that he may have been part-Belgian) '[did] not displace the killers' genocidal intent'.[70]

In its judgment at trial in the *Krstić* case, the ICTY rejected the notion that the four categories constitute 'distinct prototypes of human groups'. It declared that: 'To attempt to differentiate each of the named groups on the basis of scientifically objective criteria would … be inconsistent with the object and purpose of the Convention'.[71] Instead, the Chamber decided to identify the relevant group by using as a criterion its stigmatisation, 'notably by the perpetrators of the crime, on the basis of its perceived national, ethnical, racial or religious characteristics'.[72] While some measure of self-identification is entertained by international criminal law tribunals, 'the better view is that the group must have some form of at least perceived reality in the first place; otherwise the Convention could be used to protect fictitious national, ethnical, racial or religious groups'.[73] It also appears clear that a group cannot be defined negatively, eg as 'non-Serbs'.[74]

Most commentators believe that for a successful prosecution for genocide there must be a genocidal campaign or at least a pattern of collective violence of which the underlying offence was part. In 2004, the ICTY issued its judgment on appeal in the *Krstić* case, terming the killings of some 8,000 men and boys by the Bosnian Serb army, a non-State armed group, in the aftermath of the fall of the Bosnian Muslim enclave of Srebrenica, 'genocide'.[75] The ICTY Appeals Chamber accepted that genocide could indeed occur in a localised area and with respect to a small percentage of the population of a national minority.[76]

To be prosecuted before the International Criminal Court, the relevant ICC's Elements of Crimes require in each case that the unlawful conduct 'took place in the context of a manifest pattern of similar conduct directed against' a protected group 'or was conduct that could itself effect such destruction'. The Elements

[69] ICTR, *Prosecutor v Ndindabahizi*, Judgment (Trial Chamber) (Case No ICTR-2001-71-I), 15 July 2004, para 467.

[70] Ibid, para 469.

[71] ICTY, *Prosecutor v Krstić*, Judgment (Trial Chamber) (Case No IT-98–33-T), para 556.

[72] Ibid, para 557.

[73] Cryer, Robinson, and Vasiliev, *An Introduction to International Criminal Law and Procedure*, 4th edn, n 3 above p. 214.

[74] ICTY, *Prosecutor v Stakić*, Judgment (Trial Chamber) (Case No IT-97-24-T), 31 July 2003, para 512.

[75] ICTY, *Prosecutor v Krstić*, Judgment (Appeals Chamber), n 62 above, paras 37–38.

[76] Stahn, *A Critical Introduction to International Criminal Law*, n 39 above, p 40.

further clarify that the 'term "manifest" is an objective qualification'.[77] But the ICTY explicitly rejected the notion that this element reflected customary law or that a widespread or systematic attack – mirroring the requirements for crimes against humanity – was needed in order to prosecute genocide.[78]

As Cryer and others have observed, victim groups have sometimes sought to appropriate the term *genocide* for atrocities that may fall outside its legal definition, the wish being 'to attract the mobilizing power of the label'.[79] In November 2023, three Palestinian human rights groups appealed to the International Criminal Court to prosecute Israel for genocide perpetrated against Palestinians based on its bombardment of Gaza and denial of adequate relief supplies to the affected civilian population.[80] Such a prosecution is unlikely to proceed. That said, in mid-November 2023, many UN special rapporteurs, along with members of other special human rights procedures,[81] put their name to a letter in which they declared that grave violations committed by Israel against Palestinians in the aftermath of 7 October, particularly in Gaza, pointed to 'a genocide in the making'. They affirmed that one of the elements in this genocide was the use of powerful

[77] Elements of Crimes for Article 6, 'Introduction' and for crimes under Article 6(a) to (e) of the ICC Statute.

[78] ICTY, *Prosecutor v Krstić*, Judgment (Appeals Chamber), n 62 above, para 224.

[79] Cryer, Robinson, and Vasiliev, *An Introduction to International Criminal Law and Procedure*, 4th edn, n 3 above, p 205.

[80] 'Palestinians ask war crimes court to probe Israel over genocide allegations', *Reuters*, 10 November 2023, at: https://bit.ly/46b1LiU.

[81] Francesca Albanese, Special Rapporteur on the situation of human rights in the Palestinian Territory occupied since 1967; Margaret Satterthwaite, Special Rapporteur on the Independence of Judges and Lawyers; Dorothy Estrada Tanck (Chair), Claudia Flores, Ivana Krstić, Haina Lu, and Laura Nyirinkindi, Working group on discrimination against women and girls; Surya Deva, Special Rapporteur on the right to development; Ravindran Daniel (Chair-Rapporteur), Sorcha MacLeod, Chris Kwaja, Jovana Jezdimirovic Ranito, Carlos Salazar Couto, Working Group on the use of mercenaries; Barbara G Reynolds (Chair), Bina D'Costa, Dominique Day, Catherine Namakula, Working Group of Experts on People of African Descent; Pedro Arrojo-Agudo, Special Rapporteur on the human rights to safe drinking water and sanitation; Olivier De Schutter, Special Rapporteur on extreme poverty and human rights; Farida Shaheed, Special Rapporteur on the right to education; Damilola Olawuyi (Chairperson), Robert McCorquodale (Vice-Chairperson), Elżbieta Karska, Fernanda Hopenhaym, and Pichamon Yeophantong, Working Group on the issue of human rights and transnational corporations and other business enterprises; Siobhán Mullally, Special Rapporteur on trafficking in persons, especially women and children; Livingstone Sewanyana, Independent Expert on the promotion of a democratic and equitable international order; Balakrishnan Rajagopal, Special Rapporteur on the right to adequate housing; Ashwini KP Special Rapporteur on contemporary forms of racism, racial discrimination, xenophobia and related intolerance; Paula Gaviria Betancur, Special Rapporteur on the human rights of internally displaced persons; Mary Lawlor, Special Rapporteur on the situation of human rights defenders; Claudia Mahler, Independent Expert on the enjoyment of all human rights by older persons; Ben Saul, Special Rapporteur on the promotion and protection of human rights and fundamental freedoms while countering terrorism; Irene Khan Special Rapporteur for Freedom of Opinion and Expression; Ms Reem Alsalem, Special Rapporteur on violence against women and girls, its causes and consequences; Tomoya Obokata, Special Rapporteur on contemporary forms of slavery, including its causes and consequences. Notable by their absence from the list of signatories were the Special Rapporteur on extrajudicial, summary or arbitrary executions and the Special Rapporteur on torture and other cruel, inhuman or degrading treatment or punishment. It may be that they doubted that genocide was being committed.

weaponry with inherently indiscriminate impacts, resulting in a 'colossal' death toll and destruction of life-sustaining infrastructure.[82]

Finally, incitement to commit genocide, using the media, can also be prosecuted for using 'speech as a weapon'.[83] One of those prosecuted for the crime before the ICTR was the Chief Executive of *Radio Television Libre des Milles Collines*, Ferdinand Nahimana. The Tribunal told Mr Nahimana: 'Without firearm, machete or physical weapon, [you] caused the deaths of thousands of innocent civilians'.[84] In respect of incitement, the members of the UN special procedures who signed the open letter to the international community were perhaps on stronger legal ground. They referred to 'discernibly genocidal and dehumanising rhetoric' from senior Israeli government officials, as well as some professional groups and public figures, calling for the 'total destruction', and 'erasure' of Gaza; the need to 'finish them all'; and the desire to 'force' Palestinians from the West Bank and east Jerusalem into Jordan.[85] A senior official making such statements is potentially inciting the commission of genocide. It also raises the possibility of State responsibility for an internationally wrongful act, an issue addressed in the next chapter.

V. AGGRESSION

A serious violation of the prohibition of inter-State use of force under *jus ad bellum* is an act of aggression.[86] This crime is now capable of being prosecuted by the International Criminal Court when perpetrated by a senior government or military official of a ratifying State that has accepted the Court's jurisdiction for the 'supreme international crime'.[87] The 'crime of aggression' is thus defined in the 1998 Rome Statute (as amended) as

> the planning, preparation, initiation or execution, by a person in a position effectively to exercise control over or to direct the political or military action of a State, of an act of aggression which, by its character, gravity and scale, constitutes a manifest violation of the Charter of the United Nations.[88]

[82] OHCHR, 'Gaza: UN experts call on international community to prevent genocide against the Palestinian people', Press release, Geneva, 16 November 2023, at: https://bit.ly/3QJjKHv.

[83] Stahn, *A Critical Introduction to International Criminal Law*, n 39 above, p 49.

[84] ICTR, *Prosecutor v Nahimana*, Judgment (Trial Chamber) (Case No ICTR-99–52-T), 3 December 2003, para 1099.

[85] OHCHR, 'Gaza: UN experts call on international community to prevent genocide against the Palestinian people', Press release, n 80 above.

[86] See further on this issue Chapter 1 of this volume.

[87] The International Military Tribunal in its judgment of 1946 stated that the crime of aggression 'is the supreme international crime differing only from other war crimes in that it contains within itself the accumulated evil of the whole'. See, eg, the International Crimes Database, 'Crime of Aggression', Asser Institute, 2013, at: https://bit.ly/40CbsWH.

[88] Art 8*bis*(1), ICC Statute. The United States contests this particular definition as reflecting customary law. Thus, at the 2010 Review Conference of the International Criminal Court, Harold

In practice, however, such prosecutions are very unlikely to occur. The last time an international tribunal successfully prosecuted such 'crimes against peace' was in the trials of Nazi war criminals at Nuremburg after the end of the Second World War. Subsequent attempts have fallen foul of the lack of domestic law jurisdiction over the international crime. For instance, with respect to the unlawful invasion of Iraq in 2003, in March 2006 the United Kingdom (UK) House of Lords unanimously decided that although the crime of aggression existed under customary international law, no such crime was punishable under the law of England.[89]

More recently, there have been suggestions by States and public international lawyers that a dedicated international tribunal could be established to prosecute President Vladimir Putin and his senior military and political allies for the international crime of aggression in Ukraine that began with the Russian invasion on 24 February 2022.[90] While the elements of this international crime can certainly be sustained, we should not expect any of these individuals to see the inside of an international criminal tribunal any time soon.

Likewise, in terms of hybrid war, a prosecution for the sending by a State of 'armed bands, groups, irregulars or mercenaries' to carry out grave acts of armed force against another State[91] would still be brought against the State officials responsible and not the armed group that carried out the attack. Thus, in theory – and again it is only theory – Russian actions in 2014 in relation to the attacks on State authorities in the Donbas region of Ukraine could be punishable as a crime of aggression. The non-State armed groups, such as the People's Militia of the Donetsk People's Republic, could potentially be prosecuted for having aided or abetted the commission of the crime or acted in furtherance of a common plan. But this could not occur under the International Criminal Court in any event (ie had Russia and Ukraine accepted the jurisdiction of the Court), as such complicity by a non-State actor is explicitly excluded under the Statute for the crime of aggression.[92]

Hongju Koh, the then Legal Adviser at the US Department of State, opined that the definition of aggression 'does not truly reflect customary international law, i.e., widespread and consistent State practice followed out of a sense of legal obligation'. The main objection appears to be that no prior declaration of aggression by the UN Security Council is needed in order to prosecute aggression before the International Criminal Court. This is not persuasive. No such determination was needed under the 1974 Definition of Aggression, indeed the resolution that adopted it stipulated that the Assembly 'Calls the attention of the Security Council to the Definition of Aggression, as set out below, and recommends that it should, as appropriate, take account of that Definition as guidance in determination, in accordance with the Charter, the existence of an act of aggression'. UN General Assembly Resolution 3314 (XXIX), operative para 4.

[89] UK House of Lords, *R v Jones* [2006] UKHL 16.

[90] See, eg, European Commission, 'Ukraine: International Centre for the prosecution of Russia's crime of aggression against Ukraine starts operations today', News release, 3 July 2023, at: https://bit.ly/3ucmQMK; J Hansler, 'US announces it supports creation of special tribunal to prosecute Russia for "crime of aggression" in Ukraine', *CNN*, 28 March 2023, at: https://bit.ly/3QsQHba; and 'Switzerland supports creation of special tribunal on Ukraine', *Swissinfo.ch*, 20 September 2023, at: https://bit.ly/476TEoX.

[91] Art 8*bis*(2)(g), ICC Statute.

[92] Art 25(3)*bis*, ICC Statute.

8

State Responsibility for Hybrid Warfare

THE RESPONSIBILITY OF States for violations of international law is at the heart of accountability for the conduct of hybrid warfare, as the previous chapters have sought to demonstrate. That does not mean that all forms and methods of hybrid warfare violate international law, for that is not the case. Cyberattacks and disinformation, for instance, are now part and parcel of warfare and do not breach the law of armed conflict if they are targeted at lawful military objectives. Foreign intelligence gathering in peacetime is likely to breach domestic law but is not necessarily prohibited under international law.[1] Even the transmission of propaganda into another State 'is generally not a violation of sovereignty'.[2] Nevertheless, much of what we understand as hybrid warfare does violate at least one rule of international law.

This chapter outlines first the fundamental rules of State responsibility for such violations of international law. A primary reference in this regard is the International Law Commission's Draft Articles on Responsibility of States for Internationally Wrongful Acts, which it concluded and submitted to the United Nations (UN) General Assembly in 2001. This product of the work of the International Law Commission is hereafter referred to as the 2001 Draft Articles on State Responsibility.[3] The provisions the Commission drafted on State responsibility generally reflect customary international law today, and if codified by States (or otherwise applicable as customary law) they would apply to all and any violations of international law committed in the course of hybrid warfare.

The remainder of the chapter reviews selected key incidents and instances of hybrid warfare over the past 20 years in order to identify whether any State bears responsibility for any violations of international law perpetrated therein.

[1] See, eg, on this issue J Beim, 'Enforcing a Prohibition on International Espionage' (2018) 18(2) *Chicago Journal of International Law* Art 6, available at: https://bit.ly/3G1JfPB.

[2] International Group of Experts, *Tallinn Manual 2.0 on the International Law Applicable to Cyber Operations*, Cambridge University Press, Cambridge, 2017 (hereafter, Tallinn Manual 2.0), commentary para 29 on Rule 4.

[3] Draft Articles on Responsibility of States for Internationally Wrongful Acts, with commentaries, 2001; Text adopted by the International Law Commission at its fifty-third session, in 2001, and submitted to the UN General Assembly as a part of the Commission's report covering the work of that session, in UN doc A/56/10, at: http://bit.ly/32A30cT.

I. THE FUNDAMENTAL PRINCIPLES OF STATE RESPONSIBILITY

In the context of the 2001 Draft Articles on State Responsibility, an 'internationally wrongful act' denotes the violation by a State of a rule of international law that is binding upon it.[4] The breach may be of a rule set forth in a treaty to which the State is a party; it may be of a customary nature; it may reflect a general principle of law; or it may be a rule identified by a competent judicial body, such as the International Court of Justice, a regional human rights court, or a suitably mandated domestic court. In any event, however, not only must the rule be applicable to the State in question but the conduct in question must also be attributable to it in the circumstances prevailing at the time.[5]

Article 1 of the 2001 Draft Articles on State Responsibility says simply that: 'Every internationally wrongful act of a State entails the international responsibility of that State'. But the term 'act' is slightly misleading, for, as the commentary by the Commission's Special Rapporteur at the time observes, an act for the purpose of State responsibility may consist of 'one or more actions or omissions or a combination of both'.[6] State responsibility thus describes the circumstances and consequences for a State that violates a substantive rule of international law either through act or omission.

As the Special Rapporteur further explains, the term 'international responsibility' addresses 'the new legal relations which arise under international law by reason of the internationally wrongful act of a State'.[7] Many of the rules governing State responsibility are thus secondary rules that apply once a violation of a primary rule has occurred.[8] But, given the challenges of factual and legal attribution to a State of the conduct of a non-State armed group that it is supporting, much of the law pertaining to hybrid warfare is complicated by jurisdictional issues. Clarifying the State's potential responsibility means first determining whether it has personal jurisdiction (*ratione personae*) over any

[4] The International Law Commission chose the term 'internationally wrongful act' over others that have been applied in international law over time, such as 'tort' or 'delict'. This latter term had already been used for several decades. See, eg, Permanent Court of International Justice (PCIJ), *Phosphates in Morocco case*, 1937, PCIJ, Series C, No 84, p 494. The term delict had even been used in the Commission's own earlier work on the issue of State responsibility. For instance, in its 1978 report on the issue, the International Law Commission's Special Rapporteur at the time, Roberto Ago, had proposed a draft article whereby 'any internationally wrongful act which is not an international crime … constitutes an international delict'. Draft Article 19(4) on State Responsibility, in Report of the International Law Commission on the work of its thirtieth session, UN doc A/33/10, in *Yearbook of the International Law Commission 1978*, Vol II, Part 2, ch 3.

[5] As the 2001 Draft Articles on State Responsibility stipulate: 'An act of a State does not constitute a breach of an international obligation unless the State is bound by the obligation in question at the time the act occurs'. Art 13, 2001 Draft Articles on State Responsibility.

[6] Commentary, para 1, on Art 1, 2001 Draft Articles on State Responsibility.

[7] Ibid.

[8] Art 13, 2001 Draft Articles on State Responsibility.

given conduct before coming to the barrier of material jurisdiction and the assessment of whether an internationally wrongful act has occurred.

Should those jurisdictional requirements be met, and a violation identified, the potential consequences for a State of being 'responsible' for any given internationally wrongful act are multiple. First, the responsible State is obligated to cease the wrongful conduct if it is continuing. Naturally, if the unlawful conduct consists of an omission, this must be rectified by an appropriate act.[9] As well, should the circumstances 'so require', it will need to offer 'appropriate assurances and guarantees of non-repetition'.[10] While such assurances are normally given verbally, guarantees of non-repetition involve more substantive action – 'for example, preventive measures to be taken by the responsible State designed to avoid repetition of the breach'.[11]

Second, a longstanding general principle of law dictates that a responsible State must also make 'full reparation' for the injury caused by the internationally wrongful act.[12] In its judgment on jurisdiction in the *Factory at Chorzów* case rendered almost a century ago, the Permanent Court of International Justice declared it even then to be 'a principle of international law that the breach of an engagement involves an obligation to make reparation in an adequate form'. With respect to breach of a treaty rule, reparation is hence 'the indispensable complement of a failure to apply a convention and there is no necessity for this to be stated in the convention itself'.[13]

Reparation for an internationally wrongful act involves both 'material' and 'moral' damage.[14] Material damage concerns damage to property or other interests of the State and its nationals that is assessable financially, while moral damage includes pain and suffering and the loss of loved ones.[15] As the 2001 Draft Articles on State Responsibility further provide: 'Full reparation for the injury caused by the internationally wrongful act shall take the form of restitution, compensation and satisfaction, either singly or in combination'.[16]

The consequences of most internationally wrongful acts are primarily bilateral – that is, between a perpetrator State and a victim State. The International Law Commission perceives that inter-relationship as primarily concerning 'only the relations of the responsible State and the injured State inter se'. But in the case of international human rights law, any reparations paid by the responsible

[9] Commentary, para 2, on Art 30, 2001 Draft Articles on State Responsibility.
[10] Art 30, 2001 Draft Articles on State Responsibility.
[11] Commentary, para 12, on Art 30, 2001 Draft Articles on State Responsibility.
[12] Art 31(1), 2001 Draft Articles on State Responsibility.
[13] PCIJ, *Factory at Chorzów* case, Judgment (Jurisdiction), No 8, 1927, PCIJ, Series A, No 9, at http://bit.ly/2GaUDwF, p 21.
[14] Art 31(2), 2001 Draft Articles on State Responsibility.
[15] Commentary, para 5, on Art 31, 2001 Draft Articles on State Responsibility.
[16] Art 34, 2001 Draft Articles on State Responsibility.

State are ultimately due to the injured individual or individuals rather than the State whose citizenship they hold. That is so even though compensation may be paid to that State by the culpable State.[17]

Where, however, the internationally wrongful act involves a violation of a peremptory (*jus cogens*) norm of international law, this gives rise to obligations 'owed to the international community as a whole (obligations *erga omnes*), in which all States have a legal interest'.[18] The list of such peremptory norms certainly includes aggression, war crimes, crimes against humanity, and genocide.[19] In all likelihood it also encompasses, outside the realm of such international crimes, the prohibition of individual instances of torture,[20] of arbitrary deprivation of life,[21] and of enforced disappearance.[22] The violation of certain of these norms is discussed below.

[17] Commentary, para 3, on Art 28, 2001 Draft Articles on State Responsibility. See further on this issue International Court of Justice, *Ahmadou Sadio Diallo* (*Guinea v Democratic Republic of Congo*), Judgment (Merits), 30 November 2010. The Court subsequently awarded the sum of US$95,000 to Guinea but reiterated that this sum was intended to provide reparation for Mr Diallo's injury. International Court of Justice, *Ahmadou Sadio Diallo* (*Guinea v Democratic Republic of Congo*), Judgment (Compensation owed by the Democratic Republic of the Congo to the Republic of Guinea), 19 June 2012, paras 56–57. In the case of the bombing of the Greenpeace boat, *Rainbow Warrior*, by French State agents operating covertly in New Zealand in 1985, compensation was paid to the family of the Greenpeace photographer who was killed as well as to New Zealand. C Freeman, 'Why the French bombed Greenpeace's Rainbow Warrior: "The goal wasn't to slaughter"', *Daily Telegraph*, 2 March 2023, at: https://bit.ly/3qqQSuA; *R v Mafart and Prieur* (NZ High Court) ('Rainbow Warrior') [1987] 74 *International Law Reports* 241 at p 256. France never formally apologised for its conduct.

[18] Draft Conclusion 17(1) in International Law Commission, Report of the International Law Commission, Seventy-first session, UN doc A/74/10, 2019, ch V.

[19] International Law Commission, 'Peremptory norms of general international law (*jus cogens*)', Texts of the draft conclusions and Annex adopted by the Drafting Committee on second reading, UN doc A/CN.4/L.967, 11 May 2022, Annex, norms (a) to (d).

[20] Ibid, norm (g).

[21] 'Reservations with respect to the peremptory and non-derogable obligations set out in article 6 are incompatible with the object and purpose of the Covenant. In particular, no reservation to the prohibition against arbitrary deprivation of life of persons … is permitted'. Human Rights Committee, 'General Comment No 36 – Article 6: Right to Life', UN doc CCPR/C/GC/36, 3 September 2019, para 68. In 2015, the African Commission on Human and Peoples' Rights stated: 'The right not to be arbitrarily deprived of one's life' is 'recognised as a *jus cogens* norm, universally binding at all times'. African Commission on Human and Peoples' Rights, 'General Comment No. 3 on the African Charter on Human and Peoples' Rights: The Right to Life (Article 4)', adopted at Banjul (fifty-seventh Ordinary Session), November 2015, para 5. In 2010, Sir Nigel Rodley observed that the 'core content of the right cannot seriously be contested as *jus cogens*'. NS Rodley, 'Integrity of the Person', in D Moeckli, S Shah, and S Sivakumaran (eds), *International Human Rights Law*, Oxford University Press, Oxford, 2010, p 222. Already in 1987 in s 702(c) of the Restatement of the Law, Third, Foreign Relations Law of the United States, published by the American Law Institute, the prohibition of 'murder' as a human rights rule was described as a norm of *jus cogens*.

[22] See, among others: s 702(c), Restatement of the Law, Third, Foreign Relations Law of the United States; and Inter-American Court of Human Rights, *Goiburú and others v Paraguay*, Judgment (Merits, Reparations and Costs), 22 September 2006, para 84. In 2019, the Special Rapporteur of the International Law Commission on the question of peremptory norms noted that the *jus cogens* nature of the prohibition of enforced disappearance 'has received a large degree of support'. Fourth report on peremptory norms of general international law (*jus cogens*) by Dire Tladi, Special Rapporteur, International Law Commission, UN doc A/CN.4/727, 31 January 2019, para 125.

II. STATE RESPONSIBILITY FOR INTERNATIONALLY WRONGFUL ACTS IN HYBRID WARFARE

A. Responsibility for Aggression

As the 1974 UN Definition of Aggression makes explicit: 'Aggression gives rise to international responsibility'.[23] Responsibility for aggression as an international crime focuses on the State and its executive organs, particularly of course the armed forces. But, as Chapter one discussed, that responsibility can involve either its *sending* of non-State armed groups, irregulars, or mercenaries, which perpetrate grave acts of armed violence against another State 'or its substantial involvement therein'.[24] This use of armed groups of differing nature by a State is, of course, at the very heart of contemporary hybrid warfare.

Beginning in March 2014, Russia was deeply implicated in the insurgencies launched by the 'People's Militia' of the self-proclaimed Luhansk People's Republic (LPR) and Donetsk People's Republic (DPR). In August, Russia covertly sent into Ukraine heavy artillery and tanks to the separatists along with tens of thousands of existing or former members of Russia's armed forces.[25] This amounted not only to an international armed conflict (given their overall control of the LPR and DPR People's Militias), but also to an act of aggression for which Russia continues to bear responsibility under international law. It is clear that, as things stand, the regime headed by President Putin has no intention whatsoever of complying with the requirements of that legal responsibility, but there may come a time in which a future Russian government wishes to return to compliance with international law and accept the consequences of its earlier aggression in 2014 (let alone the war of aggression it launched openly with its own armed forces on 24 February 2022). Should such a scenario ever come to pass, there is a model for the assessment and disbursement of reparations that could be instituted.

The United Nations Compensation Commission (UNCC) was created to address Iraq's financial liability for its 'unlawful invasion and occupation of Kuwait' in 1990. In its Resolution 687, the UN Security Council reaffirmed that Iraq was 'liable under international law for any direct loss, damage – including environmental damage and the depletion of natural resources – or injury to foreign Governments, nationals and corporations as a result of its unlawful invasion and occupation of Kuwait'.[26] The Commission was established in 1991 as a subsidiary organ of the Security Council.[27] While the UNCC was 'neither

[23] Art 5(2), Definition of Aggression annexed to UN General Assembly Resolution 3314 (XXIX), adopted without a vote on 14 December 1974 (1974 UN Definition of Aggression).

[24] Art 3(g), 1974 UN Definition of Aggression.

[25] MR Gordon, 'Russia Moves Artillery Units into Ukraine, NATO Says', *The New York Times*, 22 August 2014, at: https://bit.ly/48hcRoU.

[26] UN Security Council Resolution 687, adopted on 3 April 1991 by 12 votes to 1 (Cuba) with two abstentions (Ecuador and Yemen), operative para. 15.

[27] UN Security Council Resolution 692 (1991), adopted on 20 May 1991 by 14 votes to 0, with one abstention (Cuba).

a court nor a tribunal with an elaborate adversarial process',[28] in the following two decades it disbursed total compensation of approximately US$48 billion to some 1.5 million successful claimants.[29]

B. Responsibility for Other Unlawful Use or Threat of Force

There is also international responsibility for an unlawful use of force that does not reach the threshold of gravity to constitute an act of aggression. Where, in threatening or using force against a State, a person or group acts on the instructions of, or under the direction or effective control of another State,[30] this latter State engages its responsibility for having prompted the forcible action. In this regard, the commentary on the relevant provision of the 2001 Draft Articles on State Responsibility (Article 8) explains that the standard of attribution for acting on the instructions of a State encompasses the following:

> Most commonly, cases of this kind will arise where State organs supplement their own action by recruiting or instigating private persons or groups who act as 'auxiliaries' while remaining outside the official structure of the State. These include, for example, individuals or groups of private individuals who, though not specifically commissioned by the State and not forming part of its police or armed forces, are employed as auxiliaries or are sent as 'volunteers' to neighbouring countries, or who are instructed to carry out particular missions abroad.[31]

As Trapp observes, the 'clear implication' is that *either* sending volunteers *or* instructing them on a particular mission will meet the standard for attribution.[32] In assessing State responsibility for international terrorism, the particular subject of her work on State responsibility, she refers to the 'improbability' of being able to 'prove that terrorist conduct was undertaken on the specific instructions of the respondent State'.[33] While as a general rule this may well be true, the insertion of senior Russian military personnel into positions of power and authority in the breakaway republics in Ukraine could be an emblematic exception. As discussed in Chapter three, Igor Ivanovich Girkin held the rank of colonel in the Russian Federal Security Service (FSB) but having, he claimed, 'retired' from the FSB, he served as the first Minister of Defence of the DPR. Of the regular calls he made to Moscow which were intercepted by surveillance agents, many contained specific instructions for action or at the least the validation of his proposed strategy and operations.[34]

[28] UNCC, 'Claims Processing', accessed on 3 September 2013 at http://bit.ly/2U865PM (page no longer online).

[29] UNCC Home Page, at https://uncc.ch/.

[30] Art 8, 2001 Draft Articles on State Responsibility.

[31] Commentary, para 2, on Art 8, 2001 Draft Articles on State Responsibility.

[32] KN Trapp, *State Responsibility for International Terrorism*, Oxford University Press, Oxford, 2011, p 38.

[33] Ibid.

[34] See on this issue, eg, European Court of Human Rights, *Ukraine and The Netherlands v Russia*, Decision on admissibility (Grand Chamber), 30 November 2022, para 619.

In the inter-State case before the European Court of Human Rights, *Ukraine and The Netherlands v Russia*, which was declared admissible and was proceeding to judgment on the merits at the time of writing, it was observed that:

> On 14 March 2014, a group of armed fighters, including Mr Pavlov, a Russian national with military experience in the Russian armed forces who was close to Mr Girkin, attacked the premises of pro-Ukrainian organisations in Kharkiv. Given Mr Pavlov's background, connections and very early involvement, he was another instrument of Moscow's strategy for exercising effective control over the separatist militias. His operating expenses were known to have been facilitated by ultra-nationalist Russian politician Vladimir Zhirinovsky. Funding was provided by Kremlin backers.[35]

Thus, while the burgeoning insurgency in March 2014 and onwards until the early summer might not yet be deemed an aggression, it was assuredly an unlawful inter-State use of force, which involved the State responsibility of the Russian Federation.

C. Responsibility for Violations of the Law of Armed Conflict

(i) State Responsibility for the Attacks against Israel by Hamas of 7 October 2023

Attribution to a State for the 7 October 2023 attacks by Hamas against Israel remained uncertain at the time of writing. Maddocks speculates as to the legal consequences if it were found that Iran had directed the attacks. For instance, whether, in such a scenario, Iran would be responsible in international law for the attacks against the many civilians attending the music festival being held at Re'im, five kilometres from the border with Gaza, would depend on 'whether the unlawful or unauthorized conduct was really incidental to the mission or clearly went beyond it'.[36] As she argues, 'Given the meticulous planning and coordination involved in the attack together with the scale of the killings, there appears little doubt that the targeting of civilians formed a central pillar of the operation'.

If Iran ordered the attack, it could bear responsibility for the law-of-armed-conflict violations committed during the operation unless it instructed Hamas not to target civilians or otherwise to act in a way that violated international law.[37] As she concludes, however, it seems more likely

> that the most that can be proven with certainty is Iran's ongoing military and financial support to Hamas. If the available evidence supports no greater Iranian involvement in the attack than this, Hamas's conduct in violation of international law is not attributable to Iran.[38]

[35] Ibid, para 178.
[36] Commentary para 8 on Art 8, 2001 Draft Articles on State Responsibility.
[37] J Maddocks, 'Israel – Hamas 2023 Symposium – Iran's Responsibility for the Attack on Israel', Blog post, Articles of War, Lieber Institute for Law & Warfare at West Point, United States, 20 October 2023, at: https://bit.ly/3MgwfsP.
[38] Ibid.

At the time of writing, no further evidence had been adduced to support the suggestions emanating from certain quarters that State agents of Iran had supported the planning of the attacks.[39]

(ii) State Responsibility for the Bombing of the Nord Stream Pipelines in September 2022

In a blog post published in November 2023, following reports in the media that Ukrainian divers might have blown up the pipeline while under the 'overall control' of Ukraine (which may have provided funding, training, logistics, and weapons to the divers), Alexander Lott conjectures that this would form part of the international armed conflict between Ukraine and Russia. He suggests that the actions of the divers would thereby incur the State responsibility of Ukraine for the bombing.[40]

The blog post duly refers to the International Court of Justice's judgment in the *Bosnian Genocide* case, and especially its discussion of the holding by the International Criminal Tribunal for the former Yugoslavia (ICTY) that the overall control test, if met, would institute an international armed conflict between the State exercising that control of a non-State armed group and the State attacked by that non-State armed group.

On this issue the International Court of Justice declined to confirm the overall control test as the correct one under international law.[41] Lott further suggests, however, that the overall control test was also the 'wartime' test for State responsibility for the acts of non-State armed groups engaged in hostilities against another State. On this, the Court was unequivocal in rejecting the overall control test as the threshold for determining when a State is responsible for acts committed by paramilitary units or armed groups which are not among its official organs. The Court reiterated that 'effective control' – where the supporting State gives directions or instructions for each specific act – as the one that applies.[42]

The Court confirmed that a State was responsible for the acts of its organs as well as for 'other persons or entities which are not formally recognized as official organs under internal law but which must nevertheless be equated with State organs because they are in a relationship of complete dependence on the State'.[43] This latter scenario is not applicable to the team of divers, based on the available evidence. And as the Court went on to say:

[39] See, eg, D Haynes, 'Israel says it has evidence of Iranian "involvement" in Hamas attack – but "cannot elaborate"', *Sky News*, 23 October 2023, at: https://bit.ly/40bBBLL.

[40] A Lott, 'Did an Alleged Ukrainian Attack Against the Nord Stream Pipelines Violate the Law of Armed Conflict?', The blog of the Norwegian Centre for the Law of the Sea, 21 November 2023, at: https://bit.ly/3RbKSR5.

[41] The Court did, though, declare that 'it may well be that the test is applicable and suitable'. International Court of Justice, *Case Concerning Application of the Convention on the Prevention and Punishment of the Crime of Genocide (Bosnia and Herzegovina v Yugoslavia (Serbia and Montenegro))*, Judgment (Merits), 26 February 2007 (hereafter, ICJ Bosnian Genocide Judgment), para 404.

[42] Ibid, paras 404–6.

[43] Ibid, para 406.

> Apart from these cases, a State's responsibility can be incurred for acts committed by persons or groups of persons – neither State organs nor to be equated with such organs – only if, assuming those acts to be internationally wrongful, they are attributable to it under the rule of customary international law reflected in Article 8 [of the 2001 Draft Articles on State Responsibility] ... This is so where an organ of the State gave the instructions or provided the direction pursuant to which the perpetrators of the wrongful act acted or where it exercised effective control over the action during which the wrong was committed. In this regard the 'overall control' test is unsuitable, for it stretches too far, almost to breaking point, the connection which must exist between the conduct of a State's organs and its international responsibility.[44]

This does not mean that the acts of the divers may not fall to be assessed according to the rules of the law of armed conflict. But it is not correct to say that this 'would suffice to invoke Ukraine's responsibility for the alleged activities of a group of divers that hypothetically conducted the sabotage against the predominantly Russian-owned and Russian-controlled Nord Stream pipelines if Ukraine exercised overall control over their actions'.[45]

If the divers were under Ukraine's overall control, and their actions formed part of an international armed conflict, given that the pipeline did not at the salient time constitute a lawful military objective (as Lott correctly assesses),[46] this would mean that the divers had attacked a civilian object.[47] But since the divers were seemingly not (or no longer) members of Ukraine's armed forces at the time, nor was Ukraine otherwise responsible under international law for their actions, the conduct of the divers would be more likely to be in the form of civilians directly participating in hostilities in an international armed conflict.[48] That would be so, if the International committee of the Red Cross (ICRC) is correct in its view that any non-international armed conflict between the proxy armed group and Russia is extinguished by the supervening armed conflict between Russia and Ukraine.[49] It would also mean that the exclusion for the acts of armed forces under the 1997 Terrorist Bombings Convention was

[44] Ibid.

[45] Lott, 'Did an Alleged Ukrainian Attack Against the Nord Stream Pipelines Violate the Law of Armed Conflict?', n 40 above.

[46] Ibid.

[47] Under the conventional and customary law of armed conflict, civilian objects are all objects which are not military objectives. 'In so far as objects are concerned, military objectives are those objects which by their nature, location, purpose or use make an effective contribution to military action and whose total or partial destruction, capture or neutralization, in the circumstances ruling at the time, offers a definite military advantage'. Art 52(1) and (2), Protocol Additional to the Geneva Conventions of 12 August 1949, and relating to the Protection of Victims of International Armed Conflicts (Protocol I); adopted at Geneva, 8 June 1977; entered into force, 7 December 1978 (hereafter, 1977 Additional Protocol I). Both Russia and Ukraine are States Parties to the 1977 Additional Protocol I.

[48] See generally N Melzer, *Interpretive Guidance on the Notion of Direct Participation in Hostilities under International Humanitarian Law*, ICRC, Geneva, 2009.

[49] See on the issue of extinction of a non-international armed conflict, the discussion of a proxy armed conflict in Chapter 3 of this volume above.

inapplicable, and thus the divers would be international terrorists who must be prosecuted by Ukraine.[50]

Alternatively, the acts of the divers could be the acts of an organised armed group engaged in a distinct non-international armed conflict with Russia. Here, though, a challenge of jurisdiction *ratione loci* arises. In contrast to the global reach of the law governing international armed conflict (and which certainly includes hostilities on the high seas or in the exclusive economic zone of any State),[51] non-international armed conflict is tightly circumscribed as a matter of geography.[52] There was no fighting on the high seas in the area or in the relevant exclusive economic zones at the salient time; therefore, there was no intense and regular combat such as to create hostilities falling to be considered as a distinct non-international armed conflict between the group and Russia. In such a scenario, the divers would not be civilians directly participating in hostilities in a non-international armed conflict, because there was none to which their acts could attach. Therefore, the divers would be 'only' international terrorists whose unlawful acts must be prosecuted by Ukraine. As with the previous scenario of an international armed conflict, the exclusion for purely domestic terrorism would not apply.[53]

D. Responsibility for Violations of International Human Rights Law

State responsibility is at the heart of international human rights law whose raison d'être is the protection of the individual against the power of the sovereign. As Chapter five outlined, however, potentially significant jurisdictional hurdles must be overcome to attribute State responsibility where a human rights violation concerns action taken extraterritorially. The UN Human Rights Committee has taken a broader approach to extraterritorial jurisdiction under the relevant treaty than has the European Court of Human Rights, at least as far as violations occurring during the use of force during combat are concerned. Thus, in its General Comment on the right to life, published in 2019, the Committee stated that, under the 1966 International Covenant on Civil and Political Rights,[54] the duty to respect and ensure the right to life 'includes persons located outside any territory effectively controlled by the State whose right to life is nonetheless

[50] Art 19(2) and Arts 6(1)(c) and 8(1), respectively, International Convention for the Suppression of Terrorist Bombings; adopted at New York, 15 December 1997; entered into force, 23 May 2001 (hereafter, 1997 Terrorist Bombings Convention).

[51] S Casey-Maslen, *Hague Law Interpreted: The Conduct of Hostilities under the Law of Armed Conflict*, Hart Publishing, Oxford, 2018, p 49.

[52] Ibid, pp 67–70.

[53] Art 3, 1997 Terrorist Bombings Convention, n 50 above.

[54] International Covenant on Civil and Political Rights; adopted at New York, 16 December 1966; entered into force, 23 March 1976.

affected by its military or other activities in a direct and reasonably foreseeable manner'.[55] This encompasses acts in the conduct of hostilities.

In marked contrast, as Chapter five discussed, in its judgment on the merits in *Georgia v Russia (II)*, the European Court would not find extraterritorial jurisdiction for unlawful acts by Russia in a situation of armed conflict without concluding that the accused State had effective control over the area concerned:

> The very reality of armed confrontation and fighting between enemy military forces seeking to establish control over an area in a context of chaos means that there is no control over an area. This is also true in the present case, given that the majority of the fighting took place in areas which were previously under Georgian control.[56]

Thus, only where there is an effective belligerent occupation of a foreign State, including through the medium of proxy armed groups, will the European Court of Human Rights adjudge the merits of a substantive human rights violation occurring in the context of an armed conflict. Hence, in the so-called 'occupation phase' that followed the end of the five days of hostilities between Georgia and Russia, the Court held that Russia's actions *did* fall within the material jurisdiction of the European Convention.

The European Court noted that a substantial Russian military presence remained after hostilities had ceased in South Ossetia.[57] Moreover, Russia itself provided 'numerous indications' of the extent of the 'economic and financial support' it had provided and that it continued to provide to South Ossetia.[58] Without the chaos of conflict swirling, the Court decided that the Russian Federation had exercised effective control over South Ossetia from 12 August to 10 October 2008 – the date of the official withdrawal of Russian troops – but also beyond that date. It therefore concluded that the events which occurred after the cessation of active hostilities fell within the jurisdiction of the Russian Federation for the purpose of Article 1 of the 1950 European Convention on Human Rights.[59]

The Court found an administrative practice of unlawful acts by Russia in Georgia (by which is meant repeated occurrence of human rights violations combined with official tolerance of their commission). Despite indications that, at certain times, Russian troops *did* intervene to stop acts of violence being committed against civilians and their property by South Ossetian militia

[55] Human Rights Committee, 'General Comment No 36 – Article 6: Right to Life', UN doc CCPR/C/GC/36, 3 September 2019, para 63, interpreting Art 6, International Covenant on Civil and Political Rights.

[56] European Court of Human Rights, *Georgia v Russia (II)*, Judgment (Grand Chamber), 21 January 2021, para 126.

[57] Ibid, para 164.

[58] Ibid, para 166.

[59] Ibid, para 174–75. Article 1 of the European Convention stipulates that: 'High Contracting Parties shall secure to everyone within their jurisdiction the rights and freedoms defined in Section I of this Convention'.

forces, in many cases they were 'passively present' during scenes of looting.[60] The measures taken by the Russian authorities to prevent the alleged violations thus proved to be insufficient and indeed were even officially tolerated 'as is also shown by the fact that the latter did not carry out effective investigations into the alleged violations'.[61] This gave rise to the responsibility of Russia for the manifold violations of human rights that occurred.

No such geographical jurisdictional challenges pertain to the hybrid threats emanating from China and directed at Taiwan, as Chapter five also describes. In contrast, there are considerable evidentiary barriers to be overcome if responsibility for a violation of international human rights law is to be grounded in international law. Securing the jurisdiction of an impartial forum within which affected Taiwanese could press their claims for the violation of their right to freedom of opinion through the exercise of cognitive warfare would also be a very significant challenge.

E. Responsibility for Violations of Disarmament Law

As observed in Chapter six, disarmament treaties are explicitly framed in terms of the actions of a State Party. The very first article of such treaties typically stipulates that: 'Each State Party undertakes never under any circumstances' to engage in certain conduct with respect to the weapons within the scope of the relevant treaty. In this, a disarmament treaty differs from certain law-of-armed-conflict treaties, which apply also as a matter of personal jurisdiction to a non-State armed group that is a party to an armed conflict.[62] This implies that, in the case of the 1997 Anti-Personnel Mine Ban Convention,[63] for instance, unless an armed group is under the jurisdiction or effective control of a State Party, conduct by that group contrary to the terms of the Convention will not engage the international responsibility of the State.

The situation in Ukraine, which has been a State Party to the Convention since 1 June 2006, is a complex one. But it has certainly involved multiple treaty violations. First, Ukraine failed to destroy its own stockpiles of the prohibited weapons by the legal deadline set for it by the terms of the Convention – 1 June 2010.[64]

[60] European Court of Human Rights, *Georgia v Russia (II)*, Judgment (Grand Chamber), paras 216–17.

[61] Ibid, paras 218–19.

[62] This is particularly the case with Article 3 common to the four 1949 Geneva Conventions, which stipulates that: 'In the case of armed conflict not of an international character occurring in the territory of one of the High Contracting Parties, each Party to the conflict shall be bound to apply, as a minimum, the following provisions …'.

[63] Convention on the Prohibition of the Use, Stockpiling, Production and Transfer of Anti-Personnel Mines and on Their Destruction; adopted at Oslo, 18 September 1997; entered into force, 1 March 1999.

[64] Art 4, 1997 Anti-Personnel Mine Ban Convention. See on this issue, S Casey-Maslen, *The Anti-Personnel Mine Ban Convention: A Commentary*, Oxford University Press, Oxford, October 2023, paras 4.45–4.48.

This failure already involved the responsibility of Ukraine for an internationally wrongful act. At the time of writing, the remaining stockpiles – amounting to more than three million anti-personnel mines – had still to be destroyed. In April 2023, Ukraine declared that:

> Anti-personnel mines, the presence of which was declared by Ukraine as part of the implementation of Article 4 of the Ottawa Convention,[65] are in the warehouses of the Armed Forces of Ukraine and will be destroyed in accordance with the commitments made after the cessation of hostilities and the restoration of the territorial integrity of Ukraine within its internationally recognized borders.
>
> At the same time, if the warehouses and arsenals where anti-personnel mines are stored are located in the territories occupied by Russia, or they have been subjected to air and missile strikes by the armed forces of the Russian Federation, then information about such mines can be obtained only after the territory has been liberated, cleared and carrying out relevant inspections.[66]

Ukraine's legal deadline for the clearance of all anti-personnel mines in mined areas under its jurisdiction or control was set to expire on 1 June 2016.[67] But with the hybrid warfare that began in 2014 in Crimea and the Donbas, anti-personnel mines began to be used by the separatist groups, creating a new and significant landmine threat. The mines were either supplied by Russia (a State not party to the 1997 Convention) or seized from undestroyed Ukrainian stockpiles. The overwhelming majority of the mines laid in Russia appear to be of Russian manufacture, and Ukraine noted that only 605 OZM-4 anti-personnel mines were left in the Autonomous Republic of Crimea occupied by the Russian Federation.[68]

It was clear by late 2014 that Ukraine would be unable to clear the contamination before the expiry of its treaty-mandated clearance deadline. It was initially reluctant to seek an extension to the deadline, as the treaty allows,[69] claiming that it did not have control over the affected areas owing to Russian aggression. It wrongly asserted that because it had not laid the mines, and since armed conflicts were ongoing on its territory, it was not responsible for clearance until the government's effective control of the mined areas had been restored.[70] It was

[65] This is another informal short title for the Anti-Personnel Mine Ban Convention.

[66] Report of Ukraine submitted in accordance with Article 7 of the Anti-Personnel Mine Ban Convention, dated 25 April 2022 [*sic*], Form B. The report, which covers the situation in calendar year 2022, was in fact submitted in 2023.

[67] An affected State Party may seek and be granted a maximum extension of 10 years, renewable on further request. Art 5(1), 1997 Anti-Personnel Mine Ban Convention, n 63 above.

[68] Report of Ukraine submitted in accordance with Article 7 of the Anti-Personnel Mine Ban Convention, n 66 above.

[69] Art 5(3), 1997 Anti-Personnel Mine Ban Convention, n 63 above.

[70] Communication of Ukraine, UN Ref C.N.285.2018.TREATIES- XXVI.5 (Depositary Notification), received by the depositary of the Convention on 31 May 2016, available at: http://bit.ly/2kwnstd. See on this issue: Casey-Maslen, *The Anti-Personnel Mine Ban Convention: A Commentary*, n 64 above, para 5.15.

therefore in violation of the Convention from 1 June 2016 onwards, engaging its international responsibility for another internationally wrongful act.[71]

In November 2018, however, Ukraine submitted a request to extend its mine clearance deadline by five years. The request was granted at the Convention's Seventeenth Meeting of States Parties and a new deadline set for 1 June 2021, returning Ukraine to compliance with Article 5 and more broadly the Convention. On 8 June 2020, Ukraine submitted a second request to extend its mine clearance deadline. The request was granted at the Eighteenth Meeting of States Parties and a new deadline set for 1 December 2023. Ukraine then received a further extension, this time for 10 years, at the Twenty-First Meeting of States Parties in November 2023. On this occasion, however, there was clear and reliable evidence that Ukraine had itself been using anti-personnel mines.[72] This is a serious violation of the comprehensive prohibition on use in Article 1 of the Convention.[73]

The Constitution of Ukraine stipulates that: 'International treaties that are in force, agreed to be binding by the *Verkhovna Rada* [Parliament] of Ukraine, are part of the national legislation of Ukraine'.[74] In addition, potentially, the use of anti-personnel mines in armed conflict is criminalised under Ukraine's own criminal code. It is stipulated therein that

> use of methods of warfare prohibited by international instruments, or any other violations of rules of the warfare recognized by international instruments consented to by binding by the Verkhovna Rada (Parliament) of Ukraine, and also giving an order to commit any such actions … shall be punishable by imprisonment for a term of eight to twelve years.[75]

This would render the actions of any Ukrainian soldiers who laid anti-personnel mines in the conflict with Russia not only a violation of the 1997 Anti-Personnel Mine Ban Convention, engaging State responsibility for Ukraine, but also a domestic offence attracting their individual criminal responsibility.[76]

More serious still, at the time of writing there were unconfirmed reports that Ukraine might even be planning to prosecute captured Russian soldiers for the

[71] Ibid, para 5.279.

[72] Report of the Independent International Commission of Inquiry on Ukraine, UN doc. A/HRC/52/62, 15 March 2023, para 36; Human Rights Watch, 'Ukraine: Banned Landmines Harm Civilians', Washington DC, 31 January 2023, at: https://bit.ly/3qA8eVA.

[73] Ukraine's use of mines was discussed at the Convention's Intersessional Meetings in Geneva in June 2023. On 19 June 2023, Steve Goose, the head of delegation of the civil society network the International Campaign to Ban Landmines (ICBL), described Ukrainian use as 'without doubt the most serious violation of the Convention since it was negotiated in 1997'. In response, Ukraine 'protested' the remarks by civil society, but did not deny the substance of the allegations. On 21 June 2023, it said that it had 'no information to confirm the veracity' of the allegations but did not engage on their substance.

[74] Art 9, Constitution of Ukraine, unofficial translation available at: http://bit.ly/3OAJHHT.

[75] Art 438, Criminal Code of Ukraine, unofficial translation available at: http://bit.ly/3Vt95BD.

[76] Casey-Maslen, *The Anti-Personnel Mine Ban Convention: A Commentary*, n 64 above, para 9.94.

use of anti-personnel mines on its territory – even though Russia was not bound by the terms of the Convention as a State not party – while seemingly granting impunity to the members of its own forces. Under customary international law, combatant members of State armed forces in an international armed conflict are entitled to what is known as combatant's privilege,[77] meaning that they can only be prosecuted for war crimes and not for the use of force in compliance with the law of armed conflict. It is generally understood that this privilege extends to preclude prosecution of combatants for all but customary law war crimes and those binding upon the relevant State to whose armed forces the soldier belongs.

F. Responsibility for Acts of Terrorism

As noted in Chapter four, Ukraine has brought a case against Russia before the International Court of Justice for the shooting down of Malaysian Airlines Flight MH17 on the basis of the 1999 UN Terrorism Financing Convention.[78] This includes the financing of activities prohibited under the 1971 Montreal Convention for the Suppression of Unlawful Acts against Civil Aviation. In its request for provisional measures of 16 January 2017, Ukraine argued that Russia had 'instigated and sustained an armed insurrection against the authority of the Ukrainian state, including by systematically supplying illegal armed groups and associated groups and individuals, with heavy weaponry, money, personnel, training, and other support'. Ukraine further argued that Russia 'knew that these illegal groups were not only engaged in combat against the Ukrainian authorities, but were routinely perpetrating acts of terrorism against Ukrainian civilians'. Despite this knowledge, it said, Russia 'decided to sponsor their activities, providing cash, critical weapons, and other support'. With that assistance, the armed groups have committed a series of terrorist attacks, including the shooting down of Malaysian Airlines Flight MH17.[79]

In its 'countermemorial', Russia observes that the wording in the 1971 Montreal Convention stipulates that any person commits an offence if he unlawfully *and intentionally* destroys an aircraft in service.[80] Russia rejects the notion advanced by Ukraine that intent should be given a broader meaning

[77] See, eg, GD Solis, *The Law of Armed Conflict: International Humanitarian Law in War*, 3rd edn, Cambridge University Press, Cambridge, 2021, p 37.

[78] International Convention for the Suppression of the Financing of Terrorism; adopted at New York, 9 December 1999; entered into force, 10 April 2002. The Convention is the most widely ratified of the global sectoral terrorism treaties, with 190 States Parties and 2 signatories at the time of writing.

[79] International Court of Justice, *Application of the International Convention for the Suppression of the Financing of Terrorism and of the International Convention on the Elimination of All Forms of Racial Discrimination* (*Ukraine v Russian Federation*), 'Request for the indication of provisional measures of protection submitted by Ukraine', 16 January 2017, at: https://bit.ly/3QQrLfD, para 7.

[80] Art 1(1), Convention for the Suppression of Unlawful Acts against the Safety of Civil Aviation; adopted and signed at Montreal, 23 September 1971; entered into force, 26 January 1973.

encompassing indirect intent or recklessness.[81] The public hearings on the merits in the case were held in June 2023.[82] At the time of writing, the Court was deliberating its judgment. If it finds that Russia is legally responsible for the shooting down of Flight MH17, in violation of applicable terrorism treaties, Russia's responsibility under international law for an internationally wrongful act will be engaged, including the duty to make full reparation.

G. Responsibility for International Crimes

In 2004, the ICTY issued its judgment on appeal in the *Krstić* case, terming the killings of some 8,000 men and boys by the Bosnian Serb army – a non-State armed group – in the aftermath of the fall of the Bosnian Muslim enclave of Srebrenica, 'genocide'.[83] The *Bosnian Genocide* case before the International Court of Justice, ultimately decided in 2007, concerned the potential State responsibility of Serbia and Montenegro (the successor State to the Federal Republic of Yugoslavia[84]) for those acts of genocide. An application to the Court was originally made in 1993.

The first hurdles to overcome pertained to the jurisdiction of the Court to hear the case. In its application, Bosnia and Herzegovina principally relied on Article IX of the 1948 Genocide Convention as the jurisdictional basis. This provision stipulates as follows:

> Disputes between the Contracting Parties relating to the interpretation, application or fulfilment of the present Convention, including those relating to the responsibility of a State for genocide or for any of the other acts enumerated in article III, shall be submitted to the International Court of Justice at the request of any of the parties to the dispute.[85]

Despite the lack of mutual recognition between the applicant and respondent countries at the time of filing the application, which was only rectified

[81] International Court of Justice, *Application of the International Convention for the Suppression of the Financing of Terrorism and of the International Convention on the Elimination of All Forms of Racial Discrimination* (*Ukraine v Russian Federation*), 'Counter-Memorial on the Case Concerning Application of the International Convention for the Suppression of the Financing of Terrorism', 9 August 2021, at: https://bit.ly/3srZ4vk, para 155.

[82] International Court of Justice, *Application of the International Convention for the Suppression of the Financing of Terrorism and of the International Convention on the Elimination of All Forms of Racial Discrimination* (*Ukraine v Russian Federation*), Press release No 2023/30, 14 June 2023, at: https://bit.ly/3Pana6K.

[83] ICTY, *Prosecutor v Krstić*, Judgment (Appeals Chamber) (Case No IT-98–33-A), 19 April 2004, paras 37–38.

[84] A State which existed between 1992 and 2006 and occupied part of the territory of the former Socialist Federal Republic of Yugoslavia.

[85] Art IX, Convention on the Prevention and Punishment of the Crime of Genocide; adopted at Paris, 9 December 1948; entered into force, 12 January 1951.

upon the signature in Paris on 14 December 1995 of the Dayton Agreement,[86] the Court declared that it did indeed have jurisdiction *ratione personae*. It explained that it had always had recourse to the principle according to which it 'should not penalize a defect in a procedural act which the applicant could easily remedy'.[87]

With regard to geographical jurisdiction, Yugoslavia had contested the scope of application of the 1948 Genocide Convention. The Court ruled, however, that the rights and obligations enshrined by the Convention are rights and obligations *erga omnes*. The Court stated that the obligation each State thus has to prevent and to punish the crime of genocide is not territorially limited by the Convention.[88] The Convention, and particularly its Article IX, also did not limit the extent of the obligations of the parties in time, meaning that jurisdiction was not excluded *ratione temporis*.[89]

As to material jurisdiction, Yugoslavia had asserted that State responsibility was excluded from the scope of application of Article IX. This claim was swiftly rejected by the Court, which further observed that: 'Nor is the responsibility of a State for acts of its organs excluded by article IV of the Convention, which contemplates the commission of an act of genocide by "rulers" or "public officials"'.[90] Gill praised the Court's decision on jurisdiction *ratione materiae*, declaring that:

> Article IX also clearly states that the ICJ has competence to determine questions of State responsibility for genocide or the failure to prevent genocide. The Court's decision has cleared away any remaining doubts relating to this question once and for all, and in doing so, has given Article IX of the Convention the significance it was, in my view, intended to have and deserves. Any other interpretation would have relegated the provision to having marginal importance at best. While State responsibility is distinct from criminal responsibility, there can be no doubt that a State can incur classical (civil) State responsibility by committing genocide, or failing to prevent

[86] Article X of the 1995 General Framework Agreement for Peace in Bosnia and Herzegovina stipulated that the Parties 'recognize each other as sovereign independent States within their international borders'.

[87] International Court of Justice, *Case Concerning Application of the Convention on the Prevention and Punishment of the Crime of Genocide* (*Bosnia and Herzegovina v Yugoslavia*), Judgment (Preliminary Objections), 11 July 1996, para 26.

[88] Ibid, para 31. In the later judgment on the merits, the Court stated that the substantive obligations arising from Articles I and III of the Genocide Convention (n 85 above) 'are not on their face limited by territory. They apply to a State wherever it may be acting or may be able to act in ways appropriate to meeting the obligations in question'. The obligation to prosecute individuals imposed by Article VI 'is by contrast subject to an express territorial limit. The trial of persons charged with genocide is to be in a competent tribunal of the State in the territory of which the act was committed, or by an international penal tribunal with jurisdiction'. ICJ Bosnian Genocide Judgment, n 41 above, paras 183–84.

[89] International Court of Justice, *Case Concerning Application of the Convention on the Prevention and Punishment of the Crime of Genocide* (*Bosnia and Herzegovina v Yugoslavia*), Judgment (Preliminary Objections), n 87 above, para 34.

[90] Ibid, para 32.

genocide, for more than just failure to provide for domestic legislation making it a criminal offence, or for failure to cooperate in questions of extradition.[91]

With the potential jurisdictional obstacles overcome,[92] the case moved to consideration of its merits. A further 11 years elapsed before a judgment on the merits was rendered ('an exceptionally long case' even by the standards of the Court[93]). On 26 February 2007, the International Court of Justice issued its judgment in the case, holding that Serbia had failed to prevent genocide at Srebrenica.

The Court did not find Serbia responsible for the *commission* of genocide. It nonetheless discerned a duty upon each State Party to the Convention not to commit genocide. Such a duty, which is not set forth explicitly in the 1948 Convention, is inferred from the fact that its Article I categorises genocide as 'a crime under international law' and from the expressly stated obligation to prevent the commission of acts of genocide. As it explained:

> It would be paradoxical if States were thus under an obligation to prevent, so far as within their power, commission of genocide by persons over whom they have a certain influence, but were not forbidden to commit such acts through their own organs, or persons over whom they have such firm control that their conduct is attributable to the State concerned under international law. In short, the obligation to prevent genocide necessarily implies the prohibition of commission of genocide.[94]

With respect to the relationship between Serbia (the successor State to the erstwhile Federal Republic of Yugoslavia) and the self-declared Republic of the Serb People of Bosnia and Herzegovina, later called Republika Srpska (RS), the Court found it established that Serbia was 'making its considerable military and financial support available to the Republika Srpska, and had it withdrawn that support, this would have greatly constrained the options that were available to the Republika Srpska authorities'.[95] The Court concurred with the findings of the ICTY in the *Krstić* case whereby the Army of the Republika Srpska (VRS) targeted the Bosnian Muslims of Srebrenica or the Bosnian Muslims of Eastern Bosnia. The ICTY Appeals Chamber in that case adjudged that:

> The size of the Bosnian Muslim population in Srebrenica prior to its capture by the VRS forces in 1995 amounted to approximately forty thousand people. This represented not only the Muslim inhabitants of the Srebrenica municipality but also many

[91] TD Gill, 'The "Genocide" case: Reflections on the ICJ's Decision in *Bosnia and Herzegovina* v. *Serbia*, Commentary' (2007) 2 *Hague Justice Journal* 45–49, at p 47.

[92] Serbia would again seek to raise jurisdictional objections during its later pleadings, including on the basis that it was not the successor State to the Socialist Federal Republic of Yugoslavia (SFRY) (in existence between 1918 and 1992), but this was dismissed by the Court in its 2007 judgment (ICJ Bosnian Genocide Judgment, n 41 above). Separately, the Federal Republic of Yugoslavia (1992–2006) sought to accede to the Genocide Convention in 2001, with a reservation to the application of Article IX, but this was also unsuccessful in precluding the Court's jurisdiction *ratione personae*.

[93] Gill, 'The "Genocide" case: Reflections on the ICJ's Decision in *Bosnia and Herzegovina* v. *Serbia*, Commentary', n 91 above, pp. 45–46.

[94] ICJ Bosnian Genocide Judgment, n 41 above, para 166.

[95] Ibid, para 241.

> Muslim refugees from the surrounding region. Although this population constituted only a small percentage of the overall Muslim population of Bosnia and Herzegovina at the time, the importance of the Muslim community of Srebrenica is not captured solely by its size.[96]

In seeking to ascertain whether Serbia's international responsibility was incurred in connection with the massacres committed in the Srebrenica area during the period in question, the Court considered three questions. The first was whether the acts of genocide could be attributed to Serbia on the basis that those acts were committed by its organs or persons whose acts are attributable to it under customary rules of State responsibility. In this regard, the Court held that it had not been demonstrated that the Yugoslav army took part in the massacres, nor that the political leaders of the Federal Republic of Yugoslavia had a hand in preparing, planning or in any way carrying out the massacres. While there was much evidence of direct or indirect participation by the Yugoslav army, along with the Bosnian Serb armed forces, in military operations in Bosnia and Herzegovina in the years prior to the events at Srebrenica, it had not been shown that there was any such participation in relation to the massacres committed there. Further, neither the Republika Srpska nor its army (the VRS) were de jure organs of the Federal Republic of Yugoslavia, 'since none of them had the status of organ of that State under its internal law'.[97]

The Court also recalled its holding in the *Nicaragua* case[98] to the effect that

> persons, groups of persons or entities may, for purposes of international responsibility, be equated with State organs even if that status does not follow from internal law, provided that in fact the persons, groups or entities act in 'complete dependence' on the State, of which they are ultimately merely the instrument.[99]

But it did not find that those who committed genocide at Srebrenica had such ties with the Federal Republic of Yugoslavia that they could be deemed to have been completely dependent on it.[100]

As already discussed, the Court decided that the test for whether the conduct of a non-State armed group was otherwise to be attributed to the State was whether that State had 'effective control' over its actions. This requires that the State's instructions be given in respect of each operation in which the alleged violations occurred, not generally in respect of the overall actions taken by the persons or groups of persons which committed the violations. In the view of the Court, Bosnia and Herzegovina had not proved that instructions were issued by

[96] ICTY, *Prosecutor v Krstić*, Judgment (Appeals Chamber) (Case No IT-98–33-A), 19 April 2004, para 15.

[97] ICJ Bosnian Genocide Judgment, n 41 above, para 386, citing Art 4(2), 2001 Draft Articles on State Responsibility.

[98] International Court of Justice, *Case Concerning Military and Paramilitary Activities in and against Nicaragua (Nicaragua v United States of America)*, Judgment (Merits), 27 June 1986.

[99] ICJ Bosnian Genocide Judgment, n 41 above, para 392.

[100] Ibid, para 393.

the federal authorities in Belgrade, or by any other organ of the Federal Republic of Yugoslavia, to commit the massacres, still less that any such instructions were given with the specific intent (*dolus specialis*) characterising the crime of genocide. All indications are to the contrary: that the decision to kill the adult male population of the Muslim community in Srebrenica was taken by some members of the Republika Srpska army's Main Staff, but without instructions from, or effective control by, the Federal Republic of Yugoslavia.[101]

The second issue was whether such organs or persons were complicit in genocide, which is prohibited by Article III(e) of the Convention. The Court again asked whether relevant acts – assisting genocide in particular – could be attributed to Serbia. This involved an examination of whether State organs or persons under the State's effective control furnished 'aid or assistance' in the commission of the genocide in Srebrenica, in a sense not significantly different from that of those concepts in the general law of international responsibility. It thus referred to Article 16 of the 2001 Draft Articles on State Responsibility ('Aid or assistance in the commission of an internationally wrongful act'), which it deemed to reflect a rule of customary international law. The article reads as follows:

> A State which aids or assists another State in the commission of an internationally wrongful act by the latter is internationally responsible for doing so if:
>
> (a) That State does so with knowledge of the circumstances of the internationally wrongful act; and
>
> (b) The act would be internationally wrongful if committed by that State.

Importantly, the Court deemed that the wording of the draft article indicated that the mental element of the wrongful act of providing aid or assistance to a perpetrator of the crime of genocide was that the State 'acted knowingly, that is to say, in particular, was aware or should have been aware of the specific intent (*dolus specialis*) of the principal perpetrator'.[102] This constituted a lower threshold of proof than the one proposed by the Special Rapporteur of the International Law Commission who, in his commentary on Article 16, had suggested that, to incur State responsibility under this provision, the assisting State should *intend* that the unlawful act be perpetrated by the recipient of the assistance.[103] On this legal issue, the International Court of Justice was assuredly correct.

But on the basis of the evidence furnished by Bosnia and Herzegovina, the Court was not convinced that these conditions were met with respect to Serbia.

[101] Ibid, para 413.

[102] Ibid, paras 420–21.

[103] 'The second requirement is that the aid or assistance must be given with a view to facilitating the commission of the wrongful act, and must actually do so. This limits the application of article 16 to those cases where the aid or assistance given is clearly linked to the subsequent wrongful conduct. A State is not responsible for aid or assistance under article 16 unless the relevant State organ intended, by the aid or assistance given, to facilitate the occurrence of the wrongful conduct and the internationally wrongful conduct is actually committed by the aided or assisted State'. Commentary para 5 on Art 16, 2001 Draft Articles on State Responsibility.

The Court thus held that it had not been established 'beyond any doubt' that the authorities of the Federal Republic of Yugoslavia supplied (and had continued to supply) the leaders of the Republika Srpska army, who decided upon and carried out those acts of genocide, with their aid and assistance at a time when those authorities were clearly aware that genocide was about to take place or was under way. The Court found it 'clearly decisive' that it was 'not conclusively shown that the decision to eliminate physically the adult male population of the Muslim community from Srebrenica was brought to the attention of the Belgrade authorities when it was taken'. The Court therefore concluded that Serbia's international responsibility was not engaged for acts of complicity in genocide.[104]

The third and final question posed by the Court was whether Serbia had complied with its twofold obligation deriving from Article I of the 1948 Genocide Convention to both prevent and punish genocide. In this regard, the Court stated that the obligation to prevent genocide is one of 'conduct' and not 'result'. Thus, a State

> does not incur responsibility simply because the desired result is not achieved; responsibility is however incurred if the State manifestly failed to take all measures to prevent genocide which were within its power, and which might have contributed to preventing the genocide.[105]

In addition, the Court declared that a State can be held responsible for breaching the obligation to prevent genocide only if genocide was actually committed.[106] In this respect, it referred to Article 14(3) of the 2001 Draft Articles on State Responsibility, whereby: 'The breach of an international obligation requiring a State to prevent a given event occurs when the event occurs and extends over the entire period during which the event continues and remains not in conformity with that obligation'. Of course, the Court said, this does not mean that the obligation to prevent genocide only comes into being when genocide is already being perpetrated, which would be absurd. Instead, a State's obligation to prevent the commission of genocide arises

> at the instant that the State learns of, or should normally have learned of, the existence of a serious risk that genocide will be committed. From that moment onwards, if the State has available to it means likely to have a deterrent effect on those suspected of preparing genocide, or reasonably suspected of harbouring specific intent (*dolus specialis*), it is under a duty to make such use of these means as the circumstances permit.[107]

In applying the law to the facts of the case, the International Court of Justice noted that, during the relevant period, the Federal Republic of Yugoslavia was

[104] ICJ Bosnian Genocide Judgment, n 41 above, paras 422–24.
[105] Ibid, para 430.
[106] Ibid, para 431.
[107] Ibid.

in a position of influence over the Bosnian Serbs 'unlike that of any of the other States parties to the Genocide Convention'. This was due to the strength of the political, military, and financial links between Yugoslavia on the one hand and the Republika Srpska and its army on the other, 'which, though somewhat weaker than in the preceding period, nonetheless remained very close'.[108]

The Court also recalled that it had already, two years before the massacre at Srebrenica, imposed provisional measures on the Federal Republic of Yugoslavia to ensure

> that any military, paramilitary or irregular armed units which may be directed or supported by it, as well as any organizations and persons which may be subject to its control, direction or influence, do not commit any acts of genocide, of conspiracy to commit genocide, of direct and public incitement to commit genocide, or of complicity in genocide.[109]

Serbia had been clearly put on notice. In this regard, although the Court did not find that the Yugoslav authorities knew that genocide was imminent, 'they could hardly have been unaware of the serious risk of it' once the Bosnian Serb army decided to occupy the Srebrenica enclave.

The leadership in Belgrade – and President Milošević 'above all' – were fully aware of the deep-seated hatred between the Bosnian Serbs and the Muslims in the Srebrenica region, the Court recalled. Yet Serbia had not shown 'that it took any initiative to prevent what happened, or any action on its part to avert the atrocities which were committed'. Given that, for a State to be held responsible for breaching its obligation of prevention, it is necessary only to show that the State concerned had the means to do so and that it 'manifestly refrained from using them', the Court concluded that Serbia had violated its obligation to prevent the genocide at Srebrenica 'in such a manner as to engage its international responsibility'.[110]

Having held Serbia responsible for failing to prevent genocide, the Court's decision not to award reparations against it was controversial to say the least. Here again, though, Gill praised the decision as 'probably the wisest thing to put the case to rest after fourteen years of litigation'. He wrote:

> The Court found that its declaratory rulings regarding Yugoslavia/Serbia's failure to prevent genocide; failure to cooperate with the ICTY by rendering General Mladić into its custody; and failure to carry out fully the terms of its earlier orders on provisional measures, were sufficient and appropriate reparation under the circumstances. This has the obvious effect of precluding any Bosnian claims for financial compensation for its failure to prevent the massacre at Srebrenica. While this may seem to

[108] Ibid, para 434.

[109] International Court of Justice, *Case Concerning Application of the Convention on the Prevention and Punishment of the Crime of Genocide* (*Bosnia and Herzegovina v Yugoslavia* (*Serbia and Montenegro*)), Order (Request for the Indication of Provisional Measures), 8 April 1993, para 52, dispositive A(2).

[110] ICJ Bosnian Genocide Judgment, n 41 above, para 438.

deny the Bosnian Government and more significantly the victims (and their families) a concrete remedy, it was on balance the least disadvantageous and most prudent decision on this issue which was available to the Court. Aside from the question whether any amount of financial compensation could adequately compensate the victims for what occurred, and whether the Court could realistically be expected to calculate and assess an appropriate level of compensation which would do justice to the victims, there is another aspect of this which should not be lost sight of. What would such a ruling have meant in terms of settling the overall dispute and contributing to the normalization of relations between the parties? There is no doubt that another protracted round of proceedings would have resulted from any Court decision allowing for financial compensation. Whether this would have resulted in any meaningful compensation to the victims or contributed to an improvement in the relations between Bosnia Herzegovina and Serbia is debatable.[111]

[111] Gill, 'The "Genocide" case: Reflections on the ICJ's Decision in *Bosnia and Herzegovina* v. *Serbia*, Commentary', n 91 above, pp 48–49.

Annex I: An Introduction to International Law

THIS FIRST ANNEX is intended as a backgrounder for non-lawyers as well as for domestic legal experts that are not also schooled in international law. It offers a foundation in international law that will serve as a backdrop to the eight substantive chapters and which may be useful to study before reading them.

The text briefly defines international law before outlining how it applies to hybrid warfare. Next, the sources of international law are explained. The Statute of the International Court of Justice identifies three primary sources (treaties, customary law, and general principles of law) and two subsidiary sources (the decisions of courts – case law – and the works of the world's leading international lawyers: 'publicists' in the language of the 1945 Statute of the International Court of Justice).

The 'subjects' of international law are first and foremost States, which can draft and contract international rules as well as be bound by them. Also at least partial subjects of international law are international organisations, armed groups, and private corporations. To a certain extent and in specific situations individuals are also bound directly by international law, particularly with respect to international crimes. The notion of jurisdiction in international law is then clarified, along with a description of the four key bases of jurisdiction: geographical, personal, material, and temporal. Finally, the ever-present challenge of the enforcement of international law is tackled.

WHAT IS INTERNATIONAL LAW?

International law (formally referred to as 'public international law')[1] is the body of law that regulates conduct of international concern to the subjects of international law. As already noted (and discussed below), the subjects of international law are primarily (but not only) States. A full subject of international law has the power to make rules of international law as well as the duty to obey them. Partial subjects of international law are typically rule 'takers' but not also rule 'makers'. The State operates through its organs (executive, legislative, and

[1] Private international law concerns the choice of domestic jurisdiction for the resolution of a dispute between individuals or companies from different countries.

judicial) as well as its agents (individuals who are under the 'direction, instigation or control' of those organs).[2] The acts of each of these organs and agents are normally also acts of the State itself, which may comply with or violate one or more rules of international law.

Modern international law began with the adoption by States of the Charter of the United Nations in 1945.[3] But many rules of international law pre-date the adoption of the UN Charter and continue to bind States today. International legal rules may be written in a treaty that a State decides to join, or they may be unwritten rules that States have generally accepted as binding on them (known as customary international law). The breach of any of those rules entails the responsibility of the State under international law. In many instances domestic law continues to apply in parallel to international law, but it does not override international law, nor can it ever justify or excuse a breach of international law. In so-called 'monist' States, international law is directly binding in domestic law while in others (dualist States) legislation must be adopted to give effect to each new treaty rule of international law.

HOW DOES INTERNATIONAL LAW APPLY TO HYBRID WARFARE?

Just as is the case with domestic law, international law has many different branches. Several among the many branches of international law regulate and restrict the conduct of hybrid warfare by one State against another. This may be, for instance, with respect to the use of armed force on the territory of another State (*jus ad bellum*); international law may also regulate the fighting between the armed forces of two States or between the armed forces of a State and a non-State armed group (under the law of armed conflict, also called international humanitarian law); it may apply to the violent actions of a non-State armed group (under counterterrorism law); or it may concern the treatment of individuals by the organs or agents of a State (international human rights law). The supply or use of certain weapons by State agents in hybrid warfare can breach disarmament law.

The violation of any rule of international law entails the responsibility of the State. But in addition to this State responsibility, certain unlawful acts of special gravity will amount to international crimes. In such a case the individual perpetrators may be held personally responsible under international criminal law, for instance for the commission of war crimes. They may be prosecuted in domestic courts or before an international criminal tribunal, such as the International Criminal Court.

[2] Commentary para 2, Chapter II, Draft Articles on the Responsibility of States for Internationally Wrongful Acts, International Law Commission, UN doc A/56/10, 2001 (hereafter, 2001 Draft Articles on State Responsibility).

[3] Art 2(4), Charter of the United Nations; adopted at San Francisco, 26 June 1945; entered into force, 24 October 1945 (hereafter, UN Charter).

WHERE ARE THE RULES OF INTERNATIONAL LAW TO BE FOUND?

The Statute of the International Court of Justice, which establishes that Court, was adopted along with the UN Charter in 1945.[4] The International Court of Justice, which is discussed below in relation to the enforcement of international law, is a court that resolves disputes between States or gives advisory opinions on the interpretation and implementation of international law. Whenever possible it does so by reference to what are termed the primary sources of international law. These primary sources are listed in the Statute: treaties, international custom, and general principles of law.[5] If the Court cannot find the answer to the dispute before it in any of those three primary sources of international law it may look at 'subsidiary' means in order to determine what the relevant rule is. These subsidiary means are the decisions of courts and the writings of the leading international lawyers of the day.[6]

Treaties

The first primary source of international law listed in the Statute of the International Court of Justice is treaty law. 'Treaty' is the general term used in international law today (even though the Statute itself refers to 'conventions').[7] The law of treaties is the branch of international law that governs, among other things, what a treaty is; how it may be adopted; how it should be interpreted; and how it may be amended (and even how it may be brought to an end).

Many of the rules of the law of treaties are of a customary nature, meaning that they bind all States (see below). But these rules are also codified – meaning they are written in a treaty – in the 1969 Vienna Convention on the Law of Treaties.[8] This convention defines a treaty as an 'international agreement concluded between States in written form and governed by international law, whether embodied in a single instrument or in two or more related instruments and whatever its particular designation'.[9]

Thus, to be a treaty under international law, the text must be in writing (so oral agreements are insufficient). In contrast, it does not matter whether the word 'treaty' is used in the title of the written instrument, the key issue is whether States were intending to agree on a written text that would be binding under

[4] Statute of the International Court of Justice; adopted at San Francisco, 26 June 1945; entered into force, 24 October 1945 (hereafter, ICJ Statute).

[5] Art 38(1)(a)–(c), ICJ Statute.

[6] Art 38(1)(d), ICJ Statute.

[7] Art 38(1)(a), ICJ Statute.

[8] Vienna Convention on the Law of Treaties; adopted at Vienna, 23 May 1969; entered into force, 27 January 1980 (VCLT). At the time of writing, 116 States were party to the VCLT. A further 15 States were signatories. The VCLT largely codifies customary international law on treaties.

[9] Art 2(1)(a), VCLT.

international law and thereby constitute a treaty. Examples of nomenclature that may identify a treaty are 'agreement', 'charter', 'convention', 'covenant', 'declaration', 'protocol', and even 'memorandum of understanding'.

The normal way to join a treaty – that is to say, to become a State Party[10] – is to sign and ratify it. The reason for this two-stage process is to allow a senior representative of the State (eg a minister for foreign affairs or an ambassador authorised to do so) to sign the treaty upon or following its adoption, indicating his or her State's general support for the treaty and its aims. But in many States it is the national parliament that then reviews the treaty and decides whether the State should join.

It is also possible under many treaties to 'accede' – an alternative means for a State to join. Accession to a treaty is a one-step process that effectively combines signature and ratification in a single act. Some treaties no longer allow signature once they have entered into force and so States wishing to join that did not sign beforehand *must* accede. This is the case, for instance, with the 1997 Anti-Personnel Mine Ban Convention.

Once approval has been given by the legislature and the executive of a State to ratify a treaty, an instrument of ratification (a formal letter) is sent to the treaty depositary that is authorised by the treaty to receive and register ratifications to it. For many treaties with global effect, the UN Secretary-General is the depositary.[11] But for other treaties it may be either a single State (eg Switzerland for the 1949 Geneva Conventions) or a small number of States (eg Russia, the United Kingdom, and the United States for the 1971 Biological Weapons Convention).

Once the requisite number of ratifications or accessions has been received – each treaty must specify what that number is[12] – the treaty will then enter into force, meaning it becomes fully binding on the States that have joined it up until that point.[13] After any new ratification or accession, the State becomes a party to the treaty after the period of time specified in the treaty. In the case of the Anti-Personnel Mine Ban Convention, for example, this is the first day of the sixth month after the date of deposit of the instrument of ratification or accession.

Only States Parties are directly bound by all the rules in a treaty. It is a general principle of the law of treaties that a treaty cannot bind third parties, in particular other States, without their express consent.[14]

[10] The synonym 'High Contracting Party' is also found in some treaties, such as in treaties pertaining to the law of armed conflict (e.g. the 1949 Geneva Conventions).

[11] This applied to more than 550 treaties at the time of writing.

[12] The number may differ widely. The minimum is two (this was the threshold set under the 1949 Geneva Conventions) whereas the 1992 Chemical Weapons Convention required 65 ratifications or accessions.

[13] There may be a specified time lag between the number being reached and the entry into force of the treaty.

[14] Art 34, VCLT.

The media will often loosely refer to 'signatory States' to a treaty when in fact they mean States Parties. Under international law, 'signatory State' means just that – a State that has signed the treaty but not ratified it. There are, though, still certain consequences under international law of merely signing a treaty. As the Vienna Convention on the Law of Treaties explains, a signatory State must not engage in conduct that would 'defeat the object and purpose of a treaty'.[15] This means action that is contrary to the fundamental aims of the treaty. For example, with respect to a disarmament treaty, an act that would defeat its object and purpose and therefore be unlawful would be for a signatory State to use the weapon that is being comprehensively banned. Where, however, a signatory State later declares formally in a letter to the depositary that it does not intend to become a party to the treaty, it is relieved of this obligation.

When joining a treaty, a State may often make a reservation to one or more of the provisions. This means that the State does not accept the obligation contained in certain articles. Some treaties, particularly disarmament treaties, do not allow any reservations. In general, treaty law does not allow a reservation where it is 'incompatible' with the object and purpose of the treaty.[16] Sometimes the line between a particular 'interpretation' of certain provisions by a State and a reservation in respect of them may be difficult to draw. This may lead to concern that a treaty is not being respected. One way to resolve the dispute is to refer the issue to the International Court of Justice for an advisory opinion on whether certain reservations to a particular treaty are lawful.

Just as a State can join a treaty, so in many cases it is possible to leave it. The process for leaving, known as denunciation or withdrawal, is normally set out in one of the articles of the treaty in question. Often, the withdrawing State Party must inform the other States Parties of the reason for leaving and there will be a time lag before withdrawal takes effect. It is not always possible to leave a treaty, as it depends on the wording of the treaty text. If the treaty is silent, then it will be necessary to discern the intention of the negotiating States.[17] In the case of the 1966 International Covenant on Civil and Political Rights, the UN Secretary-General, as depositary, has taken the view that it is not possible for a State Party to withdraw from it.[18]

It is not normally possible for the States Parties to a treaty to expel a particular State Party. That said, in the aftermath of its invasion of Ukraine in February 2022, Russia was first suspended and then ejected from the Council of Europe.[19]

[15] Art 18(a), VCLT.

[16] Art 19(c), VCLT.

[17] Art 56, VCLT.

[18] Treaty Section of the UN Office of Legal Affairs, *Treaty Handbook*, Revised edn, New York, 2013, at: https://bit.ly/3848R0b, p 27.

[19] Resolution CM/Res(2022)2 on the cessation of the membership of the Russian Federation to the Council of Europe, adopted by the Committee of Ministers on 16 March 2022, at: https://bit.ly/3MyttPw.

In order to be a State Party to the 1950 European Convention on Human Rights[20] a State must be a member of the Council of Europe. In March 2022, therefore, the European Court of Human Rights adopted a resolution decreeing that Russia would cease to be a State Party to the European Convention on 16 September 2022.[21]

Customary Law

State Practice and Opinio Juris

A rule of customary international law is a rule that is observed by States out of a sense of legal obligation (known by the shortened Latin formulation, *opinio juris*). To qualify as international custom, a rule must reflect State practice and associated opinion that it is binding under international law. State practice describes both what States do (or do not do) and, especially, how they say they act.[22] Treaty-making may constitute relevant State practice.[23]

The wording in the Statute of the International Court of Justice makes it explicit that the necessary practice must be general among States, but does not need to be either universal or perfectly aligned. Thus, in its judgment in a famous case, the Court declared that, for a rule to be established as customary, the relevant State conduct 'should, in general, be consistent with such rules, and that instances of State conduct inconsistent with a given rule should generally have been treated as breaches of that rule, not as indications of the recognition of a new rule'.[24]

But in order to meet the threshold, the 'general' practice must comprise so-called 'specially affected' States, a requirement set out by the Court in 1969.[25] These are States that engage in relevant conduct as well as, potentially, those which are affected by the conduct in question.[26] As an example, the International Committee of the Red Cross (ICRC) explained in the introduction to its 2005 study of customary international humanitarian law that, with

[20] Convention for the Protection of Human Rights and Fundamental Freedoms; adopted at Rome, 4 December 1950; entered into force, 3 September 1953.

[21] European Court of Human Rights, 'The Russian Federation ceases to be a Party to the European Convention on Human Rights', Press release ECHR 286 (2022), 16 September 2022, at: https://bit.ly/49E9A3G.

[22] H Thirlway, *The Sources of International Law*, Oxford University Press, Oxford, 2014, p 66.

[23] MN Shaw, *International Law*, 8th edn, Cambridge University Press, Cambridge, 2017, p 60.

[24] International Court of Justice, *Case Concerning Military and Paramilitary Activities in and Against Nicaragua (Nicaragua v United States)*, Judgment (Merits), 27 June 1986 (hereafter, ICJ Nicaragua Merits Judgment), para 186.

[25] International Court of Justice, *North Sea Continental Shelf Cases (Germany v Denmark; Germany v The Netherlands)*, Judgment, 20 February 1969, para 73.

[26] International Court of Justice, *Obligations Concerning Negotiations Relating to Cessation of the Nuclear Arms Race and to Nuclear Disarmament (Marshall Islands v United Kingdom)*, Judgment (Preliminary Objections), 5 October 2016, para 44.

respect to the legality of the use of blinding laser weapons, specially affected States include those identified as having been in the process of developing such weapons.[27] As one legal expert observes, although no individual specially affected State possesses a veto over the formation of customary law, a majority of such specially affected States can always block the formation of a customary rule.[28] It remains unclear, though, how many and which specially affected States would be sufficient to prevent the formation of a custom in a particular instance.[29]

The second of the two elements in the formation of custom is that the relevant State practice must be 'accepted as law'. The 'frequency, or even habitual character' of the acts (or omission) 'is not in itself enough'.[30] Thus, an act that is done through tradition but without that sense of legal obligation – such as rolling out the red carpet for a visiting head of State – is not a rule of customary international law. In its judgment in another famous case, the Court stated that: Not only must the acts concerned amount to a settled practice, but the States concerned must feel they are conforming to what amounts to a legal obligation.[31] As is the case with State practice, *opinio juris* does not need to be universally consistent, but it must be general and settled.

There are many customary rules of international law. Some have become customary law after being agreed upon as treaty rules while others have become custom independently of any treaty. Thus, for example, in the branch of law that governs the use of force between States (*jus ad bellum*), it is permissible for one State to use force in self-defence in response to an 'armed attack' against it. This rule is set out in the UN Charter.[32] But when it is entitled to use force in self-defence the actual force used must comply with the principles of necessity and proportionality[33] (as described in some detail in Chapter one). These principles are not found in any treaty but reflect rules of customary law.

Similarly, in the law of armed conflict, only limited treaty rules govern warfare in a non-international armed conflict (eg where there is regular and intense combat between a State and a non-State armed group). But many of the rules governing international armed conflict (hostilities between the armed forces of two or more States), which exist in both treaty and custom, have

[27] ICRC, 'Introduction', Study of Customary International Humanitarian Law, 2005, at: https://bit.ly/3RaTfvY.

[28] KJ Heller, 'Specially-Affected States & the Formation of Custom', Amsterdam Law School Legal Studies Research Paper No 2017-45, Amsterdam Center for International Law No 2017-30, 1–67, available at: https://bit.ly/3sVgT6p, at pp 65–66.

[29] S Yeini, 'The Specially-Affecting States Doctrine' (2018) 112(2) *American Journal of International Law* 244–53.

[30] International Court of Justice, *North Sea Continental Shelf Cases* (*Germany v Denmark*; *Germany v The Netherlands*), Judgment, para 77.

[31] Ibid.

[32] Art 51, UN Charter.

[33] ICJ Nicaragua Merits Judgment, n 24 above, paras 176 and 194; and International Court of Justice, *Legality of the Threat or Use of Nuclear Weapons*, Advisory Opinion, 8 July 1996, para 41.

become customary law also in non-international armed conflict. An example is the prohibition on targeting civilian objects,[34] which was not incorporated in the 1977 Additional Protocol II to the four Geneva Conventions.[35]

In general, a rule applies to every State once it has crystallised as (become) customary law. There is, however, a potential exception for a persistent objector, a State that has consistently objected to the rule prior to it becoming accepted as custom.[36] According to one of the customary rules of the law of armed conflict identified by the ICRC, the use of expanding bullets (those which expand or flatten easily in the human body) is prohibited.[37] It may be the case, but it is not certain, that the United States is in a position to claim persistent objector status to this rule. For States Parties to the 1998 Rome Statute of the International Criminal Court, however, any national or anyone else who is on their territory and who uses expanding ammunition in connection with an international armed conflict commits a war crime.[38] In 2010, the Statute was amended to include also use in a non-international armed conflict, but this applies only to States that have ratified the relevant amendment.[39]

Jus Cogens *Rules*

Certain rules of customary international law are also peremptory in nature, meaning they have an exceptional status in international law.[40] To amount to a

[34] See International Committee of the Red Cross (ICRC), Customary International Humanitarian Law Rule 7: 'The Principle of Distinction between Civilian Objects and Military Objectives', at: https://bit.ly/3tHhNU6.

[35] Protocol Additional to the Geneva Conventions of 12 August 1949, and relating to the Protection of Victims of Non-International Armed Conflicts (Protocol II); adopted at Geneva, 8 June 1977; entered into force, 7 December 1978.

[36] International Court of Justice, *Fisheries Case* (*United Kingdom v Norway*), Judgment, 18 December 1951, p 19; and see, eg, Thirlway, *The Sources of International Law*, n 22 above, pp 86–88.

[37] ICRC, Customary international humanitarian law (IHL) Rule 77: 'Expanding Bullets', at: http://bit.ly/3gvLivK.

[38] Art 8(2)(b)(xix), Rome Statute of the International Criminal Court; adopted at Rome, 17 July 1998; entered into force, 1 July 2002.

[39] Amendment to Article 8 of the Rome Statute of the International Criminal Court; adopted at Kampala, 10 June 2010; entered into force, 26 September 2012 (hereafter, ICC Statute). At the time of writing, 45 States Parties had ratified the amendment. Andorra, Argentina, Austria, Belgium, Botswana, Chile, Costa Rica, Croatia, Cyprus, the Czech Republic, El Salvador, Estonia, Finland, Georgia, Germany, Guyana, Italy, Latvia, Liechtenstein, Lithuania, Luxembourg, Malta, Mauritius, Mexico, Mongolia, The Netherlands, New Zealand, North Macedonia, Norway, Panama, Paraguay, Peru, Poland, Portugal, Romania, Samoa, San Marino, Slovakia, Slovenia, Spain, State of Palestine, Sweden, Switzerland, Trinidad and Tobago, and Uruguay. When seven-eighths of the States Parties to the Rome Statute ratify the amendment, however, it will enter into force for all States Parties. Art 121(4), ICC Statute.

[40] A peremptory norm of general international law 'is a norm accepted and recognized by the international community of States as a whole as a norm from which no derogation is permitted and which can be modified only by a subsequent norm of general international law having the same character'. Draft Conclusion 2, Fifth report on peremptory norms of general international law (*jus cogens*) by Dire Tladi, Special Rapporteur, International Law Commission, UN doc A/CN.4/747, 24 January 2022.

jus cogens rule (to use the Latin name), the rule must be accepted and recognised as such by the international community of States as a whole. General State practice is thus not sufficient for the creation of a peremptory norm of international law. The list of peremptory norms of international law is short but certainly includes aggression, war crimes, crimes against humanity, and genocide,[41] all of which may be relevant to the conduct of hybrid warfare.

Having the status of a *jus cogens* norm means that the rule is so important that it cannot be amended or circumvented by the negotiation of a treaty. Indeed, if the terms of a new treaty violate an existing *jus cogens* norm, the treaty is itself invalid.[42] Thus, for example, a treaty between two States which required them to launch a war of aggression would thus be void.

General Principles of Law

General principles of law are the third primary source of international law identified by the Statute of the International Court of Justice. They involve rules common to domestic legal regimes around the world and may be rules of purely domestic law or those that are recognised as principles of international law. It has been suggested that the right to life is a general principle of international law because of the universal prohibition of murder in every State's criminal law.[43]

Subsidiary Sources

The decisions of courts and the writings of leading international lawyers are designated a subsidiary source of international law. Thus, in justifying its decision as to a particular rule of international law the International Court of Justice may cite judgments from other courts and books or articles by international lawyers. The same is true of regional human rights courts, such as the European Court of Human Rights.

THE SUBJECTS OF INTERNATIONAL LAW

States

States are full subjects of international law with the capacity to conclude treaties and adhere to them. At the time of writing, 197 States were recognised as

[41] International Law Commission, 'Peremptory norms of general international law (*jus cogens*)', Texts of the draft conclusions and Annex adopted by the Drafting Committee on second reading, UN doc A/CN.4/L.967, 11 May 2022, Annex, norms (a) to (d).

[42] Art 53, VCLT.

[43] C Tomuschat, 'The Right to Life – Legal and Political Foundations' in C Tomuschat, E Lagrange, and S Oeter (eds), *The Right to Life*, Martinus Nijhoff, Leiden, 2010, p 16.

such by the UN Secretary-General in his capacity as treaty depositary: the 193 UN Member States, two Observer States (Holy See and Palestine), and two 'other' States (Cook Islands and Niue). Thus, 196 States are party to the UN Convention on the Rights of the Child and the only State not party (the United States) is a signatory.

Regional organisations may recognise entities as States that the UN Secretary-General does not. For example, the Sahrawi Arab Democratic Republic is a Member State of the African Union and whose sovereignty is proclaimed over Western Sahara. It is also a party to the 1981 African Charter on Human and Peoples' Rights.[44] In February 2018, the European Commission published an expansion plan that included the possibility of Kosovo's accession to membership of the European Union at some unspecified point in time after 2025.[45] Kosovo formally submitted an application for EU membership in December 2022.

International Organisations

International organisations are subjects of international law with international personality, meaning that they can draft legally binding treaties under international law as well as have obligations imposed upon them.[46] In 1986, States concluded the Vienna Convention on the Law of Treaties between States and International Organizations, but the treaty is not yet in force, with two further ratifications by States needed at the time of writing.[47] This treaty defines an 'international organization' as an 'intergovernmental organization'.[48] In 2011, the International Law Commission elaborated Draft Articles on Responsibility of International Organisations for Internationally Wrongful Acts, which contained a broader definition of an 'international organization' as 'an organization established by a treaty or other instrument governed by international law and possessing its own international legal personality'.[49]

[44] African Charter on Human and Peoples' Rights; adopted at Nairobi, 27 June 1981; entered into force, 21 October 1986. The SADR ratified the African Charter in May 1986.

[45] European Commission, 'Strategy for the Western Balkans: EU sets out new flagship initiatives and support for the reform-driven region', Press release, Strasbourg, February 2018.

[46] International Court of Justice, *Interpretation of the Agreement of 25 March 1951 between the WHO and Egypt*, Advisory Opinion, 20 December 1980, para 37.

[47] Vienna Convention on the Law of Treaties between States and International Organizations or between International Organizations; adopted at Vienna, 21 March 1986; not yet in force (hereafter, VCLTIO). The VCLTIO will enter into force once 35 States have either signed and ratified or acceded to it. At the time of writing, 33 had done so: Albania, Argentina, Australia, Austria, Belarus, Belgium, Bulgaria, Colombia, Croatia, Cyprus, Czechia, Denmark, Estonia, Gabon, Germany, Greece, Hungary, Italy, Liberia, Liechtenstein, Malta, Mexico, Moldova, The Netherlands, Palestine, Portugal, Senegal, Slovakia, Spain, Sweden, Switzerland, the United Kingdom, and Uruguay.

[48] Art 2(1)(i), VCLTIO.

[49] Art 2(a), Draft Articles on the Responsibility of International Organizations, adopted by the International Law Commission in 2011, and submitted to the UN General Assembly in UN doc

Examples of international organisations are the United Nations, the International Atomic Energy Agency (IAEA), and the North Atlantic Treaty Organization (NATO). Regional organisations are also international organisations, such as the African Union, the Council of Europe, and the Organization of American States (OAS), the world's oldest regional organisation. So-called regional economic integration organisations, such as the Association of Southeast Asian Nations (ASEAN), the Economic Community of West African States (ECOWAS), and the European Union are also examples of international organisations.

Where the relevant treaty explicitly allows, certain or all international organisations may join. Many have signed and ratified or acceded to the Vienna Convention on the Law of Treaties between States and International Organizations[50] (although their adherence does not count towards triggering the treaty's entry into force).[51] In the field of international human rights law, the Convention on the Rights of Persons with Disabilities is open to signature and 'confirmation' or accession by 'regional integration organizations'.[52] At the time of writing, the European Union was a party to the Convention, the only such body to do so.

The IAEA has been drafting treaties between itself and individual States for many decades, first with the Comprehensive Safeguards Agreement (CSA) and subsequently with the Additional Protocol to the CSA. As of 3 May 2023, the IAEA had concluded comprehensive safeguards agreements with 182 States[53] and an Additional Protocol with 141 of those States.[54] These agreements concern the ability of the IAEA to monitor nuclear material (eg uranium and plutonium) in those States with a view to ensuring that it is used only for peaceful purposes and not diverted to the development of nuclear weapons or other nuclear explosive devices.

A/66/10, at: http://bit.ly/2YOKPz7 (hereafter, 2011 Draft Articles on the Responsibility of International Organizations).

[50] At the time of writing, these were 12 in number: the IAEA, the International Civil Aviation Organization, the International Criminal Police Organization, the International Labour Organization (ILO), the International Maritime Organization (IMO), the Organisation for the Prohibition of Chemical Weapons (OPCW), the Preparatory Commission for the Comprehensive Nuclear-Test-Ban Treaty Organization, the United Nations, United Nations Industrial Development Organization (UNIDO), Universal Postal Union, World Health Organization (WHO), and the World Intellectual Property Organization (WIPO). In addition, the Council of Europe, the Food and Agriculture Organization of the United Nations (FAO), the International Telecommunication Union, United Nations Educational, Scientific and Cultural Organization (UNESCO) and the World Meteorological Organization were signatories.

[51] Art 85, VCLTIO.

[52] Art 43, Convention on the Rights of Persons with Disabilities; adopted at New York, 13 December 2006; entered into force, 3 May 2008 (hereafter, CRPD). The Convention defines a 'regional integration organization' as 'an organization constituted by sovereign States of a given region, to which its member States have transferred competence in respect of matters governed by the … Convention'. Art 44, CRPD.

[53] IAEA, 'Safeguards agreements', accessed 23 November 2023, at: https://bit.ly/2UvGxeL.

[54] IAEA, 'Status List: Conclusion of Additional Protocols', Status as of 3 May 2023, at: https://bit.ly/2xzlfTO.

Armed Groups

Non-State armed groups are a partial subject of international law, at the least when they are party to an armed conflict.[55] Thus, in 2004, the Appeals Chamber of the Special Court for Sierra Leone held that 'it is well settled that all parties to an armed conflict, whether states or non-state actors, are bound by international humanitarian law, even though only states may become parties to international treaties'.[56]

But in a decision reached the same year, the Special Court for Sierra Leone made a far more controversial finding. The Appeals Chamber concluded that the 1999 Lomé Agreement between the Revolutionary United Front (RUF) and the Government of Sierra Leone 'created neither rights nor obligations capable of being regulated by international law'.[57] Its argument was that the RUF had no treaty-making capacity so, as a logical consequence, the Lomé Agreement itself could not, by definition, be a treaty.[58]

This conclusory argument is arguably incorrect as a matter of law. Common Article 3 to the four 1949 Geneva Conventions stipulates that 'the Parties to the conflict should further endeavour to bring into force, by means of special agreements, all or part of the other provisions of the present Convention'. Thus the Convention itself foresees that an agreement between a State and a non-State actor can agree, in a manner that binds them both, to apply in non-international armed conflict the other provisions of the Convention that are normally only applicable in international armed conflict. As the ICRC wrote in 2008, special agreements

> can provide a plain statement of the law applicable in the context – or of an expanded set of provisions of IHL beyond the law that is already applicable – and secure a clear commitment from the parties to uphold that law.

This is an acceptance of binding international legal obligations tantamount to treaty-making.[59]

Private Corporations

It is generally accepted that 'bodies corporate' (to use the legal term) are partial subjects of international law and enjoy a measure of international legal

[55] See on this issue Chapter 3 above.

[56] Special Court for Sierra Leone (SCSL), *Prosecutor v Sam Hinga Norman*, Decision on Preliminary Motion Based on Lack of Jurisdiction (Child Recruitment) (Appeals Chamber) (Case No SCSL-2004-14-AR72(E)), 31 May 2004, para 22.

[57] SCSL, *Prosecutor v Kallon and Kamara*, Decision on Challenge to Jurisdiction: Lomé Accord Amnesty (Appeals Chamber), 13 March 2004, para 42.

[58] Ibid, paras 48 and 49.

[59] ICRC, 'Increasing Respect for International Humanitarian Law in Non-International Armed Conflicts', Geneva, February 2008, p 16.

personality when they are party to an armed conflict (such as a private military force like The Wagner Group). It is also accepted that the staff and directors of a private company may be held individually responsible under international criminal law for international crimes they have committed in the course of their work. This was made clear in judgments in a series of trials before the Nuremberg Military Tribunals that followed the end of the Second World War. But the extent to which private corporations are directly bound by international human rights law is far more contested.[60]

There are indications, however, that the trend is towards holding corporations responsible for human rights violations. In its 2020 judgment in *Nevsun v Araya*, the Supreme Court of Canada held that Canadian corporations may be sued in tort for violations of international human rights law that occur abroad.[61] The plaintiffs suing Nevsun claimed that they had been conscripted by the Eritrean military as 'slaves', forced to work at the defendant's mine, where they were subjected to cruel, inhuman, and degrading treatment in violation of customary international law. By five votes to four, the Court held that claims for violations of international human rights norms abroad may be brought in Canadian courts on the grounds that common law has 'adopted' custom. It declared that some norms of customary law 'prohibit conduct regardless of whether the perpetrator is a state'.[62]

In 2023, an action by practitioners of the Falun Gong religious movement, which alleged they or family members were victims of human rights abuses committed by the Chinese Communist Party and Chinese government officials and that these abuses were enabled by technological assistance of US corporation Cisco Systems, Inc, was allowed to proceed by the US Court of Appeals for the Ninth Circuit.[63] At the time of writing, it was uncertain whether the decision would be reviewed by the US Supreme Court.

THE JURISDICTION OF INTERNATIONAL LAW

The relationship between domestic law and international law is in part determined by the issue of jurisdiction. Four jurisdictional bases – geographical, personal, material, and temporal – govern whether international law applies to any given set of facts along with whether a particular tribunal has the legal mandate to assess whether international law has been complied with. Each of

[60] A State may of course own, wholly or in part, a corporation. When this is the case, the corporation will not be, or is unlikely to be, acting in a private capacity, but rather as an agent of the State, which of course is bound directly by customary and treaty human rights law.

[61] Supreme Court of Canada, *Nevsun Resources Ltd v Araya*, 2020 SCC 5, Judgment rendered on 28 February 2020.

[62] Ibid, paras 105, 111, 113, and 114.

[63] US Court of Appeals for the Ninth Circuit, *Doe v Cisco*, Decision, 19 July 2023. The Ninth Circuit appellate court covers California and 8 other US states.

these jurisdictional bases, which are considered in turn below, must be satisfied if a positive response is to be rendered to both questions.

Geographical Jurisdiction

Most branches of international law have some geographical limitations to their application. This is especially the case with international human rights law, as Chapter five discusses, but it also applies to international counterterrorism law – given the focus on domestic criminal provisions – as well as, to a certain extent, the law of armed conflict. Thus, while an international armed conflict may exist between two States anywhere in the world, a non-international armed conflict is limited to a single territory and indeed jurisdiction over the fighting is restricted to the area where hostilities are being conducted. In the words of the International Criminal Tribunal for the former Yugoslavia (ICTY): 'some of the provisions are clearly bound up with the hostilities and the geographical scope of those provisions should be so limited'.[64]

The challenge to geographical jurisdiction (*ratione loci* in Latin) is less significant in the case of *jus ad bellum* and disarmament law. Jurisdiction *ratione loci* will, however, be very relevant to an international criminal tribunal. In particular, under the Rome Statute the International Criminal Court's ability to judge certain international crimes is restricted to those perpetrated on the territory of a State Party and extends to such crimes committed elsewhere only where the alleged perpetrator is a national of a State Party.[65]

Human rights jurisdiction exists primarily on a State's sovereign territory. But such jurisdiction also extends to conduct on a State's nationally flagged or registered ships or aircraft, whether military or civilian in nature, and irrespective of where in the world they are located. The 1984 Convention against Torture requires that each State Party take effective measures to prevent acts of torture not only in its sovereign territory but also in 'any territory under its jurisdiction'.[66] Peremptory (*jus cogens*) norms apply to acts by States perpetrated anywhere in the world.[67]

[64] ICTY, *Prosecutor v Tadić*, Decision on the Defence Motion for Interlocutory Appeal on Jurisdiction (Appeals Chamber), 2 October 1995, https://bit.ly/2YR8mzd, para 68.

[65] An exception exists where a State not party makes a formal declaration giving jurisdiction to the Court but without ratifying the Rome Statute of the International Criminal Court.

[66] Art 2(1), Convention against Torture and Other Cruel, Inhuman or Degrading Treatment or Punishment; adopted at New York, 10 December 1984; entered into force, 26 June 1987 (1984 Convention Against Torture).

[67] With respect to genocide, see: International Court of Justice, *Case Concerning Application of the Convention on the Prevention and Punishment of the Crime of Genocide* (*Bosnia and Herzegovina v Yugoslavia*), Judgment (Preliminary Objections), 11 July 1996, para 31. An *erga omnes* obligation results from the peremptory nature of a rule.

Personal Jurisdiction

Personal jurisdiction (*ratione personae*) generally determines whether a State in any given case is bound by a particular treaty and whether a tribunal has the jurisdiction to hear the case based on that treaty (or another rule of international law). In the case of international human rights law, jurisdiction *ratione personae* pertains both to those who benefit from the protection of the law and to those who are obligated under international law to provide such protection.

Where a State exercises effective control over a non-State actor, it will be generally responsible under international law for the conduct of that non-State actor. This notion of effective control was set by the International Court of Justice in the *Nicaragua* case as the standard under international law with respect to US control over the *Contras*.[68] It means not just providing funds, training, and/or weapons but also giving instructions as to the conduct of specific military operations. If a foreign State does not exercise the requisite level of control over an armed group or other non-State actor, it will not normally be responsible for the acts or omissions of that group or actor that breach international law.

Material Jurisdiction

Material jurisdiction concerns the subject-matter of an international legal obligation. In the context of the International Court of Justice, a key issue is often whether a dispute exists. Thus, the Statute of the Court declares that its function 'is to decide in accordance with international law such disputes as are submitted to it'.[69] The Statute further provides that the States Parties to it may at any time declare that they recognise as compulsory the jurisdiction of the Court in all legal disputes concerning:

a. the interpretation of a treaty;
b. any question of international law;
c. the existence of any fact which, if established, would constitute a breach of an international obligation;
d. the nature or extent of the reparation to be made for the breach of an international obligation.[70]

With respect to human rights law, jurisdiction *ratione materiae* concerns the rights that are protected and the respect and protection that they require of the State. Material jurisdiction also pertains to the ambient context, such as the existence of an armed conflict or the occurrence of a natural disaster.

[68] ICJ Nicaragua Merits Judgment, n 24 above, paras 115–16.
[69] Art 38, Statute of the International Court of Justice.
[70] Art 36(2), Statute of the International Court of Justice.

Temporal Jurisdiction

Temporal jurisdiction concerns whether a given act falls within the jurisdiction of a particular court or tribunal based on when it occurred. This is particularly an issue with respect to the date on which a State became party to a particular treaty. Hence, for instance, events that took place prior to a State becoming party to a human rights treaty and which involved a potential unlawful killing may well not be subject to adjudication before the relevant regional human rights court. But, as Chapter five describes, the duty to investigate suspicious death (a 'procedural' obligation under the right to life as opposed to a 'substantive' obligation) may persist for many years, including after a State becomes party to the treaty, thereby according jurisdiction to a court that it would otherwise not have in a particular case.[71]

HOW IS INTERNATIONAL LAW ENFORCED?

A range of fora and methods exist to enforce international law, with widely varying degrees of effectiveness. Fora include domestic courts and international tribunals as well as, of course, the UN Security Council, which under the terms of the UN Charter is given primary responsibility for the maintenance of international peace and security.[72] The law may be enforced against individuals, corporations, and States, as well as (potentially) armed groups.

Domestic Courts

Many domestic courts are empowered – ie have jurisdiction – to hear complaints that international law has been violated. Indeed, in so-called monist States, international law may be directly justiciable before a court because the State is a party to a relevant treaty.[73] In certain dualist States, where the rule at issue is of a customary law nature, this will be directly applicable to a dispute in a national court. For instance, in South Africa, the Constitution stipulates that customary international law is the law of the land unless it is inconsistent with the Constitution or an Act of Parliament. As two legal experts observe: 'The result is that customary international law is directly enforceable before a South African

[71] S Casey-Maslen, *The Right to Life under International Law*, Cambridge University Press, Cambridge, 2021, para 3.15.

[72] Art 24(1), UN Charter.

[73] Under the Constitution of certain States, international obligations are directly incorporated into domestic law upon ratification. In other States, direct incorporation occurs only for 'self-executing' treaties (those that are capable of direct application based on their clear and precise formulation). The Peace and Justice Initiative, 'How does international law apply in a domestic legal system?', 2023, at: https://bit.ly/3sD0HqA; and 'Self-executing treaties', 2023, at: https://bit.ly/47LWYWj.

court, while treaty law must first be incorporated into South African legislation before it becomes enforceable in municipal law'.[74]

In contrast, States such as the United Kingdom that are 'super dualist' in nature ordinarily require domestic implementing legislation even for customary rules. Thus, for instance, as Chapter seven recalls, with respect to the unlawful invasion of Iraq in 2003 which involved British troops, the House of Lords unanimously decided in 2006 that although the crime of aggression existed under customary international law, no such crime was punishable under the law of England because the rule had not been incorporated into UK law.[75] But with respect to the European Convention on Human Rights to which the United Kingdom is party, the 1998 Human Rights Act transcribes the rights protected under international law into UK domestic law, making them directly justiciable before the High Court.

At the time of writing, an unusual case was before the High Court of England and Wales concerning an illegal armed group. Three bombing victims have sued the former Sinn Fein president, Gerry Adams, and the Provisional Irish Republican Army (PIRA) for the harm they suffered in three different IRA mainland bombings between 1973 and 1996. John Clark, a victim of the March 1973 Old Bailey bombing in London; Jonathan Ganesh, a victim of the February 1996 London Docklands bombing; and Barry Laycock, a victim of the June 1996 Arndale shopping centre bombing in Manchester, have sued both Mr Adams and the IRA for nominal damages of £1. The barrister leading Mr Adams's legal team said that the IRA was an 'unincorporated association' which was 'incapable in law of being sued'. Counsel for the claimants said a 'fundamental issue' at a trial would relate to whether they established that Mr Adams was a 'Commanding Officer of the Belfast Brigade of the IRA'. Arguments in the case came to an end on 22 November 2023 and the judge's ruling was expected in the near future.[76] While the case was being argued on the basis of domestic law, it could have ramifications for future actions under international law.

UN Security Council

The role of the UN Security Council is to maintain international peace and security. It does so first and foremost by encouraging the peaceful settlement of disputes.[77] Although the notion is not precisely defined in the UN Charter,

[74] G Ferreira and A Ferreira-Snyman, 'The Incorporation of Public International Law into Municipal Law and Regional Law against the Background of the Dichotomy Between Monism and Dualism' (2014) 17(4) *Potchefstroom Electronic Law Journal* 1471–96, at: https://bit.ly/3QKNaoA, at p 1473.

[75] UK House of Lords, *R v Jones* [2006] UKHL 16.

[76] 'Gerry Adams fights case brought by three bombing victims to establish his membership of the IRA', *Daily Telegraph*, 21 November 2023.

[77] Arts 33–38, UN Charter.

instances of threats or breaches of international peace and security are framed as a 'threat to the peace', a 'breach of the peace', or an 'act of aggression'. While in earlier decades, these tended to be limited to inter-State use of force (or the threat of such use of force), especially since the 1990s internal violence, involving war crimes or patterns of grave violations of human rights, has also been sufficient on numerous occasions to constitute a threat to international peace and security.

There are 15 members in the Security Council: five permanent members with veto power (China, France, Russia, the United Kingdom, and the United States) and 10 non-permanent members. Of these 10 non-permanent members, five are elected by the General Assembly each year for a two-year term.[78] Any member of the Council, whether permanent or non-permanent, may propose the text of a resolution. In order to pass, a resolution on a substantive matter (as opposed to one only dealing with a procedural issue) must attract nine positive votes from the 15 Council members.

If any of the five permanent members votes against the resolution – as opposed to abstaining – the resolution does not pass. At the time of writing, the most recent draft resolutions to be vetoed concerned the situation in the Middle East and specifically with respect to Palestine (Gaza).[79] On 18 October 2023, the text of a resolution proposed by Brazil[80] was vetoed by the United States. Among other things, Brazil had sought to include a call for 'the rescission of the order for civilians and UN staff to evacuate all areas in Gaza north of the Wadi Gaza and relocate in southern Gaza'. But in vetoing the resolution, the United States expressed its belief that it was necessary to allow diplomacy to 'play out, especially when Secretary-General Guterres, President Biden, Secretary [of State] Blinken and regional actors are engaged in intensive dialogue' on the issues on which the Council was deliberating. The United States also expressed its disappointment that the draft resolution made no mention of Israel's right of self-defence.[81]

A week later, a draft resolution on the same issue was put forward by the United States[82] but this time was vetoed by both China and Russia. China explained that its objection to the draft resolution was that it was

> evasive on the most pressing issue of ending the fighting and never calls for an immediate ceasefire in clear and unambiguous language. At this moment, a ceasefire is not only a diplomatic term, but means the life and death of many more civilians. It is irresponsible and extremely dangerous for a Security Council resolution to be ambiguous

[78] For 2024, the 10 non-permanent members were Algeria, Ecuador, Guyana, Japan, Malta, Mozambique, the Republic of Korea (South Korea), Sierra Leone, Slovenia, and Switzerland.

[79] The comprehensive list of vetoed resolutions is available on the UN website at: https://bit.ly/38gGXL5.

[80] See UN doc S/2023/773.

[81] Statement of the United States, 9442nd meeting of the UN Security Council, New York, 18 October 2023, UN doc S/PV.9442, at: https://bit.ly/3GfUXWO, pp 3–4.

[82] See UN doc S/2023/792.

> on issues of war and peace. It is tantamount to paving the way for large-scale military action and giving a green light to further escalation of war.[83]

China further stated that it 'in no way' denied Israel's 'security concerns' but it opposed the attempt to establish 'a new narrative on the Palestinian-Israeli issue, ignoring the fact that the Palestinian territories have been occupied for a long time, and avoids the fundamental issue of independent statehood for the Palestinian people'.[84]

UN General Assembly

The UN General Assembly may on occasion identify or warn about violations or abuses of international law by or in a State, but it has no real enforcement powers. The exception to this general rule is the Uniting for Peace resolution, adopted during the Korean War,[85] and which has been referred to in situations where the Security Council is deadlocked. A leading international lawyer has, however, described Resolution 377 A (V) as having 'a potential that could subvert the well-equilibrated balance of power within the United Nations'.[86]

In February 2023, at its Eleventh Emergency Session, the General Assembly deplored 'in the strongest terms the aggression by the Russian Federation against Ukraine in violation of Article 2(4) of the Charter'.[87] A total of 141 Member States voted in favour of Resolution and seven voted against – Belarus, the Democratic People's Republic of Korea (North Korea), Eritrea, Mali, Nicaragua, Russia itself, and Syria. Among the 32 abstentions were China, India, Pakistan, and South Africa. The Assembly repeated its demand that Russia 'immediately, completely and unconditionally withdraw all of its military forces from the territory of Ukraine within its internationally recognized borders'.[88]

International Court of Justice

The International Court of Justice focuses on resolving disputes between States peacefully. It also identifies the responsibility of States for breaches of

[83] Statement of China, 9453rd meeting of the UN Security Council, New York, 25 October 2023, UN doc S/PV.9453, at: https://bit.ly/3sPHRwh, p 5.

[84] Ibid.

[85] UN General Assembly Resolution 377 (V), adopted on 3 November 1950 by 52 votes to 5 (The Byelorussian SSR, Czechoslovakia, Poland, the Soviet Union, and the Ukrainian SSR) with 2 abstentions (Argentina and India).

[86] C Tomuschat, 'Uniting for Peace', UN Audiovisual Library of International Law, New York, 2008, at: https://bit.ly/3sWSXj3, p 4.

[87] UN General Assembly Resolution ES-11/1 ('Aggression against Ukraine'), adopted on 23 February 2023 by 141 votes to 7 with 32 abstentions, operative para 2.

[88] UN General Assembly Resolution ES-11/1, operative para 4.

international law, including whether reparations should be made (and, if damages are payable, how much that should be). This issue is covered in more detail in Chapter eight. In the wording on the ICJ's website:

> The International Court of Justice acts as a world court. The Court's jurisdiction is twofold: it decides, in accordance with international law, disputes of a legal nature that are submitted to it by States (jurisdiction in contentious cases); and it gives advisory opinions on legal questions at the request of the organs of the United Nations, specialised agencies or one related organisation authorised to make such a request (advisory jurisdiction).[89]

The States Parties to the Statute of the Court may 'at any time declare that they recognize as compulsory ... the jurisdiction of the Court'.[90] This gives those States the right to bring any one or more other States that have also accepted this obligation before the Court. They also undertake to appear before the Court as respondents in proceedings brought against them by one or more other such States. The declarations are deposited with the UN Secretary-General. At the time of writing, 74 of the 193 UN Member States had recognised the compulsory jurisdiction of the International Court of Justice.[91] All other States are also entitled to bring cases before the Court but the respondent State must accept the Court's jurisdiction on an ad hoc basis (unless it is laid down in a treaty, as is the case, for instance, with the 1948 Genocide Convention).[92]

Under the terms of the UN Charter, each UN Member State undertakes to comply with the decision of the Court in any case to which it is a party.[93] Should any party to a case fail to comply with a judgment rendered by the Court, the other party may have recourse to the UN Security Council, 'which may, if it deems necessary, make recommendations or decide upon measures to be taken to give effect to the judgment'.[94]

[89] International Court of Justice, 'Jurisdiction', at: https://bit.ly/3MXxA84.

[90] Art 36(2), Statute of the International Court of Justice.

[91] Australia, Austria, Barbados, Belgium, Botswana, Bulgaria, Cambodia, Cameroon, Canada, Costa Rica, Côte d'Ivoire, Cyprus, Democratic Republic of Congo, Denmark, Djibouti, Dominica, the Dominican Republic, Egypt, Equatorial Guinea, Estonia, Finland, The Gambia, Georgia, Germany, Greece, Guinea, Guinea-Bissau, Haiti, Honduras, Hungary, India, Iran, Ireland, Italy, Japan, Latvia, Lesotho, Liberia, Liechtenstein, Lithuania, Luxembourg, Madagascar, Malawi, Malta, the Marshall Islands, Mauritius, Mexico, The Netherlands, New Zealand, Nicaragua, Nigeria, Norway, Pakistan, Panama, Paraguay, Peru, the Philippines, Poland, Portugal, Romania, Senegal, Slovakia, Somalia, Spain, Sudan, Suriname, Swaziland, Sweden, Switzerland, Timor-Leste, Togo, Uganda, the United Kingdom, and Uruguay.

[92] 'Disputes between the Contracting Parties relating to the interpretation, application or fulfilment of the present Convention, including those relating to the responsibility of a State for genocide or for any of the other acts enumerated in article III, shall be submitted to the International Court of Justice at the request of any of the parties to the dispute'. Art IX, Convention on the Prevention and Punishment of the Crime of Genocide; adopted at Paris, 9 December 1948; entered into force, 12 January 1951.

[93] Art 94(1), UN Charter.

[94] Art 94(2), UN Charter.

International Crimes

As Chapter seven discusses in detail, there are four 'core' international crimes for which individuals may bear criminal responsibility under international criminal law. These are: war crimes (by far the most common), crimes against humanity, genocide, and aggression. Each may be relevant to hybrid warfare.

Just as in domestic law, there are typically two elements to any international crime that must be successfully established for a conviction to be secured before a domestic court or an international criminal tribunal. There must be a culpable act (often known by its Latin name, *actus reus*) and an associated culpable state of mind (the *mens rea*).

With respect to the *mens rea*, it may have to be proved not only that the individual accused intended to commit the unlawful act (eg murder, torture, rape) but also that he or she did so with an underlying intent or knowledge. In the case of crimes against humanity, this involves the accused knowing that the act was committed as part of a widespread or systematic attack directed against any civilian population (whether or not he personally wanted to further the attack).[95] In the case of genocide, a perpetrator must have the specific intent (known by the Latin tag *dolus specialis*) to 'destroy, in whole or in part, a national, ethnical, racial or religious group, as such'.[96]

The crime of aggression is generally defined as a serious violation of the prohibition of the use of armed force by a State against the sovereignty, territorial integrity, or political independence of another State. Its prosecution is unusual for an international crime as, under the Rome Statute of the International Criminal Court, which has had material jurisdiction over the crime since 2017, the planning, preparation, initiation or execution of aggression may only be perpetrated 'by a person in a position effectively to exercise control over or to direct the political or military action of a State'.[97]

[95] Art 7(1), ICC Statute.
[96] Art 6, ICC Statute.
[97] Art 8 *bis* (1), ICC Statute.

Annex II: Glossary of Abbreviations and Key Terms

Accession	A one-stop process for a State to become party to a treaty.
ADIZ	Air defence identification zone
Actus reus	Unlawful criminal conduct whether by act or omission.
Agent (of a State)	A person or entity that is acting on behalf of a State.
APMBC	Anti-Personnel Mine Ban Convention
Armed conflict	An international legal term classifying certain situations of armed violence. International armed conflict is hostilities between States while non-international armed conflict is sustained and intense fighting between a State and an organised non-State armed group. Once an armed conflict exists, the **law of armed conflict** applies.
AI	Artificial intelligence
CAR	Central African Republic
CBRN	Chemical, biological, radiological, and nuclear
CCM	Convention on Cluster Munitions
Codification	Existing rules of international law that are written into a treaty
CRPD	Convention on the Rights of Persons with Disabilities
Disarmament law	The branch of international law that prohibits the production, stockpiling, transfer, and use of specific weapons.
DPP	Democratic Progressive Party (Taiwan)
EEZ	Exclusive economic zone
FSB	Russian Federal Security Service

Hybrid warfare	The integrated use by one State of regular and irregular armed forces to employ forcible and non-forcible measures in and against another State with the aim of destabilising and potentially overthrowing its government and critically weakening its armed forces. Hybrid warfare occurs in the context of an international armed conflict between two or more States and may involve an armed attack in violation of *jus ad bellum*.
Hybrid threats	The use by one State against another of unlawful or unfriendly forcible and non-forcible measures, but which do not amount to an armed attack or an international armed conflict. Their aim is to destabilise and potentially overthrow its government and to undermine other State institutions. Hybrid threats, which may amount in certain circumstances to the threat or use of force under international law, may include (but are not limited to) cyberattacks, intimidation, disinformation and misinformation, and economic and military pressure.
IAEA	International Atomic Energy Agency
ICC	International Criminal Court
ICCPR	International Covenant on Civil and Political Rights
ICESCR	International Covenant on Economic, Social and Cultural Rights
ICRC	International Committee of the Red Cross
ICTR	International Criminal Tribunal for Rwanda
ICTY	International Criminal Tribunal for the former Yugoslavia
IHL	International humanitarian law (also known as **the law of armed conflict**).
International counterterrorism law	The branch of international law that defines when international terrorism has been perpetrated, both in peacetime and during armed conflict
international crime	A serious violation of international law attracting individual criminal responsibility
International criminal law	The branch of international law that governs the prosecution of individuals for international crimes.

International human rights law	The body of international law that protects individuals and peoples against violence and abuse and requires those in power to recognise and facilitate their fundamental rights.
International law	The body of law that regulates conduct of international concern by the **subjects** of international law
IRA	Irish Republican Army
JIM	Joint Investigative Mechanism (UN)
JNA	Yugoslav National Army
Jurisdiction	The legal power or responsibility over people or States
Jus ad bellum	The branch of international law that regulates inter-State use of armed force
Law of armed conflict	The branch of international law that regulates hostilities between State armed forces or between State armed forces and an organised armed group and offers protection to those in the power of the enemy, in particular when they are in detention
Law of law enforcement	The branch of international law that regulates the use of force in policing and other forms of law enforcement
Mens rea	The mindset associated with unlawful conduct (***actus reus***) necessary to secure a conviction for a crime under both domestic and international law.
NAM	Non-Aligned Movement
NATO	North Atlantic Treaty Organization
NPT	Treaty on the Non-Proliferation of Nuclear Weapons (1968)
OAU	Organization of African Unity
OCHA	Office for the Coordination of Humanitarian Affairs
ODIHR	Office for Democratic Institutions and Human Rights (OSCE)
OHCHR	Office of the United Nations High Commissioner for Human Rights
OIC	Organisation of Islamic Cooperation

Organ (of a State)	A formal entity forming part of the executive, legislature, or judiciary of a State.
OSCE	Organization for Security and Co-operation in Europe
OTP	Office of the Prosecutor (ICC)
PCIJ	Permanent Court of International Justice
PLA	People's Liberation Army (China)
Public international law	*see* **International law**
Ratification	The process by which a **signatory State** becomes a party to a treaty
RS	Republika Srpska
SADR	Sahrawi Arab Democratic Republic
SCSL	Special Court for Sierra Leone
Signatory State	A State that has signed *but not ratified* a treaty and which is not a **State Party**
State	A sovereign entity that has a defined territory (notwithstanding border disputes), a population, a government, and the ability to conclude treaties
State Party	A State that has joined a **treaty** and which is legally bound by its provisions.
Subjects (of international law)	Persons or entities that are directly regulated by **international law**. A full subject of international law has the capacity to conclude and join a **treaty**.
Treaty	A written international agreement between States that is governed by international law. (Titles that may be used to designate treaties include charter, convention, covenant, declaration, and protocol)
UK	United Kingdom
UN	United Nations
UNCC	United Nations Compensation Commission
US	United States

VCLT	Vienna Convention on the Law of Treaties
VCLTIO	Vienna Convention on the Law of Treaties Between States and International Organizations or Between International Organizations
VR	Virtual reality
WHO	World Health Organization
WMD	Weapons of mass destruction

Index

www.ingramcontent.com/pod-product-compliance
Ingram Content Group UK Ltd.
Pitfield, Milton Keynes, MK11 3LW, UK
UKHW020844290926
15470UKWH00004B/1536

9 781509 979578